Greene and Cornwallis
in the Carolinas

To Uncle Lee
+ Aunt Sue,

Thanks so much
for your support!

Love,
Jeff

Greene and Cornwallis in the Carolinas

The Pivotal Struggle in the American Revolution, 1780–1781

JEFFREY A. DENMAN *and*
JOHN F. WALSH

McFarland & Company, Inc., Publishers
Jefferson, North Carolina

Library of Congress Cataloguing-in-Publication Data

Names: Denman, Jeffrey A., 1959– author. | Walsh, John F., 1989– author.
Title: Greene and Cornwallis in the Carolinas : the pivotal struggle
in the American Revolution, 1780–1781 / Jeffrey A. Denman, John F. Walsh.
Description: Jefferson, North Carolina : McFarland & Company, Inc., Publishers, 2020 |
Includes bibliographical references and index.
Identifiers: LCCN 2019045388 | ISBN 9781476667232 (paperback) ∞
ISBN 9781476637051 (ebook)
Subjects: LCSH: Greene, Nathanael, 1742–1786. | Cornwallis, Charles Cornwallis,
Marquis, 1738–1805. | United States—History—Revolution, 1775–1783—Campaigns. |
North Carolina—History—Revolution, 1775–1783. | South Carolina—History—
Revolution, 1775–1783.
Classification: LCC E237 .D46 2020 | DDC 973.3/3—dc23
LC record available at https://lccn.loc.gov/2019045388

British Library cataloguing data are available

ISBN (print) 978-1-4766-6723-2
ISBN (ebook) 978-1-4766-3705-1

Front cover artwork "Major General Nathanael Greene
Saves the American Army," Halifax County, Virginia,
February 14, 1781 (painting by Werner Willis)

Printed in the United States of America

*McFarland & Company, Inc., Publishers
Box 611, Jefferson, North Carolina 28640
www.mcfarlandpub.com*

To the memory of Janet V. Denman (1933–2017),
whose resolute spirit in the face of adversity
helped inspire this work

To Elizabeth C. Denman,
who supported this venture from its inception
and provided moral support

To Marie and Peter Walsh,
whose unwavering love and support
helped make this work possible

Acknowledgments

A work like this or any other is never done in isolation. There are so many people connected to it and we want to thank all those who have provided assistance in the years that it has taken to complete this book.

We would like to thank Warren Smith, the reference librarian at the Walpole Public Library in Walpole, Massachusetts, who got us every book we needed for research from anywhere in the country; Kathie Ludwig and Paul Davis of the David Library of the American Revolution; the Norman Leventhal Map Center at the Boston Public Library; Independence National Historical Park in Philadelphia; the Harvard Library; the South Carolina Historical Society; Barbara Bass of the Halifax County Historical Society in Virginia; Princeton University Press; New-York Historical Society; Rhode Island Historical Society; University of South Carolina Library; Steve Tuttle of the South Carolina Archives; Morristown National Historical Park; United States Military Academy Department of History; Nathanael Greene Homestead in Coventry, Rhode Island; Jack Kessler and Tom Greene for their tour of Nathanael Greene's birthplace and for opening up their homes; Pelican Publishing.

We thank the following for reviewing drafts of the chapters: Carl Borick, John Buchanan, Mark Lender, James Kirby Martin, Benjamin Carp, William Fowler, Rich Strum, Geoff Tegnell, and a special thanks to Jim Piecuch for his review and comments along the way.

We thank the staff at the battlefield sites of Kings Mountain, Cowpens, Guilford Courthouse, and Ninety Six; the South Carolina Archives; North Carolina State Archives; the Maryland Historical Society; Massachusetts Historical Society; Tim Potts, for his advice and counsel; Stephanie Regan of the University of Massachusetts–Boston for copy editing of the manuscript; John Padula, technology specialist at Baker School in Brookline, Massachusetts, for technology assistance in the final stages of assembling the manuscript, and of course, Elizabeth C. Denman, who has endured long conversations about Nathanael Greene for several years.

Table of Contents

Preface

The American Revolution in the South has been largely forgotten in the historical record for many adult students of history. The concept of this project struck me after my own teaching of the American Revolution unit at my school in 2009. In our textbook, there was only one paragraph dedicated to the southern theatre of war. I thought that very odd and began developing materials around that topic for my students. As my class was watching a film clip from an American Revolution series, watching Nathanael Greene and Charles Cornwallis battle each other until Cornwallis moved to the coast of Virginia, I realized that the people and events of that theatre of war were strangers to my students, and to most adults for that matter. Not many people I have crossed paths with have ever heard of anything important happening in the American South during the Revolution. Thus, a project was born.

The neglect of the southern theatre is not surprising. Most of the literature that is found in bookstores deals with the northern campaign. George Washington transcends the Revolution and Thomas Jefferson's Declaration of Independence is world-renowned. Lexington and Concord, Bunker Hill, Valley Forge, Trenton, and Princeton and are all incredible stories. The amount of primary source documentation that has resulted from the Revolution makes for excellent reading, and the subsequent books that have been written on this subject are clearly important.

But it is not the whole story. Many books have been written about the southern campaign and many of those have been cited in this work. However, this story narrows the scope and primarily follows the two protagonists, Nathanael Greene and Charles Cornwallis, from Greene's arrival in Charlotte in December 1780 to the evacuation of Charleston. This work has primarily used their letters and those of their chief lieutenants to tell the incredible story of American victory against overwhelming odds and British failures against an inferior force. With the preponderance of primary source material on Greene and Cornwallis, additional material from their letters has been used to enhance and build on the material thus far produced in the literature. It is important to keep the narrative moving and eliminate unnecessary detail to make the story readable and promote further and deeper exploration of the topic for the avid student of the Revolution. Yorktown has been covered extensively elsewhere, and since Cornwallis's actions were far removed from Greene at this point, it is not included here in vast detail.

Nathanael Greene is an interesting study. Since the beginning of the Revolution, Greene's fortunes had ebbed and flowed. In this book, we begin at a low point for Greene: his tenure as Quartermaster General and the fallout near the end of his term. He masterminds an incredible campaign in the Carolinas, forces Cornwallis's hand, and with the

Revolution won, sinks into the depths with a financial boondoggle that haunted him until his premature death in 1786. His story is a tragedy of sorts.

Cornwallis, on the other hand, despite famously surrendering his army at Yorktown to effectively bring the war to a close, enjoyed a long and successful military career following his return to England. It was the events of the grueling southern campaign that helped to prepare him. The southern campaign is one of the few blemishes on a remarkable military career. It was his encounter with Greene that thwarted the general's attempts to win one his greatest prizes.

The Carolinas that Greene walked into in 1780 presented a complex society of a wide variety of ethnic groups, religious orientations, and allegiances. It was also a divided society, with most of the influence coming from the tidewater and a disenfranchised backcountry with little political or economic power. The story begins with a picture of the backcountry, so the reader can grasp the complexities that existed in places far removed from Charleston. It is difficult to appreciate the story without understanding the previous several decades leading up to the Revolution. Geography, settlement patterns by various ethnic and religious groups, and loyalism play an integral part. It was not an easy task to ameliorate bad feelings, win the hearts and minds of the populace, and defeat British forces while always fighting with few resources, but that was what Greene had to do. Greene had learned much from the northern campaigns that he had been involved with, and as Washington's chief lieutenant, he gained the necessary skills to wage war against the most powerful empire on earth.

Arguably, the American Revolution was won in the South. Cornwallis ended up in Yorktown with his back to the Chesapeake as a direct result of the events in the Carolinas. And an ugly campaign it was. It was a nasty civil war, with neighbor fighting neighbor, rapes, pillaging, burnings, hangings, and the dreaded tar and feathering. It was an era before plantation houses and cotton fields, when the South was an oasis of undeveloped land. Native Americans were on the frontier, and the backcountry and the people who inhabited it come to the forefront of our story.

Lastly, the British strategy to invade the Carolinas sealed the fate of their campaign in the Revolution. Basing their strategy on the assumption that southerners would rally to the Crown and the South would be won over was a fatal flaw. Nathanael Greene saw to it that Cornwallis would never accomplish his goals. The partisans, who lurked in the swamps and the woods, had a deleterious effect on Cornwallis and his troops as he chased Greene throughout the Carolinas to no avail. Paradoxically, with every British victory in the South, a little piece of the army fell away until the whole deck of cards crumbled.

Cowpens, Kings Mountain, and Guilford Courthouse should stand in the pantheon of pivotal battles that changed the face of America. But sadly, these places hold only regional importance to the general population. If we are to understand our history completely, we need to expand our own thinking and begin to look at those other important people who made key historical contributions to the republic. Washington, Jefferson, and Hamilton are larger-than-life figures, but they aren't the only ones. The Revolution was won and lost by thousands of soldiers from both sides of the Atlantic whose voices survive in memoirs, letters, and pension statements. When the dust settled at Yorktown, the British Empire was irrevocably changed, accompanied by the dawn of a new era in the place we call America.

—Jeff Denman

Introduction

Modern attempts to understand what eighteenth-century soldiers experienced are always a challenge, but retracing the steps of soldiers helps to understand the severity of their travails as well as the significance of the victories they experienced. As I traveled throughout the Carolinas visiting many of the sites of the conflict, I was taken with the enormous distances traveled by soldiers from one place to another. When I drove from Guilford Courthouse to the banks of the Dan River at Boyd's Ferry, I was left only wondering how these men performed these incredible tasks day after day. I pondered the fatigue they felt, and the generally poor food and medical care as well. Living in New England, it is easy to imagine frigid nights, but sleeping in a tent, or sometimes without one, with no modern amenities or comfort to keep away the cold, is unimaginable. Soldiers of the eighteenth century were a different breed. Modernity has not done us any favors in terms of "roughing it," and we will never truly know how these men were able to sustain themselves over a long period of time.

At the same time, the thrill of small victories along the way is not that hard to imagine. Standing on the banks of the Dan River where Boyd's Ferry used to run, I could imagine the relief that the common soldier must have felt that the swollen river was now between the British and the ragtag American army, finally bringing some degree of relief when Cornwallis turned back to Hillsborough to begin his retreat from the banks of the river. But then again, it was winter in the Carolinas.

Soldiers' pension applications are filled with vivid descriptions of battles and other horrific and emotional scenes. Michael Graham was at the Battle of Long Island and recalled the "confusion and horror" of the scene with "artillery flying with the chains over the horses' backs, our men running in almost every direction."[1] Some, like Richard Wallace, thought about the effects of their own actions and how they might affect the outcome of the war. Wallace swam across frigid Lake Champlain to deliver a message he thought important, especially when he "reflected that the lives of many of my countrymen might depend upon the success of my effort, I resolved at every hazard to go forward, and if I perished I should die in the best of causes."[2] And some succumbed to fear, like Garret Watts at Camden, who admitted that he "was amongst the first that fled" after the "discharge and loud roar soon became general from one end of the lines to the other."[3]

All of these stories are human and reflect the courage and also the frailties of the common soldier. I thought about the British soldier during my sojourn in the Carolinas as well. Being thousands of miles from home, in a climate that wreaked havoc on them, especially in long, brutal summers, and with a dwindling supply line and little hope in sight, must have plagued at their inner workings. Working against an enemy that at times they never saw coming added to their general fatigue. Lurking in the woods and hiding behind trees and stone walls; the enemy defied the traditional eighteenth-century European methods of warfare.

Winter was the setting for many of the most memorable scenes from the Revolution, from Washington's crossing of the Delaware on Christmas of 1776 to the beleaguered rebel army freezing at Valley Forge. Three years after the attack on Trenton, the war was about to take a major turn. On December 26, 1779, a British fleet under the command of General Henry Clinton set sail from New York and headed south. The passage was not an easy one. As the ships were battered by storms and impeded by ice, morale on board dropped. This was remembered by John Robert Shaw of the 33rd Regiment of Foot: "We set sail in very gloomy spirits–our prospects were gloomy indeed–the very elements seemed to conspire against us, and threaten us with destruction. By the heaving and rolling of the ship, all the beds in which we lay broke loose from the sides of the vessel to which they were fastened, and the ships were so agitated by the wind and waves that she changed her position, so that the gunnels ran under water, and the guns on the same side broke loose on the quarterdeck."[4]

The storms scattered the fleet and greatly delayed their progress. Although most of the troops eventually arrived safely, the voyage did result in significant losses. "Few ships arrived at Tybee in Georgia before the end of January," remembered Banstre Tarleton; "some were taken, others separated, one ordnance vessel foundered, most of the artillery, and all the cavalry horses perished. This accident greatly deranged and impeded the intended attack on Charles town."[5]

The intended target of the British was Charleston, which itself had seen better times. The closing months of 1779 had seen a resurgence of smallpox after a two-decade absence. A letter written to the commander of the American forces there explained, "[N]ew discoveries are made every day of the small-pox; the persons are immediately removed to the pest house."[6] The American army defending the city was greatly outnumbered and needed the assistance of the local militia. The militia, however, was reluctant to enter the infected city. "They declare against going into town; from what I can understand, they are afraid of the small pox breaking out, when they are cooped up, which they say, will be worse to them than the enemy."[7] Without consistent militia assistance, Major General Benjamin Lincoln's troops were in trouble and war was returning to the South.

With all these factors at play, and with all the human frailties we carry with us, it would take extraordinary leadership to pull together a large group of men from differing backgrounds and lead them in a cause that would encounter severe hardship, fatigue, hunger, and disease along the way. Over the next two years, the brutality of the war in the southern department would test the combatants to the limit. Over the course of many engagements, two exceptional leaders would emerge. Charles Cornwallis of the British and Nathanael Greene were about the square off in what would become the deciding campaign of the Revolution.

Note to Reader: The original spelling of most of the primary source documents that are referred to in this book has been maintained except in rare cases where understanding might be compromised. In the few cases where this is not done, modern spelling is used.

PART I

Prelude

1

The Backcountry

The world that Nathanael Greene rode into in late 1780 was anything but a simple rural society. The geography of the land in the backcountry was different from that of the north, and there existed a more complex relationship between myriad religious and ethnic groups as well as a contentious relationship with those who dominated politics on the coast. Understanding the nature of society and all that had happened in the last several decades leading up to the Revolution would challenge any military leader who had arrived on the scene for the first time. The colonial history of the Carolinas is varied and complex, and it would be impossible to cover it all in one chapter, so the focus will be on the major political and economic events from the beginnings of major migrations to the backcountry to the beginning of the Revolution, a period of time spanning approximately four decades.

South Carolina's geography and people presented a unique challenge to living there as well to those administering it as a political entity. The low country, beginning on the coast, extended approximately eighty to one hundred miles inland and was particularly ideal for rice plantations.[1] Rising more than two hundred feet above the coastal plain was the Piedmont.[2] Here lay the sand and the pines of what became known as the fall line, the head of navigation, intersected by numerous creeks and rivers, which contained fertile lands along the major rivers and on the plateaus that separated the river valleys.[3] The fall line was considered the beginning of the backcountry that extended west to the Appalachian Mountains. However, approximately eighty miles inland, running parallel to the coast, were the sandhills, which geologically form a more realistic line of separation between the backcountry and the low country. The locations of rapids shift with the seasons and the water level, and no abrupt break marks the landscape.[4]

The river systems in the Carolinas are a confusing network of waterways, but of major importance is that the rivers divide the land into narrow districts with mostly swamps as borders. There are three major river systems in South Carolina: the Pee Dee, Santee, and the Savannah, which all begin on the eastern slopes of the Blue Ridge Mountains in North Carolina.[5] Numerous other rivers and streams dot the region and are tributaries to the state's primary river systems.[6] There were few bridges, and rivers were only passable at a few fords; otherwise, boats would be required for crossings. The rivers were subject to severe fluctuations depending on weather conditions, and as the future would show, the movement of armies and overall strategy would depend on the ability to get men across a river.[7]

Following two pages: **From *The Papers of General Nathanael Greene*, Vol. VII: 26 December 1780–29 March 1781 edited by Dennis M. Conrad and Richard K. Showman. Copyright 1994 by the University of North Carolina Press. Used by permission of the publisher, www. uncpress.org.**

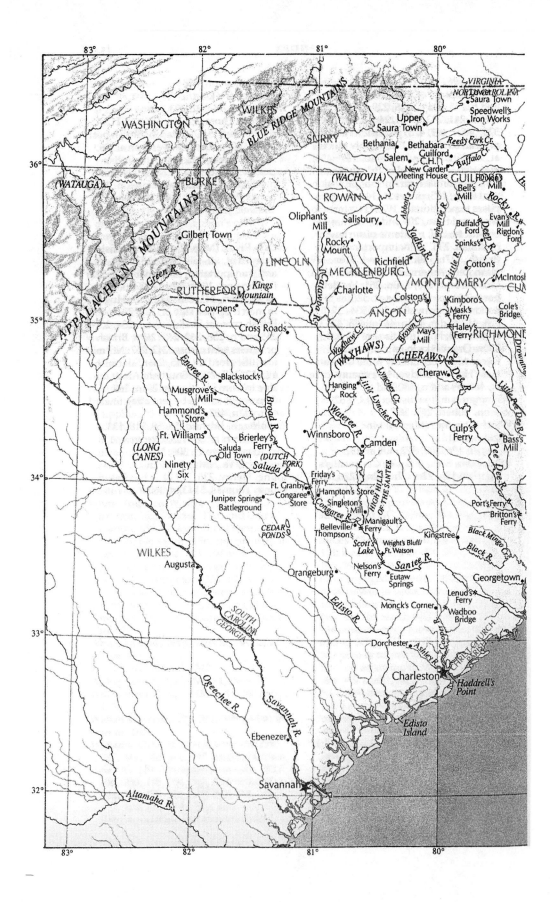

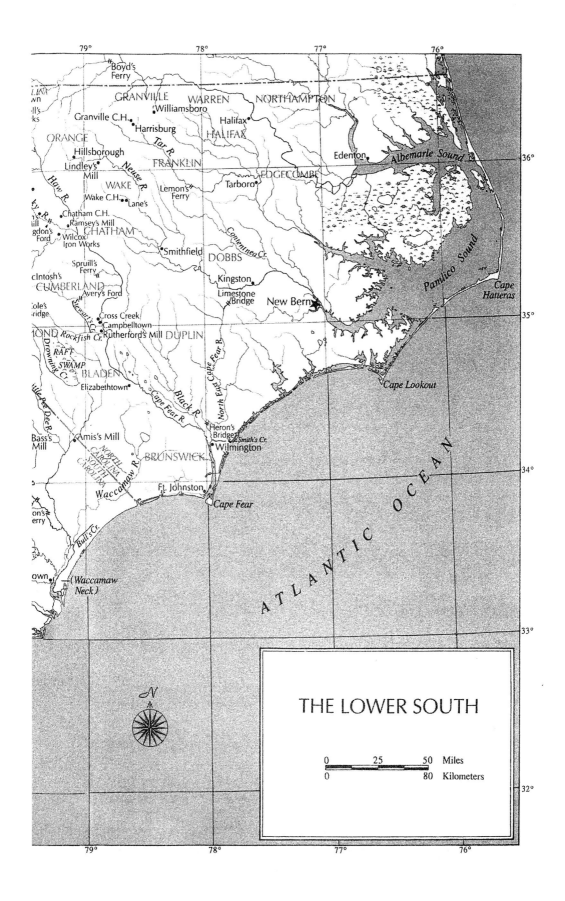

79°   78°   77°   76°

Boyd's
Ferry

GRANVILLE   WARREN   NORTHAMPTON
Williamsboro
CAROLINA
wn
ll's
ks   Granville C.H.   Halifax
ORANGE   Harrisburg   HALIFAX
Hillsborough   Tar R.   Edenton   Albemarle Sound
Lindley's   FRANKLIN   36°
Mill   Neuse R.   EDGECOMBE
WAKE   Lemon's   Tarboro
Haw R.   Wake C.H.   Ferry
y R.   Lane's
ill R.   Chatham C.H.
gdon's   Ramsey's Mill   CHATHAM   Contentnea Cr.
Ford   Wilcox   Smithfield
Iron Works   DOBBS   Pamlico Sound
Spruill's   Cape
cIntosh's   Ferry   Kingston   Hatteras
CUMBERLAND   Avery's Ford   Limestone   New Bern
ole's   Bridge   35°
ridge   Cross Creek
IOND   Stewart's Cr.   Campbelltown
Rockfish Cr.   Rutherford's Mill   DUPLIN

RAFT   Cape Fear Lookout
Drowning   SWAMP
C.   BLADEN
Elizabethtown   Cape Fear R.
lle Pee Dee R.   Black R.   North East Cape Fear R.

Bass's   Amis's Mill   Heron's
Mill   Bridge   Smith's Cr.
NORTH   BRUNSWICK   Wilmington
CAROLINA
SOUTH   34°
CAROLINA
Waccamaw R.   Ft. Johnston
Cape Fear
on's
erry   Bull's Cr.
ATLANTIC   OCEAN
own   (Waccamaw
Neck)

33°

N

THE LOWER SOUTH

0   25   50   Miles

0   80   Kilometers

32°

79°   78°   77°   76°

In what became known as the Piedmont, society was based on farming, where the average landholders held about 150 acres and grew corn, potatoes, peas, beans, cabbage, and pumpkins, as well as some barley, rye, and oats.[8] The Piedmont was a place of rolling hills and lush valleys, with dozens of streams teeming with fish and plenty of wild game.[9] The economy of the Piedmont was not limited to agriculture. Artisans such as blacksmiths, carpenters, shoemakers and weavers were also common. The store became a central focus of the countryside, often operating a tavern as well.[10] Profits were hard to come by because of the difficulty of land clearance and the transport of goods to market, so many men who would emerge as leading slaveowners and political leaders began life in the backcountry not only as planters but tavern keepers, millers and surveyors.[11] Slavery existed in the Piedmont, but did not compare to Charlestown, which had 53 Africans to every three whites. Some owned a few slaves, but many owned none at all.[12] By 1768, the low country, with its rice cultivation and indigo, held about 86 percent of the colony's taxable wealth and more than 90 percent of its slaves.[13]

What a farmer produced depended on where he lived. For instance, the rolling land between the North and South Forks of the Edisto, near Orangeburg, was used primarily for cattle, since the rivers were closed off from the coast and thus agriculture became a disadvantageous pursuit.[14] Navigation on the Edisto was severely limited, and the land route to Charleston was equally problematic, with poorly constructed roads that the assembly gave no aid in building or maintaining. These roads were under public care and the labor needed to maintain them made a bad situation worse.[15] In Fredericksburg, near the Wateree, the needs of the small farmer and planter depended on the location of the settlement. Slaveowners and those who had large families settled the river bottom south of the fall line where they found rich soil, while small farmers settled in the center and northern part of the township where corn was produced.[16] In the eastern townships, indigo brought great wealth to the region, and thus with it, slave labor. The militia census of 1757 finds 155 slaves from sixteen to sixty years of age listed from Williamsburg, indicating a total population of over 600 people.[17]

Transportation of goods from the interior to the coast was a hazardous and troublesome process. In a land of rivers and creeks, few bridges existed to connect the opposite shore of a river.[18] Rivers exited the Piedmont over rocks, and thus navigation was too difficult.[19] Transporting goods over land was equally hazardous. Roads that ran parallel to the river needed to cross some small creeks, some deeper than others. Routes to the coast ranged from one hundred to three hundred miles, and thus the products of the backcountry could provide little competition to the products from other parts of the state. Therefore, the Piedmont remained an isolated series of outposts disconnected from the coast until modern transportation methods of the day began to be developed.[20]

South Carolina's neighbor to the north, North Carolina, figured prominently in this story and had its own unique features of geography and settlement, which deserve some mention. North Carolina has three regions: from east to west, the Coastal Plain extends inland from the ocean about 150 miles; then rises the Piedmont Plateau, marked by gently rolling hills; followed by the Appalachian Mountains in the westernmost part of the state.[21] It was the Piedmont with which farmers were most impressed. The soil was generally good, with plentiful rainfall for crop production and abundant pasture for livestock.[22] Forests with stands of pine and hickory provided families with wood for building, and whenever possible, colonists settled along creeks and rivers to take advantage of rich topsoil deposited from frequent river flooding.[23] Indians who had deserted their villages had cleared fields for agriculture, which farmers took advantage of, growing rye, barley, oats, and vegetables, while also utilizing the space for livestock and fruit trees.[24] Herman Husband, a farmer from Maryland on a trip to North Carolina in 1754, noted that it had "wholesome pleasant air, good water, fertile land, and beyond expectation according to its appearance, a moderate and short winter and for 7 or 8 months in the year dureing [*sic*] my stay there free from all kind of troublesome insects."[25]

North Carolina's chief rivers are the Catawba, Yadkin and Pee Dee, which rise in the mountains to the west and flow southeast into South Carolina. Notably, these rivers, along with other streams in the colony, ran through deep cuts in clay soil and the steep banks filled rapidly during heavy rains, which in fact would affect both armies in the coming conflict.[26] On smaller, swifter streams, small industry sprang up, developed particularly by the Scots-Irish and the Germans, who were already skilled in constructing grist mills and tanneries.[27] Slavery had a less significant impact in the Piedmont than in the eastern part of the colony or in the backcountry of Virginia or South Carolina. Most African-Americans who lived and worked on large plantations or small farms in the eastern part engaged in providing labor for the maritime and forest industries or as personal servants and craftsmen.[28]

It is the migration of people into the backcountry that had a significant impact on events leading up to the Revolution. In the early 1730s, then South Carolina Governor Robert Johnson began to encourage the settlement of the backcountry as a possible buffer "from slaves, Indians, and the agents of competing European governments."[29] It began to be peopled by Germans, Swiss, Dutch, Irish, Scots, Scots-Irish, Welsh and English.[30] From a religious perspective, there were Presbyterians, Reform Presbyterians, Lutherans, Baptists, Anglicans, French Huguenots, and Quakers, to name a few.[31] Governor Johnson created eleven townships near the rivers with fifty acres designated for each person. Each township formed a parish, and when a parish reached a population of one hundred families, they were to elect two members to the assembly. Settlers had the lands rent-free for the first ten years, and thereafter had to pay four shillings per year.[32] With such attractive offers, immigrants from Germany, Holland, Switzerland, Ireland, Scotland and Wales flocked to South Carolina between 1730 and 1750.

Between 1750 and 1760, a wave of Scots-Irish flooded in via the mountains of Pennsylvania and Virginia.[33] Political leaders and landowners in the South sought settlement by English, German, and German-Swiss Protestants whose reputation for being industrious and orderly preceded them.[34] In 1740, few Europeans lived in the backcountry. By the American Revolution, nearly four decades later, nearly one-half of the total population of the colony lived there.[35] They came via the Great Wagon Road, which began across the Schuylkill River from Philadelphia, west to Harrisburg and then south along the Shenandoah Valley into the Piedmont of North Carolina, finishing in present-day Camden.[36] Since most of these settlers came through the "back door," their settlements were not a westward connection to the low country, and the sections were isolated from one another. This was going to cause major problems in the colony in the years to come, but the massive migration was going to cause conflict with the Native Americans specifically.

Life in the backcountry was filled with dread from the threat of violence by neighboring Indians, namely the Cherokee. In 1760, this dread came to fruition as Cherokees attacked white settlers all over the backcountry. Starting in 1730, South Carolina had initiated a plan for frontier settlement that organized townships in such a way as to provide Charleston a bulwark against enemies to the west. Unfortunately, the new migrants settled where they wanted to, in lands that were claimed by the Cherokee and Catawba.[37] The Scots-Irish, whom we will visit shortly, chose to settle in places that were claimed by the Cherokee. The war ended in 1761, and a new wave of immigration began to populate the backcountry once again. By 1775, over 50,000 people populated the interior, more than double the population in 1759.[38] Meanwhile, English and Scottish Presbyterians, Baptists, and French Huguenots settled near Charleston. Most of these settlers ended up dominating the colonial government, creating friction with the established Church of England in the region.[39]

Two problems greeted the newcomers in Carolina. The first was that the Church of England was essentially the state church. It is interesting to note that the cultural diversity of the backcountry and the direct challenges from dissenting religious groups helped lead to the disestablishment of religion throughout the republic in the years after the American Revolution, which would be a difficult road.[40] Secondly, the inability of the government in the low country to provide law and order to the backcountry settlements created issues with administration and justice.[41] While they recognized the King as the rightful leader, they did, however, demand their rights to practice their own religion on terms of their own choosing.[42]

A discussion of some of the ethnic and religious groups that settled in the backcountry is important for understanding the nature of the relationships between different ethnic groups and between the Charleston elite and some of those groups that would eventually help shape the character of the colony. The Scots-Irish were descendants of Scots Protestants who were the original settlers in northern Ireland in the seventeenth century. They had come with a social and religious order all their own, very unlike those on the coast.[43] In the early 1700s, the Irish woolen trade collapsed because of the protection granted to English manufacturers, and depression ensued in Ulster.[44] In Scotland, the linen trade met with stiff competition from Ireland, and the resulting unemployment caused distress for many.[45] As one person put it, "The ... town of Paisley can not now support those ingenious mechanics who have raised it to its present greatness, but they are forced to abandon their friends and country and seek subsistence in a distant clime, which they cannot in their own."[46] Social conditions resulting from economic decline also affected the area. Petty theft became rampant. James Hogg, who rented a farm, lost so much property from petty theft he was forced to emigrate to North Carolina, bringing with him 280 people. "The people in my neighborhood were extremely addicted to theft and pilfering, the constant attendants of slavery and poverty."[47]

Their own history became a motivation for emigration as well. The Ulster Scots believed the state should not interfere in their religious practices as long as they conducted themselves in a peaceable manner. They despised class differences, especially the rule of a privileged class over the rest of society.[48] With the Scots-Irish came the Presbyterian Church. Until this time, the southern colonies were mostly Episcopalian, and the Presbyterians supported separation of church and state.[49] Ulster Scots settled in all thirteen American colonies, primarily in Pennsylvania and the high country of Virginia and the Carolinas, because these areas were open to settlement prior to French expulsion from North America.[50] The Scots-Irish became the most dominant ethnicity in the colonies south of New York.[51] They had come into conflict with the Indians and the Quaker government in Philadelphia, which precipitated their move southward into the Carolinas, where they eventually settled above the fall line in an arc from present-day Lancaster

County to Abbeville County on the Savannah River.[52] Many settled in the Waxhaws, one of the largest Scots-Irish settlements in South Carolina, near the North Carolina-South Carolina border. Cheap and valuable land was the main attraction, and each male head of household could claim one hundred acres for himself and an additional fifty acres for each member of the household and each servant.[53] The Scots-Irish could claim a miserable history with the English and were persecuted for their Presbyterian beliefs and practices.[54] They were tightly connected to kin and usually emigrated in groups with relationships going back to Ulster in the old country. They could be very antagonistic to other religious groups, which helped stir the fires of sectarian animosity in the backcountry.[55]

The Moravians were another backcountry group that demonstrated the diversity of the region and left a unique imprint on their role in the American Revolution. The Moravians were part of an evangelical church dating back to the fifteenth century, the oldest Protestant sect, and were considered clannish, separating themselves from others by worshipping and working together and viewing everyone else as a stranger.[56] With pacifism at the core of their beliefs, the Moravians refused to fight against the Spanish in Georgia in the 1730s and left for a large area of the Piedmont of North Carolina, where they lived apart from other settlers and spoke German instead of English.[57]

Fearing that "it looked as though men were going to divide our land and drive us out, the Brethren felt it necessary to send deputies to the Assembly at Hillsborough, and petition that we might be permitted to retain our ancient Privileges, and that we might be protected in the possession of our property."[58] Fortunately for the Moravians, "it was well received … [with the Assembly] saying that our Rights and Liberty had been granted by an Act of Parliament, that through us agriculture, trade and manufactures had been improved and extended in the western part of the State, that through our peaceable and orderly behavior we had won great respect and reputation, that in an especial manner we had proved our willingness on all occasions to aid and assist the common cause, so far as our religious scruples permitted."[59] Ironically, economic hardship due to lack of connections with the outside world forced the hands of the Moravians. They began operating stores or taverns and exporting pottery, leather goods and foodstuffs to port cities like Charleston.[60]

Their political loyalty on the eve of revolution lay with the Americans. With the signing of the Declaration of Independence, the Moravians recognized the Continental Congress as the supreme power in the land, and thus began supporting the fledgling American government.[61] Even before the Declaration, a diary entry for January 6, 1776, detailed a test of loyalty: "This evening Mr. Sporgen's brother came with a secret message from Capt. Heinrich Herman and other leaders of the Loyalist party, to find out in what way and how far we would unite with them, and what money and other things we would let them have, offering to stand by us and protect us to the full extent of their power. We absolutely refused to have anything to do with such an undertaking, which would be most dangerous for us."[62] As pacifists, the Moravians were exempt from military service provided they made a cash payment in lieu of personal service.[63] But even as pacifists, they were more than willing to provide aid to the American army.

True to their beliefs, the Moravians served their God best when serving others, caring for the sick and wounded, for example, after the Battle of Guilford Courthouse.[64] But they had just come to America to live simply. War intervened, and although they were exempt from military service, they did not feel it was right to pay for substitutes to fight in their places, so they petitioned the state assembly to share in the cost of the war and were relieved of the triple taxes they had to pay because of it.[65] Initially they were looked at suspiciously in terms of their motives, but the Moravians were finally recognized as dutiful citizens of the state and became an important cog whose money and supplies were essential for the welfare of the state in general and the soldiers of the battlefield in particular.[66]

During the latter part of the colonial period, many Quakers, made up of different ethnicities, migrated toward the southern colonies, most likely for economic reasons.[67] In North Carolina, for example, one of the few forms of organized religion that existed within the state was the Society of Friends.[68] Even so, in the early 1700s the Quakers were able to exert some political influence in the state, but only temporarily; for most of the colonial period, Quakerism was very distant from public affairs and focused mostly on an inward spiritual life.[69] The lack of unity in their relationship with the state government caused some problems for the Quakers. As they were exempted from military service, they were subject to heavy fines or an increase in taxes. So the struggle within the Quaker position was whether paying fines or taxes was contributing directly to the war effort, which violated their pacifist approach.[70] Many Quakers refused to pay taxes, so the state in turn seized their property instead.[71] The North Carolina government collected these monies with little objection, reasoning that the pacifist nature of some of the non-resistant sects would render them inadequate soldiers, and granting them full exemption from military service.[72]

In 1776, the Declaration of Independence threw the Quakers into great turmoil. It is a key part of their faith to obey civil law, except when it violates their conscience.[73] In 1772, the yearly meeting "asserted its loyalty and attachment to George III … and gave forth their testimony against all Plottings, conspiracies, and Insurrections against the King and Government, whatsoever as works of darkness."[74]

Both sides poorly treated the Quakers during the war, and both sides fought for the support of the Quakers at the same time.[75] They suffered from the violence that raged around them, both financially and through the loss and destruction of property. But they remained true to their faith and principles. After the Battle of Guilford Courthouse, the Quakers were involved in caring for wounded soldiers and the burial of the dead. Greene himself sent a letter to the Quakers of New Garden, stating he would protect them whenever possible, mentioning at the end of his letter that the only way to end the war was "for the people to be united."[76] The response Greene received was direct, but demonstrated the true Quaker spirit. They replied, "We are able to assist as much as we would be glad to, as the Americans have lain much upon us, and of late the British have plundered and entirely broken up many among us, which renders it hard, and there is at our meeting house … upward of one hundred now living, that have no means of provisions except what hospitality the neighborhood affords them."[77] At the end of the letter, the Friends reiterate their duty: "As we have none to commit our cause to but God alone, but hold it the duty of true Christians, at all times to assist the distressed."[78]

In the fall of 1766, Charles Woodmason, a newly ordained Anglican minister, left Charleston and headed to the backcountry to begin work in the primitive settlements scattered throughout this region. He traveled thousands of miles each year, moving from one settlement to another, performing his religious duties while chronicling life in the backcountry. Although his journals provide great depth to the daily lives of these people, he nonetheless brought his own prejudices to his writings. He was from England, and was a planter, merchant and parish official.[79] According to Woodmason, the backcountry was a land of primitive and backwards people, far removed from the wealth and status of the low-country elite.[80] The social and political order that he observed in England was not fulfilled in the backcountry upon which he now thrust himself. Here, he was faced with religious denominations who stymied him, particularly the Presbyterians and Baptists, who challenged his every move.[81] Woodmason found sectarian differences stark in the backcountry, and his own contempt for non–Anglicans made it worse. Baptists disliked Woodmason and his church, and he liked the Presbyterians even less, who generously returned the favor.[82]

His observations offer a window into not only living conditions, but the lack of religion. "Officiated in the Presbyterian Meeting House to about 200 Hearers, Chiefly Presbyterians. Offer'd to give Sermon twice on ev'ry Sunday. Rejected."[83] Along the undefined border of North and South Carolina, Woodmason described scenes of domestic life. "As in many Places they have nought but a Gourd to drink out off Not a Plate Knife or Spoon.... It is well if they can get some Body Linen, and some have not even that. They are so burthed'd with Young Children, that the Women cannot attend both House and Field—And many live by Hunting, and killing of Deer—There's not a Cabbin but has 10 or 12 Young Children in it...."[84] Woodmason related that the parents of Irish Presbyterians "let them [children] run thus wild, than to have them instructed in the Principles of Religion by a Minister of the Church of England."[85]

Itinerant preachers were nothing new to the backcountry. The region was inundated with preachers from many sects. "Preached ... in my way back at Lynch's Creek to a great Multitude of People assembled together, being the 1st Episcopal Minister they had seen since being in the province—They complain'd of being eaten up by Itinerant Teachers, Preachers and Imposters from new England and Pennsylvania.... And among the Various Plans of Religion, they are at Loss which to adapt, and consequently are without any Religion at all."[86] Woodmason was so frustrated at what he experienced that he wrote a letter to the Bishop of London on October 19, 1766, in which he remarked, "If more Ministers are not provided, and do not come over soon, We shall have all the late German, French and Irish settlers, become followers of the New Lights or join other Sectaries, and the interests of the Church be entirely lost for they are already at a very low Ebb."[87]

Much has been written about the immorality of life in the back settlements. There was a lack of sexual mores, and many couples bore illegitimate children, which in this rural society left no stigma. The Sabbath was not observed consistently, and drunkenness and gambling were a part of life on the frontier. However different rural life could be, the family unit remained intact.[88] In the backcountry, the slaveowner and the yeoman farmer worked the land, and transportation of goods to market in Charleston was by land and was a major issue. Woodmason observed in his diary, "All the Creeks being full, and impassable; for no Bridges are yet built in the Country—Nor are there any ferries or Boats—We pass at the Fords when the Waters are low—and when up, all Communication is cut off."[89]

Differences between the coastal elite and the backcountry became painfully apparent. Political leaders on the coast were completely absorbed in their own affairs and their own advancement. The backcountry was a more primitive agricultural society, where the individual took a higher priority than the community, a region of hard work and poverty compared to the wealth and leisure of the coast.[90] The area was less dependent on slave labor, more self-sufficient and less tied to foreign markets, although it did aspire to a more fully developed market economy with credit, circulation of money and goods, slavery, and staple agriculture.[91] Settlers in the backcountry, even though very individualistic, were in favor of political institutions that would promote not only economic development, but social development as well in the form of churches, schools, and towns, and eventually a higher degree of political clout with the low country.[92] Desiring a small government and a high degree of autonomy, they found themselves with quite the opposite situation, paying higher taxes, and meeting demands for military service, declarations of allegiance, and eventually military action.[93]

The American Revolution was not only a struggle between the colonists and the mother country over power and authority but one between the local aristocracy and the rising middle class of small farmers, shopkeepers, and artisans in conjunction with disenfranchised laborers and servants of the lower class.[94] Those in the backcountry were also kept at a distance from the colonial powers in Charleston. With all courts and administrative offices in Charleston, all settlers had to process legal documents there, and by 1770, the lack of a regional court system had been duly noted, as these trips were at significant cost to the individual.[95]

The backcountry was never fully satisfied with the policies of the ruling class. Its issues were clear—unfair representation in the colonial assemblies, religious discrimination, the neglect of courts and schools, and inequitable taxation.[96] With the population increasing by the early 1760s, participation was repressed at both the provincial and local levels, as the Whig elites in the east were uneasy about including such unsophisticated and unrefined settlers in the governing process.[97] In South Carolina, high property qualifications for holding office just perpetuated the coastal elite's firm control of government, and although representation from western districts was mandated by the South Carolina constitution during the war, it made little difference.[98]

The backcountry never achieved the same level of economic or social importance of the low country until after 1800, when cotton took over in the Piedmont and created plantations and their accompanying wealth that were so characteristic of the low country.[99] However, in 1768, economic conditions had improved for the backcountry, and a *Boston Chronicle* news dispatch noted that "the northwestern, north and northeastern parts of this province, have lately been so greatly improved that we are informed, the quantity of hemp made last year is nearly doubled this; that the inhabitants now manufacture most of their linens ... saw mills are erecting in various parts; and the produce of goods has been so great this year and that we may soon expect, from Camden alone, 2,000 barrels of flour."[100]

The 1760s saw the development of further tensions that created havoc in the backcountry of South Carolina. Political leaders on the coast were busy responding to Parliament's encroachments on their own affairs, and were not attending to the needs of settlers by providing for frontier forts.[101] In addition, the increasing population in the backcountry necessitated the need for social order that was not forthcoming. The need for courthouses, schools and jails conflicted with the coastal elite who did not want to establish these institutions. Thus, cattle and horse thieves roamed the countryside stealing from the permanent settlers.[102] The justice of the peace was responsible for maintaining law and order, but with all the responsibilities that came with the office, stopping frontier banditry was nearly impossible.[103] Permanent settlers complained that these people paid no taxes nor rent for property, and lived like Indians, utilizing a hunter-gatherer lifestyle and stealing from other white settlers.[104] The Indians were no longer a threat, but now social ties began to break down, and even though squatters, poachers and petty thieves were an issue, organized bands of vigilantes posed a greater threat to the region.[105] The Regulator Movement in South Carolina was born as political and social conflicts in the backcountry challenged the powers of the low-country elite.

With support from thousands of settlers, Regulators became the primary enforcers in the backcountry, working to subdue those who threatened law-abiding citizens and their property, banding together to respond to a wave of crime that engulfed the backcountry in the mid–1760s.[106] An extract of a letter published in a newspaper from Pine Tree Hill (Camden), dated May 14, 1767, noted that "on the 6th instant, a number of armed men, being in search of Horse Stealers, robbers, &c., discovered a parcel of them in camp on Broad River, where an engagement soon ensued, and the Thieves were put to flight, and though none of them were taken, it is reasonable to suppose, from the quantity of blood on the ground, that some of them were killed. They left behind them ten horses, thirteen saddles, some guns, &c."[107]

The predatory excursions of the bandits became very organized as they moved through the backcountry. "The gang of villains from Virginia and North Carolina … we hear are more formidable than ever as to numbers, and more audacious and cruel in their theft and outrages. 'Tis reported that they consist of more than 200, form a chain of communication with each other, and have places of general meeting; where … they form plans of operation and defence, and (alluding to their secrecy and fidelity to each other), call their places Free Mason Lodges."[108] From the *South Carolina and American Gazette* of August 7, 1767, a victim of the bandits described how "he is then tortured to produce money he has not, and is happy, if he, his wife and helpless children are not sacrificed to the rage and disappointment of those vile miscreants."[109] The assembly of South Carolina received a shocking grievance in late 1767: "Our large Stocks of Cattel are either stolen and destroy'd—our Cow Pens are broke up—and All our valuable Horses are carried off—Houses have been burn'd by these Rogues, and families stripp'd and turn naked into the Woods."[110] By June 1768, the Regulators controlled the colony from fifty miles inland all the way to Cherokee country and became a major intrusion in individual lives, going as far as intervening in family affairs, collecting debts, and settling old scores with old enemies.[111]

The complaints about the lack of ministers, poor schooling, and the justice system mounted as the burden on the settlers became unbearable. Woodmason in his journals remarked, "And no Marriage Licence can be obtain'd but in Charlestown—And ev'ry Person must repair to get Married, that would marry judicially and according to Law—for We have not Churches wherein to publish Banns, or Ministers to Marry Persons, Wherefrom, the Generality marry each other, which causes the vilest Abominations, and that Whoredom and Adultery overspreads our Land."[112] Woodmason defended the Regulator movement and saw the backcountry as a legitimate part of South Carolina society. While his statements can be seen as somewhat exaggerated, the essence of his statements have some merit.[113]

He feared that without an education or some type of trade, there would be more hunters and foragers who would disrupt civil society. "Through the Non-Establishment of Public Schools, A great Multitude of Children are now grown up, in the Greatest

Ignorance of everything, Save Vice.... They will learn no Trade, or Mec[h]anic Arts whereby to obtain an honest Livlihood, or practice any means of Industry."[114] The legal system frustrated Woodmason as well. "For can We truly be said to be try'd by our Peers when few or No Persons on this North Side of Santee River are on the Jury List? The Juries of ev'ry Court are generally compos'd of the inhabitants of Charelstown or its Environs."[115] Woodmason was concerned that those on juries knew nothing of the geography of the backcountry or the concerns of its people and had to "decide on Matters of which they [have] no proper Conception."[116] And with Charleston the only place to transact legal affairs, "the inhabitants were consequently forced, either to submit to the grievous delay and ruinous expense of prosecuting their claims there, and carrying criminals to Charles-Town, or to take the redress of their grievances into their own hands."[117]

There are several salient points that need to be made regarding the South Carolina Regulation. Farmers, millers and storekeepers who were advancing economically were becoming the new backcountry planter class in the mid–1760s, and hunter-gatherers were becoming outsiders as they became squatters on land without securing it through proper channels.[118] But it should not be implied that farmers and hunters were always two separate and distinct groups, because many yeoman farmers were unable to conquer the frontier and were forced into a life of hunting and foraging for their survival.[119] Farmers living a marginal existence could be subject to droughts, which could result in foraging expeditions through the countryside and subsequent thievery.[120] In the end, Regulators were not only seeking order in the backcountry, but a specific type of order that was consistent with the needs of the rising planter class.[121] Given the diversity of ethnic and religious backgrounds in the backcountry, farmers and planters were united in their grievances to rid the backcountry of those who offended the new social order.[122]

By 1769, Regulators were able to persuade the Assembly to pass the Circuit Court House Act, which established courthouses and jails in Orangeburg, Ninety-Six, Camden and Long Bluff. That same year, there is no mention of Regulator happenings, but that did not mean the end of grievances. There were still no public schools in the backcountry, and controversies surrounded the location of the construction of the courthouse in St. David's Parish, for example.[123] But by 1769 the Regulator movement was over. A group called the Moderators helped stall the vigilante movement of the Regulators, and when the governor issued a general pardon to most Regulators in 1771, it was finally the end of a chaotic and violent decade in the backcountry.[124]

North Carolina had its own "Regulator" movement, which differed from the one in South Carolina. North Carolinians in the backcountry were protesting corruption and credit policies from local merchants that they felt were unreasonable.[125] Tax lists from Orange, Randolph, and Montgomery Counties suggest that the Regulation was not a movement of just poor subsistence farmers but included members from all ranks of society.[126]

In August 1766, the Sandy Creek Association in Orange County formed and the Regulator movement in North Carolina was underway.[127] Corruption was rampant as provincial treasurers profited from public taxes. County clerks and registers charged exorbitant fees, which did not appear to take place in the east.[128] Even before the Sandy Creek Association was born, complaints were being aired. "There is a Law that provides that a Lawyer shall take no more than Fifteen Shillings for their Fee in the County Court.—Well, Gentlemen, which of you has had your Business done for Fifteen Shillings? They exact Thirty for every Cause."[129] Feelings ran deep as the long-term effects of this malfeasance were unacceptable. "But as these Practices are contrary to law, it is our Duty to put a Stop to them before they quite ruin our Country, or that we become willing Slaves to these lawless Wretches, and hug our Chains of Bondage, and remain contented under these accumulated Calamities."[130] Lawyers extracted large sums from their clients, and Scottish merchants in particular, with strict credit terms that resulted in more cases of debt, and thus became the targets of increased hostility.[131] A variety of protest methods were used by the participants, including lawsuits, civil disobedience, limited acts of violence, petitions to the governor, direct pressure on local officials, finally resulting in a military confrontation.[132]

One account describes the homegrown justice perpetrated by the Regulators. "Sundry persons ... have combined together in traitorous Conspiracies, and committed several Riots and Routs; and particularly that a number of the said Inhabitants ... did enter the House of the Honble Francis Corbin Esq ... and with Force, carried him about 70 or 80 miles from his Home, and held him in Duress, until he, by giving them a Bond of a most unusual nature, procured his Releasement."[133] One Ralph McNair testified that on October 9, 1770, he saw a number of men "who were chiefly armed with wooden cudgels or cow skin whips wherewith they assaulted and beat John Williams Esq."[134] He also witnessed a band of men "pursuing Colonel Edmund Fanning till he took shelter in the store of Messrs Johnston and Thackerston which they instantly beset, demolishing the windows and threw dirt and stones or brickbats into the house in order to force him thence."[135]

To further aggravate circumstances, sheriffs would seize property because of delinquent taxes, and then sell it later to friends or political associates.[136] But what is remarkable about these events is that none of the local officials in the backcountry had any experience in public office prior to moving to North Carolina other than tax assessor or constable, which might explain the tendency toward corruption.[137] Almost all the local officials were migrants from other colonies, so their attachment or identification with the region was not strong. Moreover, many felt that holding political office was a way to make money, although not always by legal means and with a limited view of the level of responsibility that public office demanded.[138] Herman Husband, a successful farmer and influential leader during the Regulation movement, echoed the thoughts of many. "Who can justify the Conduct of any Government who have countenanced and encouraged so many Thousands of poor Families to bestow their All, and the Labour of many Years, to improve a piece of waste Land, with full Expectation of a Title, to deny them Protection from being robed [sic] of it all by a few roguish Individuals, [who] have never bestowed a farthing thereon?"[139]

In 1768, Presbyterian ministers were trying to prevent the spread of further violence and unrest. They wrote a letter to Governor William Tryon stating, "We cannot but express our abhorrence of the present turbulent and disorderly spirit that shows itself in some parts of this Province, and we beg leave to assure your Excellency that we will exert our utmost abilities, to prevent the infection spreading among the People of our charge, and among the whole Presbyterian Body in this Province as far as our influence will extend."[140]

Governor Tryon responded to a petition by the Regulators on May 21, 1768, where he condemned their actions. "The Grievances Complained of by no Means warrant the Extraordinary Steps you have taken, in Assembling yourselves together in Arms, to the Obstruction of the Court of Justice, to the Insult of Publick Officers, and to the injury of private Property."[141] But his lack of movement on the issue further fanned the flames. In September 1768, Tryon used force when he sent 1400 militiamen to protect the superior court at Hillsborough.[142] But intimidation and violence were emblematic of the times. In a letter from Superior Court in Hillsborough in 1770, Tryon received word that on September 29, "at about 11 O'Clock the Court was opened, and immediately the House filled as close as one Man could stand by another; some with Clubs, others with Whips and Switches, few or none without some Weapon!"[143] The letter continued, "Mr. Williams an Attorney of that Court was coming in and advanced near the Door when they fell on him in a most furious Manner with Clubs and sticks of enormous Size and 'twas with great Difficulty He saved His life by taking Shelter in a Neighboring store House."[144]

The state assembly inflamed matters further and brought the issue to the breaking point in 1771 when it passed a riot act that made riotous behavior a felony, and offenders could be tried in any of the state's six courts, even possibly charged with treason.[145] Even though Tryon was in fact concerned about corruption, he had to preserve order in the province, as he had to prove to London that he could administer the province properly.[146]

On March 19, 1771, Tryon informed his colonels of militia, "I ... am determined ... to March with a Body of Forces taken from several Militia Regiments into the Settlements of the Insurgents, to reduce them to Obedience, who by their Rebellious Acts and Declarations have set the Government at defiance and interrupted the Course of Justice by obstructing overturning and shutting up the Courts of Law."[147] On May 16, the Battle of the Alamance took place, and was a fairly swift affair. "The Action begun before Twelve OClock on Thursday the 16 about Five Miles to the westward of great Alamance River, on the Road leading from Hillsborough to Salisbury."[148] The action was short, "but after an Hour the Enemy took to Tree Fighting and much annoyed the Men who stood at the guns which obliged Me to cease the Artillery for a short Time and to advance the first line to force the Rebels from their Covering."[149] Tryon reported that "after the Battle near 100 of the Rebels (who stiled themselves regulators) were found dead on the field of Battle. Several of the Reg. leaders were taken prisoner who were afterwards tried at Hillsborough condemned & Executed, which restored peace to the Country."[150] The Battle of the Alamance was the final nail in the coffin of the Regulators.

The backcountry never had their grievances redressed, nor did they ever gather again for political gain.[151] John Adams's reaction to Tryon's march noted the nonsensical British response. "This established in the minds of those regulators such a hatred towards their fellow-citizens, that in 1775, when the war broke out, they would not join them. The King has since promised them pardon for their former treasons, upon condition they commit fresh ones against their country."[152] The *Boston Gazette* complained that "the people in that province have been intolerably oppressed; and the government instead of duly attending to their repeated complaints, and redressing their grievances, have encouraged numbers to enlist as soldiers, and under the command of their late humane Governor, to stain their fields with blood."[153] But in the first great sectional struggle of the colony, the east had triumphed over the west and consolidated its power over the next three-quarters of a century. Alamance was a struggle at the local and provincial level and was unrelated to differences with Great Britain, even though political rights and individual liberty were at stake.[154]

A new governor of North Carolina took office in August 1771, and Josiah Martin immediately discerned that some of the Regulators' concerns were legitimate.[155] He expressed concern for the embezzlement of public taxes, not only with his assembly but with royal officials as well, suspended a customs collector at Port Currituck, and charged county clerks with overcharging for fees.[156] Martin urged lawmakers to consider various judicial reforms, but the assembly turned him down when they met in January 1773.[157] Governor Martin, while angering some of the leadership of the colony, attempted to re-structure the court system, the tax system, and the office of sheriff, sympathizing with former Regulators.[158] As a result of the Regulator riots, North Carolina remained a divided province on the eve of war. The backcountry remained divided on its allegiances.[159] Although there is scholarly disagreement about the nature of the Regulation movement in North Carolina, it can be safely said that North Carolinians fought against abuses of the laws, while South Carolinians lacked essential social and political infrastructure and clamored for more.[160]

The very complex system of alliances found in the backcountry cannot be explained solely on the basis of ideology, ethnic backgrounds or economic status. Rebels and loyalists both had storekeepers, planters, slaveholders and non-slaveholders in each camp.[161] Many former Regulators felt uneasy about resisting British rule because they had taken an oath of allegiance to the King after Alamance. They also felt that joining the other side would mean collaborating with former enemies. When the war came, many Regulators chose to sit it out, while others became Loyalists.[162] However, it was Whigs rather than loyalists who became the key element of the new planter class.[163]

The concept of who was a loyalist and who was not was a very complicated issue on the eve of Revolution and remains so to this day. Many historians have attempted to dissect this thorny problem and have arrived at differing conclusions. Loyalists came from all different classes, political leanings, and races of people.[164] Many in the backcountry had loyalist leanings because they came from ethnic and religious minorities that had more to fear from the ruling elite in South Carolina than from the British government that ruled from across the Atlantic.[165] Many loyalists chose a side based on who was in power at a particular time, and many chose only when it was politically expedient or for one's own personal survival.[166] Many Scottish immigrants who lived throughout North Carolina gave their allegiance to Great Britain for fear of losing land that had been granted by royal authority and from fear of reprisals if they took the other side.[167] Many Germans felt the same way.

Loyalist writers from the time felt those instigating revolution were reckless in their attempts to separate from the mother country, and that mob rule would be the result of such efforts.[168] Author Peter Moore contends that looking at how local neighborhoods formed may inform how allegiances were formed as well. His portrayal of the Waxhaw settlement located in the lower Catawba River Valley along the North Carolina–South Carolina border merits scrutiny as to how and whether partisans remained loyal to the Crown or joined the patriot movement.[169] The first settlers of the region, the Scots-Irish, moved into the creek and river bottoms on the east bank of the river beginning in 1750 and occupied the best parts by the mid–1760s.[170] They had migrated from the northern colonies. The second wave of settlers arrived just before the Revolution and moved west-ward from the port of Charleston and settled the more remote higher ground in the eastern half of the settlement.[171] The recent immigrants were more likely to live in the upper eastern part of the Waxhaws settlement. Recent immigrants were also more likely to join the British than their more established neighbors to the west.[172] The possible explanation of this phenomenon has a link to geography and migration routes. The settlers who migrated

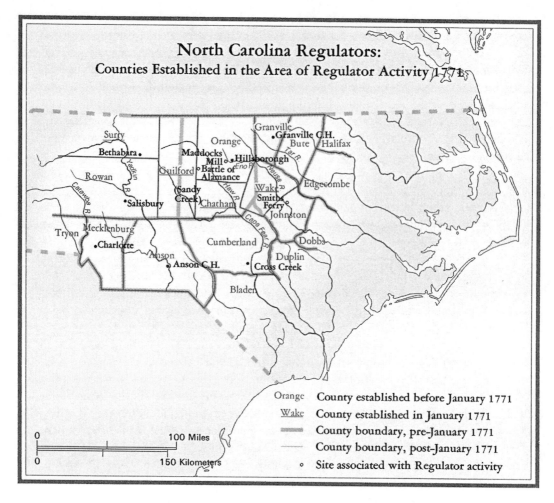

Above and opposite: **Mapping the Responses to the North Carolina and South Carolina Regulation (republished with permission of Princeton University Press, from *Atlas of Early American History: The Revolutionary Era, 1760–1790*, edited by Lester J. Cappon).**

overland from other northern colonies had established kinship links that better integrated them, while those who entered the port of Charleston lacked those connections, and further separated by class and distance, failed to be integrated into the established community.[173] Moore contends that "recent immigrants were shunted to the geographic, social, and political periphery of the community."[174] In the end, the failure of the integration of the entire community also had the deleterious effect of creating Whig and British sympathizers within the same community, and thus creating differences and animosities that the war only deepened.[175]

Those who switched sides also had a motive for doing so. Many who failed to achieve the military rank that they felt they deserved, switched sides to satisfy the sense of their own self-worth.[176] According to Robert Gray, a colonel in the royal militia, "The establishment of the King's government naturally & unavoidably occasioned an entire change of civil and military officers throughout the province, whilst their predecessors in office were stripped of their consequence and sent home.... The pangs of disappointed ambition

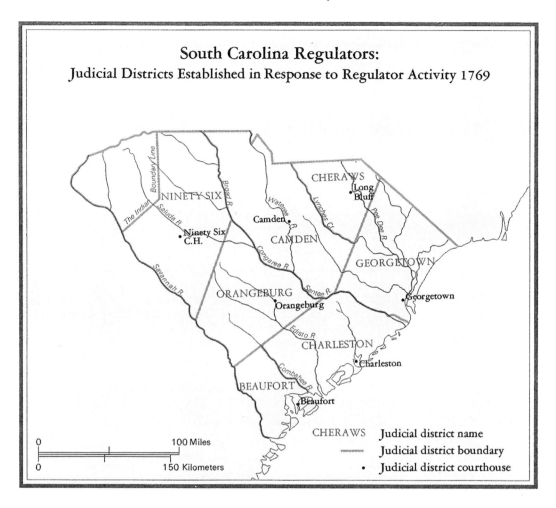

South Carolina Regulators:
Judicial Districts Established in Response to Regulator Activity 1769

soon made these men view all our transgressions with jaundiced eyes and … they were in general, especially the militia officers, determined to avail themselves of that opportunity to reestablish themselves in power."[177] Many remained disaffected, and some areas in the backcountry wanted nothing less than to be left alone.[178]

The onset of hostilities between Britain and the colonies caused consternation for those in the backcountry, even though the Regulator movement had ended. However, in North Carolina, class tensions and the inability to unite common interests after the Regulation created a new set of issues. Many poor and middling farmers preferred neutrality and disliked any central authority. As the war escalated, and pressure from the Whigs increased, the opportunity to rise up when the British army was present ignited a vicious civil war. Disaffection had turned to loyalism, and the war took on a new meaning—a preference for local authority and control of the valuable resources of the backcountry, such as grain, livestock, horses, arms, and defense of the land itself, which so many had worked so hard to tame.[179]

As the military conflict got underway, the Committees of Safety became the real transitional government in the colonies, and they were interested in measuring support for the Patriot cause.[180] The backcountry was probed for support for the patriots, who now were in control in the low country, to encourage support and to prevent wavering in support of independence.[181] Whig militias became the enforcers of social and political control in the backcountry, and this created even more disorder, as neutral inhabitants found themselves under intimidation and were transforming into loyalists, further deepening resentments among the disaffected.[182]

The British had always overestimated loyalist support, and to confirm his belief that the loyalists would be of great value in the coming campaign to take the southern colonies, George Germain, Secretary of State for the Colonies, dispatched James Simpson, former royal Attorney General for South Carolina, to determine the efficacy of loyalist support in the backcountry.[183] Simpson correctly assessed the tension in the backcountry. "There are many who left the Town and settled in the Country, where they found themselves ... resentful for their past Injuries, they are clamorous for retributive Justice, and affirm that the Province will never be settled in Peace until those People whose persecuting spirit hath caused such calamities to their fellow subjects shall receive the punishment their Iniquities deserve."[184] He was convinced that "with respect to the lower Class of people ... they will without trouble submit quietly to the Government that supports itself."[185] His fatal mistake was his summation of what this all meant: "[T]he obvious consequences which appear to me are that it will be very practicable to re-establish the King's Government in S. Carolina."[186]

With the opening salvos of war in Massachusetts, South Carolina was counting on the unity of the population in the coming days and months, and the backcountry became a prime target of both British and patriot forces for the allegiance of its diverse inhabitants.[187] The British invasion of South Carolina in 1776 failed miserably, and a new constitution was signed as patriot morale soared.[188] Down at the coast, the British moved southward in 1778, and Colonel Archibald Campbell captured Savannah. The call for loyalists went out, but the attempt failed. Patriot militias were on the prowl and threatened anyone who did not return to the rebel camp within three days.[189] Rebels had passed laws so severe that even the most ardent loyalist would not rise up.

Conflict still ensued, and legislation passed by the General Assembly in 1777 and 1778 was used by the Patriot minority to force men from neutrality.[190] Oaths became a way to enforce political conformity, but they also divided families and communities. Loyalist and patriot militias, against orders from their respective commanders of regular forces, used plunder and the destruction of property to instill fear.[191] As British forces spread to the North Carolina border in 1780, loyalist uprisings spread quickly, and those who were neutral now had to choose sides.[192] The end result was a devastated landscape and people who knew no bounds to this violent cycle.

But in 1780, difficulties for the Americans began to mount. The American commander Benjamin Lincoln had moved his troops into Charleston, which occupied the narrow peninsula between the Ashley and Cooper Rivers, being unduly influenced by political leaders. As Charleston came under siege, only a fraction of reinforcements arrived to help the beleaguered commander. The second invasion of South Carolina was going to be different. Nathanael Greene was going to be facing a stacked deck by the end of the year. Even though the British were far superior in manpower and firepower, and were by far the greatest force, their strategy would be called into question. Even though the British knew loyalist support was essential, and Parliament was less inclined to reinforce their troops in America, the opportunity for success in the southern colonies was far from certain.

2

British Strategy
and the Fall of Charleston

As the stalemate in the war in the north dragged on, the British began to rethink their American strategy. One of Germain's undersecretaries, William Knox, proposed several plans for retaking the south after being petitioned by the governors of Georgia and South Carolina in 1777.[1] A campaign in the south presented several advantages. Mild southern winters would enable the British to retain all conquered territory, unlike the north, in which cold weather forced retrenchment for the winter. There would be better coordination between army and naval forces with several navigable rivers south of Chesapeake Bay. A smaller population would require fewer troops to hold posts. After taking the southern colonies, the British would interrupt trade that was carried on through southern ports, crippling an important revenue stream for the colonies.[2] "The conquest of those provinces is considered by the King as an object of great importance in the scale of the war," Germain wrote to Henry Clinton, "as their possession might be easily maintained and thereby a very valuable branch of commerce would be restored to this country and the rebels deprived of a principal resource for the support of their foreign credit and of paying for the supplies they stand in need of, as the products of those provinces make a considerable part of their remittances to Europe."[3]

Curiously, the civilian population became the focus of their planning. The war could not be won unless loyal and even neutral civilians were organized by the army. There were some in the British government that felt the South was the most vulnerable point in the American colonies. Its population was not just centered on the coast, but scattered throughout the interior. South Carolina was mostly African-American with a pervasive fear of slave insurrections, an unpredictable Native American population on the western frontier, and a contentious relationship between the coastal elite and the backcountry.[4]

Thus, "it is the King's intention that an attack should be made on the southern colonies with a view to the conquest and possession of Georgia and South Carolina. The various accounts we receive from those provinces concur in representing the distress of the inhabitants and their general disposition to return to their allegiance."[5] An important goal was to secure British Florida's northern border; with it, the southernmost state of Georgia would also be secured, and each state north of it would be subsequently taken.[6]

As the war pressed on, and as the government's majority in Parliament began declining, the administration felt that the loyalists in the southern colonies were the best hope of securing support.[7] But political and military considerations made an incompatible combination as a basis for waging war. In order to secure political support for the war, strategy became linked to loyalist support.[8] Also, opposition to sending troops to America was growing. Not only were new taxes proving difficult to raise, but the focus on the war that was developing in the European sphere was replacing the attention to the war three thousand miles from the home islands.[9]

Once the French had become allies of America, many in Great Britain felt that America was already a separate nation and not a colony. The French entry into the war meant an expansion that would place the British and French colonies, especially the Caribbean, West Africa and India, at risk through military conflict. America began its descent down the priority list of where military resources were redistributed, especially to the West Indies and to Britain itself.[10] Some Britons believed that the French entry into the war was a chance to unify the British empire and focus all animosity on the traditional enemy of Britain.[11] The entry of Spain into the war in June 1779 posed another serious threat. Britain insisted, however, that they continue the war against their combined enemies. So tapped out were their resources that the Spanish entry into the war in the South had the effect of reinforcing Britain's commitment to the South, where loyalists could be employed to compensate for the forces being diverted to attack Spanish posts.[12]

By the late summer of 1779, Henry Clinton firmly believed that the loss of Charleston would be fatal to the American cause, and with the stalemate growing in the North, Clinton began thinking more and more about the importance of the South. South Carolina would have to be occupied and Charleston held the key. Georgia would fall as well, and more importantly, the whole area could be overrun before Washington could send any reinforcements there.[13] The only way that Britain was to achieve success in the South was to remain superior in land and sea power. Reinforcement and supply were essential, and the only way to hold this advantage was by sea power.[14] But doubt and worry began to creep into Clinton's thinking. Clinton became skeptical about the support of loyalists in the region and was unsure whether the fall of Charleston would provide the loyalist support he needed.[15] The question of whether the sea lanes would remain open concerned him as well, as the British had not effectively contained French threats in the recent past. In 1779, Admiral d'Estaing had sailed to the aid of the American rebels, moving north from the Caribbean to Georgia unchallenged.[16]

With Charleston as the main goal of the southern plan, Clinton was told by Sir James Wright, the last British Royal Governor of Georgia, that "the reduction of the province of South Carolina is certainly a matter of the utmost importance in every point of view and its weight in the scale of the rebellion very considerable."[17] He added that "the port of Charleston has carried on more trade than all the other colonies together ... [and] that they have seen ... 100 wagons in town at a time from the northern colonies as far as from Philadelphia, and that at least 250 wagons were continually going backwards and forwards."[18] Wright was "of the opinion that if South Carolina is thoroughly reduced it will give a mortal stab to the rebellion, and I am firmly persuaded it will in a great measure break the spirit of it."[19]

Wright's advice to Clinton was specific and contained a warning as well. "If a body of the King's troops were to march from Augusta [Georgia] into Carolina ... it would not only give an opportunity to all well-affected subjects to join the King's army ... prevent the Carolinians from escaping or retreating from Charleston or the plantations in the middle part of the settlements ... and its probable that it might so divide their measures as to make South Carolina fall an easy conquest to His Majesty's arms."[20] His experience in Georgia prompted him to mention what would happen if the interior of South Carolina was not cleared of rebels. "But if no army goes there, when Charleston is forced it is feared that the people will retire back and that province will be much in the same situation with this [Georgia]. You may be possessed of the town and seacoast but the rebellion will still continue and be kept up and the loyal subjects harassed and ruined as they have been here."[21] This was a forward-thinking point by Wright, and is what in fact occurred in 1781–1782.

Clinton was waffling on what to do and was sold on the idea of using every available man for taking Charleston. After submitting his views to his council, they recommended a diversion into the backcountry, and Clinton accepted their decision.[22] Clinton now had to make a decision about how to get the main body of his force to Charleston. When he met with his council, they recommended the ocean route, and he complied with their recommendation.[23] Acquiescing to his council was not an accident. Clinton's first foray into Charleston had resulted in some blame on his part, and he had no intention of repeating that. Thus, he would have a ready-made excuse if events did not result in success. His council would be his scapegoat.[24]

With George Washington bottled up in New Jersey, Henry Clinton, the British commander charged with carrying out the southern strategy, sailed for Charleston on December 26, 1779. He left approximately 15,000 troops in New York with Lieutenant General Wilhelm von Knyphausen and sailed south with approximately 8,000 more. With Clinton on the voyage south was his second in command, Lord Cornwallis, who would be the military commander responsible for bringing the Carolinas back into the British fold. Clinton wanted to use his two bases, New York and Charleston, as the centers of the British position in North America. An army in the South would be able to remain afield as long as it would remain in contact with Charleston and have access by sea to New York. By incrementally expanding its hold on territory, loyalists would have the time and means to emerge and expand into militias that could hold territory and enable British soldiers to move on to new areas.[25]

In the diary of Lieutenant Christian Friedrich Bartholomai, an Ansbach Jaeger deployed to Charleston, three propositions for conducting the war in America were near the beginning of his commentary. The first was that "the war in America must be conducted primarily from the sea for the most part the operations of the army are dependent upon the activity of the fleet." His second and third propositions demonstrate a haunting preview of events to come. "The army can accomplish nothing of importance without the support of the fleet, and may, above all, not venture very far inland without risking great danger."[26] Bartholomai explained further that "enough for subsistence can not be found deep in the countryside."[27] His reasoning was based on simple logistics. Cities and villages were widely separated and "it is impossible … to obtain subsistence even for a corps of several thousand men."[28]

But with all the assumptions made about the southern campaign, the Loyalists were the key to success. Henry Clinton knew better than anyone that the assumptions made about the new southern strategy were faulty. He knew what was to come, but duty called, and it was his job to carry out the King's orders.[29] The capture of Charleston in 1780 whetted the British public's appetite about the return of America to the fold, but by the end of the year, it was clear that America was not a singular branch of the British nation, but part of a faction united against Britain.[30]

Charleston by the eighteenth century was a plantation-based economy much like Barbados a century before.[31] The migration to South Carolina was chiefly due to overcrowding on the island itself, and more importantly, these migrants brought with them their wealth and experience from Barbados.[32] The Barbadians introduced slavery to South

Carolina before rice became a staple crop, and soon there were four blacks to every one white with the aristocracy in firm control. But rice became a major export from Carolina, for in 1707, the late Governor of Carolina, John Archdale, wrote, "Seventeen ships this year came ladened from the Carolinas with Rice, Skins, Pitch, Tar, etc., in the Virginia fleet."[33] By 1765, with Charleston established as an important economic engine, the population was about six thousand white people and seven to eight thousand enslaved Africans.[34] Charleston had become the fourth largest city in the colonies and by far the most important port in the South. Ships from Europe, Africa, the West Indies and coastal cities of North America docked there.[35] The British, in assessing their strategy, correctly assessed the economic strength of South Carolina, as its staple crops of rice and indigo created fortunes for those involved in the export business, such as wealthy planters and merchants Henry Laurens, William Henry Drayton, and Charles Cotesworth Pinckney.[36]

Charleston sat at the end of a long, marshy peninsula with the Ashley River on the west and the Cooper River on the east. There were no heights on the peninsula. "The city itself … consists of 1,020 houses, which are built along broad unpaved streets intersecting one another at right angles, each house having a garden and standing twenty to one hundred paces from any other. The warm climate makes the open spaces necessary. They permit the cool breezes to play through the city and the houses and thus make the heat of June, July, August and September at least tolerable."[37]

Captain Johann Hinrichs, a captain in the Jaeger Corps, was a highly educated, intelligent, and observant officer who was interested in politics and also spoke of the economic conditions in the colonies. His diary is filled with observations about his experiences and many details about the city of Charleston and its surroundings. Of its harbor he wrote, "[It] is very good except for the fact that, at the inlet, from Lighthouse Island to Sullivan Island, it is surrounded by a sandbank (the Bar). There are five channels through the Bar. The deepest, the Ship Channel, has twelve feet of water at low tide and twenty-one and one-half at high tide and does not permit the passage of ships heavier than an English 40-gun ship without their being lightened. At some places the Bar is covered with only three to four feet of water."[38] In Charleston proper, Hinrichs noted that "the English churches, of which St. Philip's in Meeting Street is the oldest, show wealth and good taste," and that "there are a German Lutheran church, several Presbyterian meetinghouses, a synagogue, a public library, etc."[39]

Josiah Quincy of Boston, who visited Charleston in 1773, reported in his memoir a very glowing description of the city. "I can only say, in general, that in grandeur, splendor of buildings, decorations, equipages, numbers, commerce, shipping, and indeed in almost everything, it far surpasses all I ever saw, or even expected to see in America."[40]

Hinrichs, when describing the geography of the region, was not as flattering as he was in his observations of the city of Charleston. "The entire coast from Cape Hatteras southward is flat, marshy land, for the greater part still uncultivated and suited for the growing of rice only, a habitat of snakes and crocodiles, strewn with bodies of stagnant water and covered with impenetrable woods."[41] Outside of the city, "the endless forests, which cover the entire country, deprive the soil of the beneficial rays of the life-giving sun and fill the whole atmosphere with unhealthy miasmas, which affect the germination and growth of every living organism."[42] Hinrichs, like other astute observers of the importance of Charleston to the rebellion, believed that "since no other province makes such excessive profits by contraband trade, which is facilitated by the situation of her harbor and the many small rivers and islands around the capital … no group of people was more warmly interested in this rebellion than the merchant population of South Carolina. It is quite different with the inhabitants of the country, who here go under the name of 'back-country people.'"[43]

After a brutal voyage from New York, during which most of the horses died and the shortage of provisions created havoc for man and beast, the British arrived at the rendez-vous point off Tybee Island at the mouth of the Savannah River on February 1.[44] Clinton's plan to capture Charleston seemed to be well-designed. Lincoln's force on the Neck was undermanned. To make matters worse for Lincoln, morale had plummeted as a British force took control of Savannah, and with d'Estaing sailing away, Lincoln had been left to defend the port city with not much hope of any significant reinforcement from Washington.[45] Clinton decided to land his army south of the city, as the area north of the city was too shallow and too close to American lines. Going overland and using transports to move across waterways, Clinton decided to lay siege lines across the peninsula formed by the Ashley and Cooper Rivers.[46]

After making repairs from the hazardous voyage, the British entered North Edisto Inlet on February 11 and disembarked their troops on John's Island, some thirty miles south of Charleston.[47] This fact was not lost on the defenders who reported "that between forty & fifty Sail of the Enemy's Ships … were landed in force."[48] Clinton's first action was to occupy and control Stono Ferry that connected John's Island with James Island, and then he quickly moved to seize Wappoo Cut, a creek that separated James Island from the mainland. On March 7, he crossed the cut and established batteries on the west bank of the Ashley River.[49]

Responsible for the defense of Charleston was General Benjamin Lincoln, head of the Southern Department, commanding approximately 3,600 troops, mostly militia.[50] Lincoln had believed that an attack on the rear of the town was probable, and in August 1779 had set about improving fortifications and requesting more men, which included Continental troops and cavalry, and asking Governor Rutledge to draft members of the South Carolina militia.[51] It was not until December that Congress, along with Washington's help, sent the entire Virginia line as well as the North Carolinians, totaling 3,300 men, south to reinforce Lincoln.[52] Lincoln had decided to defend Charleston and had drawn back Continental troops from Augusta. It was clear that he had no intention of attacking the British, but was going to risk everything to defend the city.[53] Even though the Continental Congress had not specifically ordered Lincoln to defend the city, sending him reinforcements held the implication that holding the city would be the best solution.[54] A line of fortifications was set up that extended from the Ashley River to the Cooper River.

Across the Neck was a canal, and behind it lay a series of redoubts covered by double abatis, constructed by 600 slaves impressed by Governor Rutledge.[55] On the west side of the peninsula were small redoubts mounting four to nine guns each, and on the Cooper River side were seven, each mounting three to seven guns. Fort Moultrie and Fort Johnson, located on either side of the entrance to the harbor, were ready to prevent a British incursion into the harbor. The American navy, commanded by Commodore Abraham Whipple, consisted of nine ships, a far cry from the overwhelming British force.[56]

One of the most important defensive advantages Lincoln had for the defense of Charleston was the Bar. It was a large sandbar that sat in front of Charleston harbor, and there were only a few channels that ships could pass in order to reach Charleston. It required great skill to cross it, and Lincoln wanted to use it to foil any attempt the take the city. Unfortunately, his dealings with Whipple made the task more difficult than it needed to be.[57] The correspondence from Lincoln to Whipple indicated the nature of the difficulty Lincoln had in trying to secure the harbor. On January 30, 1780, Lincoln told Whipple, "Your duty will be, if possible to prevent the enemy from entering the harbor; if that should be impracticable, you will in the next place oppose them at Fort Moultrie." He then added, "You will have the internal part of the bar, and the adjacent shoals sounded and buoyed by some of your officers and the best pilots you can obtain."[58]

Whipple disagreed with Lincoln about defending the bar and thought that it was impractical for fear of running his own ships aground. On February 7, the commanders of the boats wrote to Whipple telling him "that when an easterly wind is blowing; and the flood making in (such as opportunity as the enemy must embrace for their purpose) there will be so great a swell in five fathom hole, as to render it impossible, for a ship to ride moving athwart, which will afford the Enemies ships ... the advantage of Passing us."[59]

A week later, Lincoln let Whipple know the consequences of not commanding the entrance to the harbor. "Yet, I am so fully convinced that the probable services, which they will render there, should the enemy attempt to come over the Bar, and the evils consequent on their getting into this Harbour, that the attempt ought to be made, and that the measure thereby can be justified—for the safety of this Town lyes in reducing the enemy's attempt on it to a land attack."[60] Whipple and his subordinates concluded that it would be better to take a position near Fort Moultrie and contest a British attempt to gain the harbor in that manner. Lincoln was now facing the loss of Charleston's most important defensive asset in an otherwise poor position. Interestingly, the Continental Congress had stipulated that Whipple was under the command of Lincoln, yet when Whipple did not follow Lincoln's orders, he was not removed from duty, possibly for fear of losing the support of Whipple's commanders.[61]

Nonetheless, one British soldier, Lieutenant John Peebles, noted in his diary that the Americans had begun preparing the gauntlet. "The Rebels have blown up the Lighthouse at Chas Town bar & spoil'd other marks for entering the harbor, & making other preparations for a serious defense. we can't properly invest the place unless the men of war get in & destroy their ships &c."[62]

On March 7, Clinton crossed the Cut and established batteries on the west bank of the Ashley River. On the 9th, Clinton wrote to Lord George Germain, "My intention is to pass to the neck of Charleston as soon as possible. The enemy I find have collected their whole force to that place. This is said not to exceed 5000 men at present but reinforcements are daily expected."[63] Recognizing that the rebels had made the defense of Charleston their primary goal, Clinton added, "I have determined on my part to assemble in greater strength before it and with this view have called immediately to this army a corps I had left in Georgia with order by a march to Augusta to try the temper of the back settlements and draw off some opposition from this point. They will pass the Savannah River and join me by land."[64] Clinton was never convinced of the strength of loyalism in the backcountry, and his doubts surfaced in his letter to Germain. "It will remain to be proved if we have that number of friends in the interior part of the country there has formerly been such strong reasons to believe in. In this case it is to be expected the reduction of the province will immediately follow that of the capital."[65]

Concerns were growing on the American side. Approximately 1500 North Carolina and Virginia Continentals didn't arrive until April 7, and the British threat was looming. Governor Rutledge requested the South Carolina militia help defend Charleston, but that fell on deaf ears as the militia feared an outbreak of smallpox in the city, as had happened the previous November.[66] Lieutenant Colonel John Laurens, son of one of the wealthiest men in

America, Henry Laurens, and former aide-de-camp to Washington, wrote th
the 14th with the latest news and problems in the defense of Charleston. He relat
ington that the government did not want to defend the bar as it was impractical,
will "form a line of battle in such a manner as to make a cross-fire with Fort Moult
called the Middle Grounds being on the right of the ships, and the fort advanced on \ .u left."[67]
Also, "the attention of the engineers has been distracted by different demonstrations on the
part of the enemy, and they have not perfected the line across Charleston Neck."[68]

Lachlan McIntosh, a veteran American military commander, recorded on March 12
that he "found the enemy had possession of James Island since the latter end of Feby. And
were now erecting a work upon Bunkers Hill, behind Fort Johnsston. We saw their Fleet,
Transports, Store-ships, Merchant Men &ca in Stonoe River, through Wappoe Cut, from
Fergusons House in Trad Street & some Men of War over the Barr. Our Horse skirmished
near Ashly Ferry."[69] Samuel Baldwin, recording events in his diary, had even bleaker news.
"In the afternoon [March 21], the inhabitants and troops in town were surprised to see the
ships quit their station near the fort [Fort Moultrie] and come up to the town."[70] On the
24th, the news got worse as "this day the term of service of the greater part of the North
Carolina militia being expired, they marched homewards in the evening to the number of
seven or eight hundred, or more."[71]

The small American fleet did not prevent a British entrance into the harbor, but
found a position called Shute's Folly at the mouth of the Cooper River between the town
and the island. Several of the ships were sunk there to create an obstacle to British shipping and preserve a lifeline to the North. The rest of the fleet took position behind this
log-and-chain boom.[72] On the 19th, Johann Ewald, a Hessian officer, recorded in his diary
that "yesterday the fleet ... awaits a favorable wind to cross the bar and ... should ... a
severe storm come up which would force this fleet to go far out to sea, it could plunge us
into a very great disaster and tear the entire undertaking to pieces."[73] His skittishness was
wasted, for on March 20, the British crossed the bar unopposed, since Whipple had not
risked any of his ships to possible British fire.[74]

Lincoln had established General Isaac Huger at Monck's Corner, thirty miles north
of Charleston, to keep his lines of communication open and a possible avenue of escape,
and with 500 men in his charge, Huger was having his own problems.[75] Francis Marion, to
become known as the "Swamp Fox" for his daring maneuvers as a guerrilla fighter in the
southern campaign, wrote Lincoln in early March: "[W]e have not but twenty five rounds of
cartridges per man for the light Corps nor no Ammunition for the Militia now come in."[76]

Marion's military life began in 1761 as a lieutenant in a militia company. He rose to a
position of respect in his community, became a delegate to the South Carolina Provincial
Congress in 1775, and helped drive the royal governor from that state. After all organized
resistance in the South was destroyed, Marion began his career as a guerilla. After Kings
Mountain, Marion was such a menace that Cornwallis detached his notorious cavalry
commander Banastre Tarleton to get rid of him. He could not. Marion had an excellent
grasp of strategy and tactics as well as demonstrating personal bravery.[77] "Never avoiding
danger, he never rashly sought it; and acting for all around him as he did for himself, he
risked the lives of his troops only when it was necessary," recalled Henry Lee.[78] Lee described Marion as "about forty-eight years of age, small in stature, hard in visage, healthy,
abstemious, and taciturn."[79] The area between Camden to the coast and between the Pee
Dee and Santee Rivers was his theatre of operations.

Tarleton, on the other hand, would prove to be much more formidable as the war progressed. Tarleton came from a wealthy family, and had been educated at the University of Liverpool and Oxford. He was preparing to study law when a cornet's commission was purchased for him; he left for America, where he remained fairly undistinguished until the events of 1780 would begin to define him. According to author Christopher Ward, he was unmatched in his capacity to move rapidly, attacking with daring and vigor. As a man he was cold-hearted, vindictive and ruthless.

The British moved ever closer. On March 29, Lieutenant Anthony Allaire, a loyalist, wrote in his diary, "Sir Henry Clinton, with the British and Hessians, grenadiers, Light Infantry, and Yagers, passed over Ashley river to Charleston Neck, early in the morning. Spent the day in viewing Charleston and found it not a little like New York; for Ashley and Cooper Rivers form a bay exactly like New York."[80] Clinton had crossed at Drayton Hall, thirteen miles from Charleston and the former home of William Henry Drayton. Drayton, a wealthy planter from South Carolina, had been elected to the Continental Congress and had been a Revolutionary leader. The crossing was unopposed because Lincoln did not have enough troops. Samuel Baldwin observed that "the enemy, it is said, have crossed Ashley River in three different places."[81]

Johann Ewald noted on April 1 that "since yesterday we have been occupied with transporting heavy pieces, munitions, entrenching tools, gabions, fascines of different lengths, and provisions from Linning's Creek over the Ashley River to Gibbes Ferry."[82] On the 8th, at "about four o'clock this afternoon the fleet hove in sight, coming up under full sail … and passed Fort Moultrie—the Rebel fort that they boasted of on Sullivan's Island, which no fleet could ever pass. They were but a few minutes passing."[83] At that moment, the British had cut off Charleston Neck, and their fleet in the harbor had prevented an evacuation by sea. The Cooper River remained the only access point for the Americans. The British began sealing off all avenues of escape so as to begin the siege of Charleston.[84]

After the crossing was completed, the British marched down the Dorchester Road toward Charleston, reaching the Quarter House in the evening, now just six miles from Charleston.[85] "On the night of the 1st of April broke ground within 800 yards of the rebel works," Clinton wrote to Germain.[86] Clinton had to consider the American fortifications on the Charleston Neck. One of the keys to the defenses was an almost continuous series of redoubts and forts that spanned the peninsula. The main defensive line consisted of a ditch in front of a double-palisaded parapet, which would be difficult to penetrate.[87] The Americans had also dug a canal that was eighteen feet across and six to eight feet deep between the two tidal creeks on the Ashley and Cooper sides of the peninsula and were able to control the depth of the water in the canal by the use of sluices on the Cooper River side.[88] It was going to be a formidable obstacle in the event they had to storm the works.

In Charleston, "the besieged were busy transporting cattle and all kinds of chattel from the city to the shore. Moreover, many families are leaving the city out of fear of famine," noted Johann Ewald.[89] Clinton also took care of the last escape route of the Americans. Clinton detached Lieutenant Colonel Webster to "counter the designs of the Americans, and to break in upon the remaining communications of Charles Town."[90] According to Tarleton, "[T]he Americans had joined a body of militia to three regiments of Continental cavalry, and the command of the whole was intrusted to Brigadier-General Huger. This corps hold possession of the forks and passes of Cooper River, and maintained a communication with Charles Town, by which supplies of men, arms, ammunition and provision might be conveyed to the garrison during the siege, and by which the Continental troops might escape after the defences were destroyed."[91]

The Americans were taken totally by surprise. "General Huger, Colonels Washington and Jamieson, with many officers and men, fled on foot to the swamps close to their encampment."[92] Clinton remarked in his letter to Germain that "the surprise and defeat of the collected cavalry and militia of the rebels and the possessing Biggins Bridge over Cooper by Lieut. Colonel Tarleton with the horse, the Legion, and Major Ferguson's detachment, gave the command of the country to Colonel Webster … forbidding by land all further access to the town from Cooper to the inland navigation. An armed naval force which the Admiral sent into Sewee Bay and another stationed in Spencer's Inlet completed the investiture to the sea."[93]

On April 10, "Major Crosbie carried in a Summons for the Town to surrender & the Garrison to become prisoners of war, they sent back a written answer, declining to accept these terms & soon after began a smart fire."[94] "His Duty and inclination Led him to hold out to the last extremity."[95]

By the 12th, Lincoln had decided to meet with his staff. Lachlan McIntosh made note of this important meeting:

> With every information he [Lincoln] could obtain of the numbers & Strength of the Enemy &ca. &ca. [he was compelled] to take up the Idea, & Consider of the Propriety of evacuating the Garrison when without hesitation I gave it as my own opinion that as we were so unfortunate as to suffer ourselves to be penned up in the Town, & cut off from all resources in such Circumstances, we should not loose an hour longer in attempting to get the Continental Troops at least out, while we had one side open yet over Cooper River, upon whose safety, the Salvation not only of this State but some other will (may) probably depend & which I think all the other Gentn. seemd to acquiesce in.[96]

Lincoln asked them to consider the option, but a British artillery barrage from the Neck quickly ended the meeting.[97] Samuel Baldwin recorded in his diary that "this morning at 10 o'clock the enemy began to cannonade the town and have continued firing almost incessantly during the day." He also mentioned that "a nurse and a young child that was in her arms were both killed by a ball. Another woman and two or three soldiers have also been killed."[98]

On April 20, Lincoln was forced to gather his council to discuss the present situation. With only two options left, evacuate the town or offer favorable terms, Lincoln sought to capitulate to Clinton, but his terms were rejected because they would allow Lincoln to move his garrison out of the town. Clinton resumed firing on the town.[99]

Cornwallis was now on the scene, and Clinton had appointed him the new commander east of the Cooper. Cornwallis closed the last escape route of the Americans. The post at Lampriers Point, the key to communication and the movement of troops on the Cooper, was lost. Anthony Allaire noted on April 28 that "intelligence being received the Rebels had left the fort at Lempriere's Point, and gone to Charleston, we got in motion and marched down to discover the fact. We arrived about four in the morning, and found the fort occupied by the Navy."[100] Johann Ewald added that "four guns, a great amount of ammunition, and a number of small vessels have fallen into the hands of Lord Cornwallis. Now the besieged are surrounded on all sides."[101]

The month of May began the death struggle for Charleston. On the front lines, "fatigue … was so great that, for want of sleep, many faces were so swelled they could scarcely see out of their eyes."[102] By May 7, "Fort Moultrie surrendered to the British Forces—this fort by many people was reckoned impregnable yet the want of provision and the weakness

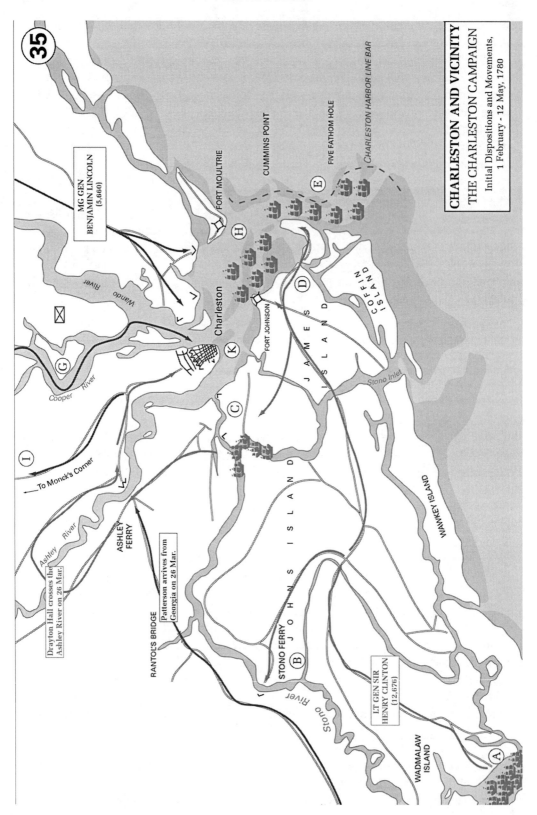

CHARLESTON AND VICINITY
THE CHARLESTON CAMPAIGN
Initial Dispositions and Movements,
1 February - 12 May, 1780

of the Garrison obliged it to surrender, greatest of the regt. which was posted there being ordered to reinforce the Town."[103]

The next day, Anthony Allaire noted, at "six o'clock in the morning, Sir Henry Clinton sent in a flag, and demanded the surrender of Charleston. General Lincoln requested cessation of hostilities till eight o'clock ... and the truce continued until four o'clock Tuesday evening when Sir Henry Clinton receiving a very insolent request, sent in word that he plainly saw that gen. Lincoln did not mean to give up the town; that the firing should commence at eight o'clock in the evening, at which time began a most tremendous cannonade... and an incessant fire of musketry all night."[104]

John Peebles, noting the contents of an intercepted letter in his diary entry for May 10, said that "it appears that they have given up all hopes of keeping the place, or of getting away, now that their retreat is cut off by Lord Cornwallis & must soon surrender for want of provision, which corresponds with the information of the deserters."[105] Civilians were suffering as American troops ravaged the city, searching private homes for food while other foraging parties pulled apart fences for palisades and took slaves for military operations within the city.[106] Exhaustion and militia who refused to do their duty were beginning to create problems for the defenders.[107] "The robberies of Excesses of all kinds committed by the Soldiers in this Town Puts the Soldier under the disagreeable Necessity of ordering an immediate punishment to be inflicted on every Soldier found strolling in any part of the Town without written pass from the Command Officer of the Corps he belongs to for that purpose the Brigadier will order patrols in the several parts of the Town as often as they may judge proper."[108]

On May 12, it was all over. The articles of capitulation were signed, and Major General Alexander Leslie led British troops into the city to handle the surrender.[109]

Descriptions of the defenders and of the town are poignant and portray the state of the American cause at this point in time. "The rebels appeared thin, miserable, ragged and very dirty. Their officers appeared to be primarily young people and poorly dressed, each in a different colored uniform and with different facings, which gave the officers of their army the appearance of comedians about to commence a show, together with their troops, without shoes, made a very comical scene," wrote Lieutenant Bartholomai of the Ansbach Jaegers.[110] Another account by Johann Ewald described the garrison as consisting of "handsome young men whose apparel was extremely ragged, and on the whole the people looked greatly starved."[111] John Peebles saw the town the day after the surrender and observed "all disorder & confusion there yet—many very good houses in town some hurt with shot & some burnt & those burnt near two years ago are not rebuilt. The streets are all sand except her [*sic*] & there a piece of brick pavement as the sides."[112]

Even north of town, in Dorchester, a village on the Ashley River twenty miles from Charlestown, the war played its hand. "Every house has the appearance (tho' deserted) of the inhabitants having lived in affluence & luxury, but this wanton Rebellion has broke in upon

Opposite: **Legend: (A) Feb., British land on Simmons Is.; (B) 16 Feb., British occupy Stono Ferry; (C) 6 March, Supply depot established on James Is. abandoned; (D) 11 March, British occupy Fort Johnson and Cummins Point; (E) 20 March, British fleet enters Five Fathom Hole covered by guns at Cummins Point; (G) 7 April, Woodford's Virginia brigade arrives via Cooper river; (H) 8 April, British fleet passes Fort Moultrie and enters harbor; (I) 13 April, American cavalry defeated at Monck's Corner; (K) 11 May, GEN Lincoln surrenders. 12 May, garrison lays down arms.**

their pleasures, & their comforts too, & reduced many wealthy people to shifting circumstances, & the poor negroes to a starving condition in many places hereabout."[113] As evidence of division among the Americans, when military stores were being collected, Captain George Rochfort of the British army told the defenders that "you had a great many rascals among you who came out every night and gave us information of what was passing in your garrison."[114]

The British had achieved a total victory. Lincoln lost approximately 5500 men captured; Continental troops were to be prisoners of war, and militia were allowed to go home on parole. Ewald reported that "we captured four hundred guns, including twenty brass cannon and a number of mortars and howitzers, and large stores of rum, coffee, rice and indigo."[115] But Ewald made another important observation in his diary, one that would foretell of the shifting sands of British fortunes. On May 20, he wrote, "Yesterday and today two thousand of the captured militia were paroled to their homes under the condition that they do not serve again until they have been exchanged. This transaction, which really borders of the ridiculous—doing something beneficial for a person of which he has no idea—was arranged only to avoid sustaining these guests. However, this economy will cost the English dear, because I am convinced that most of these people will have guns in their hands again within a short time."[116]

British casualties as reported by Clinton were 76 killed and 189 wounded, with American casualties similar.[117] The army and navy had performed well, the physical geography of Charleston allowed it to be cut off, and its citizens lacked the necessary support role in the war effort.[118] It was clear that Lincoln had mismanaged the siege as well. He should have evacuated Charleston before the British fully surrounded the city. He did not have enough troops to hold Charleston and attack the British on both the Ashley and Cooper River fronts. Whipple failed to defend the Bar and allowed the Royal Navy access to the harbor that they otherwise should never have had.[119] The evacuation of Lampriers Point on the Cooper River gave the British easy access to an important American position, while Brigadier General Isaac Huger and the cavalry failed to prevent the British from establishing a foothold in the area east of the Cooper River.[120]

The siege of Charleston was the high point of Clinton's leadership. He not only used his favorite tactic (envelopment), but the enemy helped him to carry it out. He was a hands-on administrator, exposing himself to enemy fire but carrying out his tasks with a deadly efficiency. He never won the love and admiration of his men, but they were handled with skill and put into the best possible situation for success.[121] But even with this total victory, negative thoughts about the future were never far away. Clinton still had doubts about the loyalists and was not sure whether the surrender of Charleston would be enough to win the backcountry.

Others shared his concerns. A writer in the British army sent a letter to a friend in London worried that "our victories have been dearly bought, for the rebels seem to grow stronger by every defeat.... I wish our ministry could send a Hercules to conquer these obstinate Americans, whose aversion to the cause of Britain grows stronger every day."[122] A Hessian, Captain von der Malsberg, was not convinced about the thoroughness of the British victory, either. "Time will show what effects the capture of Charlestown will have on the system of war, but I do not believe that anything will be settled at present; everything will probably be dependent upon the success or non-success of the English fleets."[123]

Clinton believed that the entire colony of South Carolina was firmly under British control. However, his relationship with Cornwallis was never good, and events to come would challenge that relationship and the nagging question of French sea power that still lingered.

3

The Long Road
to Kings Mountain

Two months before the fall of Charleston, wealthy planter Henry Laurens opined in a letter to Richard Henry Lee, Revolutionary War statesman and signer of the Declaration of Independence, that the state of affairs in South Carolina was as grim as ever. "I must now retire & weep for the distresses of my Country.... Women & Children scattered & wandering, a sickly season approaching, disaffected Brethren committing Murders & every violence, Negroes absconding, the Enemy arming them, Commerce arrested, agriculture greatly interrupted, a scene which melts such a heart of mine."[1] He had also wondered when the relief from his neighbor to the north, Virginia, was going to materialize.

After the fall of Charleston, the cold reality of a subdued South Carolina weighed heavily on many minds. In early March 1780, Laurens complained to Richard Henry Lee: "The Country will now be left open to them.... we have no army to oppose them; it is reported that they have detached 2000. Men to march towards Camden.... we have no troops but General Caswell's Brigade & Col Beauforts [Buford's] & the shattered remains of our horse."[2] Laurens's son John wrote to his father two weeks after the surrender of Charleston, complaining about the problems inside the besieged city prior to the fall: "Besides the force of the Enemy without, we had to struggle at home against incapacity in some very important persons, treasonable neglect of duty in the Staff departments, and almost a general disaffection of the Citizens."[3]

A group of 350 Continental soldiers under the command of Colonel Abraham Buford had been heading to Charleston before it fell, and once news of the British victory reached them, they decided to head back to Hillsborough, North Carolina, to regroup. With Buford's group were Governor John Rutledge and other important government officials from Charleston. Cornwallis decided to send Tarleton after Buford. On the afternoon of May 29, Tarleton came upon the rear of Buford's unit and later described the action in a report to Cornwallis: "After a march of 105 miles in 54 hours, with the corps of cavalry, the infantry of the Legion mounted on horses, and a three pounder, at Wacsaw [Waxhaw] near the line which divides North from South Carolina the rebel force commanded by Colonel Buford, consisting of the 11th Virginia and detachments of other regiments from the same province, with artillery and some cavalry were brought to action."[4] According to Tarleton, "The attacks were pointed at both flanks, the front and reserve by 270 cavalry and infantry blended, and at the same instant all were victorious, few of the enemy escaping except the commanding officer by a precipitate flight on horseback."[5]

Dr. Robert Brownsfield recorded in a letter he wrote later: "Tarleton, having arranged his infantry in the centre and his cavalry on the wings, advanced to the charge with the horrid yells of infuriated demons."[6] Buford, "now perceiving that further resistance was hopeless, ordered a flag to be hoisted and the arms to be grounded, expecting the usual treatment sanctioned by civilized warfare."[7] But the Americans were cut to pieces. Men who tried to surrender were cut down. Many suffered multiple wounds. Those who had been wounded and were lying on the ground were stabbed or hacked to death. Many who asked for "quarter" were cut down. When it was over, approximately 113 Americans were killed and 150 were wounded. The phrase "Tarleton's Quarter" would forever stand for unrestrained, cold-blooded murder.

Tarleton attributed the massacre to the loss of the cavalry's commanding officer, "which stimulated the soldiers to a vindictive asperity not easily restrained."[8] He was specifically referring to himself when his horse was shot from under him. Tarleton also blamed Buford for the loss of life by "committing a material error in ordering the infantry to retain their fire till the British dragoons were quite close; which when given, had little effect either upon the minds and bodies of the assailants, in comparison with the execution that might be expected from a successive fire of platoons or divisions, commenced at the distance of three or four hundred paces."[9]

With the Charleston victory firmly in hand, the British began plans for the subjugation of South Carolina. British confidence was at an all-time high. From the most common citizen to the most influential member of society, the locals pledged allegiance to the British.[10] Clinton was heading back to New York, and Cornwallis was tasked with the elimination of resistance in South Carolina. But it was Clinton's proclamation on June 3, just before he set sail for New York, that rattled the cages of many in the backcountry. In essence, he said that all those who failed to return to their allegiance would be considered enemies of the state. No one would be allowed to sit out the war in neutrality. After the defeat in Charleston, many people had taken loyalty oaths, hoping that these oaths and subsequent protections would mean that the British would leave them alone and allow them to sit out the remainder of the war in peace.[11] But Clinton created a firestorm within the state, motivated partisan actions, and produced widespread antipathy to British rule, thus escalating tensions in the backcountry and increasing resistance to the British presence in the state.[12]

However, Clinton was not a visionary and had a completely different view of the matter. "The ... proclamation ... had soon the most happy effects, as numbers with their arms came in every day to headquarters from the remotest parts of the province, many of them bringing in their former oppressors."[13] He added, "I must say I had every reason to believe, from the state of the province at that period, that the measure would be attended with the happiest effects."[14] Unlike a commander who owns his decisions, Clinton absolved himself of responsibility for his actions: "But, as I did not remain there myself to watch its progress and assist its operation, I shall not take it upon me to disprove the evil consequences ascribed to it since, as from the powers I gave Lord Cornwallis I cannot think myself responsible for them."[15]

Clinton believed that suppressing the rebellion would involve "occupying a few strong posts in the upper country, and the putting of arms into the hands of the King's friends for their defense against the straggling parties of rebels who might be still lurking amongst them."[16] Thus, Clinton ordered Cornwallis "to march up the north side of Santee River to Camden, where I understood a body of rebel troops were collecting with the intention of making a stand there; and I directed Lieutenant Colonel Balfour to move with another corps up its southern shore towards the district of Ninety-Six, while a third was put in motion on the Savannah River in Georgia."[17]

Cornwallis was charged to "regard the safety of Charleston and the tranquility of South Carolina as the principal and indispensible objects of his attention. When the necessary arrangements were completed … I left His Lordship at liberty … to make a solid move into North Carolina, upon condition it could be at the time made without risking the safety of the posts committed to his charge."[18] Clinton also advised Cornwallis "to send a few troops to establish a small post in Cape Fear River … as such a measure might probably prove in the meantime an encouragement and succor to the King's friends on the upper parts of that river … and strike terror into the lower counties, which were by far the most hostile."[19]

Charles Cornwallis was an experienced military man with impeccable credentials as a leader. He was born in London in 1738, to a family of either Irish or Cornish descent; the Cornwallis family had been well established in both London and Suffolk County for nearly four centuries by the time of his birth.[20] He received his education at Eton but was not long destined for an academic life. By the age of eighteen, he had settled on a military career and secured his first of many commissions as an ensign in the First Guards in December 1756.[21] He then became a member of the House of Commons in 1760 and fought in the Seven Years' War, moving up to lieutenant colonel and being cited for bravery on the battlefield.

Like many of the British officers in the Revolutionary War, Cornwallis gained his military experience on European battlefields, beginning at Minden in 1759. He and his regiment distinguished themselves at the Battle of Villinghausen in 1761, during which the Prussian-British alliance inflicted heavy casualties on a larger French army. After his father's death in 1762, Cornwallis took his place in the House of Lords.

While never wavering from his sense of duty to the king, Cornwallis showed serious reservations about the treatment of the colonies. He was particularly opposed to the schemes of taxation levied on the colonies and steadfastly voted against these measures.[22] Often supporting constitutional rights for the Americans, he was nonetheless promoted to major general by King George III in 1775. A sense of duty motivated Cornwallis to serve in America, and he was promoted to lieutenant general in 1778 and began serving under Major General Clinton.

Service in America brought frustration to Cornwallis, as well as some military successes. After a failed attempt to capture Charleston in 1776, Cornwallis and Clinton sailed north to join William Howe at New York, which resulted in a resounding success. However, following Washington's crossing of the Delaware for a surprising victory at Trenton, Clinton blamed Cornwallis for the failure to defeat Washington afterwards. Cornwallis had postponed a late afternoon attack on the Americans, only to find the next morning that Washington had escaped. Tension between the two lasted throughout the war and created a lack of cohesion in administering the conflict. Cornwallis saw success at Brandywine and Germantown in 1777, but few victories were in hand from that point forward.

However, events moved quickly for Cornwallis. In the fall of 1778, Cornwallis went back to England to care for his ailing wife, who died in February 1779. Though consumed with grief, Cornwallis returned to America. With Howe replaced by Clinton as commander in chief, Cornwallis was now second in command, and with the fall of Charleston,

Cornwallis was now directed to conduct the southern campaign. The entry of France into the conflict caused Cornwallis's eyes to shift to the southern colonies. Cornwallis began to believe that victory in America would hinge on the British ability to gather and reinforce southern loyalists as well as blockading ports that the approaching French fleet could use to land troops and supplies.[23]

Committed to the army, Cornwallis was also devoted to his family. Care for the family fell to Cornwallis after his father's death, and Cornwallis saw to it that his brothers and sisters were taken care of in terms of careers and marriages. Cornwallis, by all accounts, was devoted to his wife and two children. To most Americans, Charles Cornwallis is best remembered for his October 1781 surrender to George Washington, which effectively brought an end to hostilities between Great Britain and America. Despite this, Cornwallis enjoyed a long and distinguished career extending nearly five decades and spanning three continents as a soldier and a politician.[24] Perhaps ironically, he first landed in the Carolinas in May 1776 before rejoining the main British army in the North.

The British, after the fall of Charleston, had penetrated into the countryside establishing forts at Georgetown, Beaufort, Camden, Rocky Mount, Augusta, and Ninety Six in their determined effort to bring royal government to South Carolina. Unfortunately for them, they antagonized the countryside, and by the summer of 1780, most men came down on the side of resistance.[25] Tarleton's massacre of prisoners at the Waxhaws had a significant effect. Tarleton also burned a church at Indiantown, while Major James Wemyss of the 63rd Regiment of the British army invaded the area between Georgetown and Cheraw. Using a scorched-earth policy, he burned his way through seventy miles of territory at times about fifteen miles wide, including the destruction of Presbyterian churches, which aroused the passions of the Scots-Irish.[26]

Women in the backcountry were not immune to the escalating conflict. Some were tortured for information, while others, along with their children, watched in horror as their husbands were executed. The partisan Francis Marion observed "women and children sitting in the open air around a fire, without a blanket, or any clothing but what they had on."[27] Eliza Wilkinson wrote a terrifying account of a raid on her house by two British soldiers: "It was terrible to the last degree; and what augmented it, they had several armed Negroes with them, who threatened and abused us greatly. They began to plunder the house of every thing they thought valuable or worth taking; our trunks were split to pieces, and each man, pitiful wretch, crammed his bosom with the contents of our apparel, etc., etc., etc."[28] Wilkinson also mentioned that they entered the house "with drawn sword and pistols in their hands" to add to the horror of this encounter.[29]

Colonel Robert Gray, a Loyalist, mentioned in his account written during the war, that in areas controlled by the rebel partisans, "tories ... hid themselves in swamps, from whence they made frequent incursions upon their enemies." He noted that "both parties equally afraid of the other dared not sleep in their Houses, but concealed themselves in swamps, this is called lying out."[30] Hit-and-run tactics characterized the warfare in the backcountry. They tended to be small affairs, and many encounters may not have been recorded.[31] Francis Marion, known as the "Swamp Fox," was an impressive guerilla. Marion, a man small in stature but not in talent, could strike the enemy and just as quickly disappear into a swamp to fight another day. Tarleton once pursued him through dense swamps for twenty-six miles and could not catch him.[32] Marion's steady and deliberate attacks on the British, in concert with other partisan groups, gradually tore at the fabric of the supply system from Charleston to the backcountry. Cornwallis was facing an uphill battle on more than this front.

As the fires of the American Revolution began to rekindle in the south, violence became a serious issue as a variety of groups began to reinterpret the standards of what constituted proper warfare. The lack of centralized power in the state meant that militias were acting with little oversight and thus had to scour the countryside for supplies because of lack of support from the now nonexistent state government.[33] It also meant that militia units were more likely to mistreat prisoners as they created their own rules on how to deal with them.[34] In North Carolina, both enrolled and volunteer militias failed to function as units with a righteous cause, becoming vigilante groups using retaliation as an instrument of irregular warfare.[35]

Meanwhile, Cornwallis faced many issues in South Carolina. The loyalists presented a specific set of problems. Cornwallis had decided to organize the militia into two classes: men over forty who would primarily guard their own districts and manage paroles, and younger men who would serve in the field for six months. He thus utilized all his soldiers for battling the enemy and avoided using troops for policing in the various localities.[36] As Cornwallis moved into the interior and his supply lines began to be strained, he entrusted the tasks of procuring supplies to loyalist militia foraging parties.[37] This went poorly for the earl, as some people were only partially paid for their cattle, and filed claims for recompense after the war.[38]

Cornwallis faced other social and political issues as well, particularly in the area of who was to become a British ally. If the British had sought out Indian allies, it would have alienated many loyalists. If they rejected slave and Indian support, they might have to deal with an alliance between those two groups and the Whigs who they were trying to defeat. Since the British placed their major focus on the loyalists, they never fully utilized the three groups, which together could have united to eliminate the rebellion once and for all.[39] Cornwallis attempted to create useful militia to secure the province and promote domestic tranquility, but it suffered from ineffective leadership and proved little help to Cornwallis.[40] Nonetheless, Cornwallis made his way toward Camden.

By the early summer of 1780, Congress had yet to appoint a commander of the Southern Department. George Washington would have selected his trusted subordinate Nathanael Greene, but Congress did not consult Washington.[41] Congress instead selected Horatio Gates, who was officially appointed on July 13, 1780. Gates had been the hero of Saratoga in 1777, arguably the most important victory of the American cause to date. But Gates had some baggage of his own. He had allegedly tried to replace Washington as commander-in-chief after a string of disastrous setbacks for the Americans, but the ever-vigilant Washington had become suspicious of Gates and never trusted him again. Gates certainly had his supporters, and still enjoyed popularity, but Washington's judgment of him would prove to be true as Gates moved south to secure an American victory against a well-trained British army.

When Gates assumed command of the army on July 25th, he found an appalling situation as he rode into camp at Deep River in North Carolina. Troops were not getting regular rations and flour was in short supply. The main cavalry was at Halifax refitting, and the army was scattered with the main body made up of 1,500 Delaware and Maryland Continentals in camp, and with North Carolina militia at Moore's Ferry on the Yadkin River with Major General Richard Caswell.[42] Gates's announcement that his men should be ready to march immediately stunned his officers.[43] If there ever was a time where Gates could apply his organizational skills, this was it. The British were not pressuring him and he had time to organize his men so they could become an effective fighting force.[44] On the 27th, they were on the move.

Not only were his soldiers not ready for combat, but the route they decided to take to Camden was devoid of food and forage, though it was shorter than the route proposed by Major General Baron de Kalb, and by Colonel Otho Williams, deputy adjutant to Gates.[45] De Kalb was a German who had served in the French army and later offered his services to the American army. Claiming to be of aristocratic background, de Kalb was a true fighter and a tough soldier. He was a large man, about six feet tall, and even though he was sixty years of age, he could be found marching on foot with the common soldier. His endurance and stamina were legendary, but unfortunately for de Kalb, Congress would never approve of a foreigner being in command of an American army.

Williams had served since the beginning of the war, and had marched from Maryland to the camp at Boston as a lieutenant of a rifle corps in 1775. He participated in the failed expedition to Quebec, and in 1776, was in a rifle corps fighting at Fort Washington. After his capture in that engagement, he was exchanged and made colonel of the 6th Maryland Regiment, which marched with de Kalb to South Carolina.[46]

De Kalb and Williams wanted to march by way of Salisbury, Charlotte and the Waxhaws, where food and forage could more easily be obtained and the civilians were more aligned with the American cause.[47] But Gates would hear none of it. Ignoring the need for cavalry, Gates was underestimating the value that British cavalry would bring to the battle, especially the talents of Banastre Tarleton.[48] Also a factor in Gates's decision-making process was intelligence he had received from partisan leader Thomas Sumter. Gates learned from Sumter that the British were only using Camden as a springboard for an invasion of North Carolina, and a quick strike from the Americans would possibly reverse the intentions of Cornwallis, and thus patriot forces would have an opportunity to regroup.[49]

Sumter, though considered bold and imaginative, posed several challenges for Greene later in his administration of the war effort. Sumter was considered a poor tactical commander, who attacked when odds were against him, failed to reconnoiter situations, and was unable to coordinate a battle.[50] Henry Lee felt he was "determined to deserve success, he risked his own life and the lives of his associates without reserve. Enchanted with the splendor of victory, he would wade through torrents of blood to attain it."[51] It did not help that Sumter raised new troops by paying them with plunder from loyalists, which helped to touch off vicious civil strife.[52] Sumter's territory ranged between Camden and Ninety Six.

Lack of a unified state of mind between commanders contributed to this pending disaster. As Baron de Kalb moved into North Carolina with his Maryland and Delaware continentals, he was forced to stop at Deep River in North Carolina. Lacking provisions as well as cooperation with Richard Caswell, de Kalb's men were virtually abandoned as Caswell refused to link up with de Kalb or communicate with him on a regular basis.[53] But the advance continued.

On August 7, Gates united with Caswell's North Carolina militia fifteen miles east of the British outpost on Lynches Creek and reached Rugeley's Mill on August 15, where the only provision available was molasses.[54] Given the lack of forage en route to Camden, Gates had the pressing problem of how to feed these men. His troops were marching in stifling, excessively humid weather and were forced to gather whatever supplies they could find along the way. The land itself "was by nature barren, abounding with sandy plains, intersected by swamps, and very thinly inhabited.... the little provisions and forage which were produced on the banks of its few small streams were exhausted or taken away by the enemy," wrote Otho Williams.[55] Sumter wrote Gates requesting a body of men to harass the British supply column coming from Ninety Six. Gates, not knowing the enemy strength nor his own, sent 100 Maryland Continentals, 300 North Carolina militia, and two artillery pieces to Sumter.[56]

Gates's plans and his intentions for moving toward Camden remain mysterious. Few of his inner circle were privy to his exact plans, and his papers do not reveal his purposes on the night in question.[57] Otho Williams had many unanswered questions about the campaign. The state of the army's readiness, the poor provisions available to the army on the route of the march, and the seemingly poor advantages given the American army during the battle plagued Williams for the rest of his life.[58] Historians can only speculate why Gates moved toward Camden the way he did. Possibly he wanted to establish a defensive position that he could fortify, and thus force the enemy from their position or force a retreat because of the threat of partisan bands like Sumter and Marion threatening British supply lines.[59]

The men had been living "chiefly on green apples and peaches which rendered our situation truly miserable, being in a weak and sickly condition," wrote William Seymour in his journal.[60] The green corn on which they were also subsisting did not help the situation. But Gates was about to engage the British army with troops who were exhausted, sick and half-starved, although he outnumbered the British by a nearly 2:1 margin. Numbering 3,052 rank and file soldiers fit for duty, Gates had estimated he had 7,000, but when Williams reported that the number was far lower than Gates's estimate, Gates replied, "There are enough for our purpose."[61]

A major cause of confusion over the relative strengths of the armies was the way the two sides counted troops. The Americans only counted rank and file fit for duty, that is, infantrymen with muskets or cavalry with sabers. They omitted officers, noncoms, musicians, and staff. The British counted everyone present, regardless of their rank or assigned duty. In any case, Gates's command was an army of walking scarecrows, barely able to function. Fifteen miles to the south lay the British army under the command of Lord Cornwallis with approximately 2,200 men ready and concentrating for the fight that was inevitable, and Gates did not know he was there.

Both sides had decided on a night march. Cornwallis had "determined to march at ten o'clock on the night of the 15th and to attack at day break."[62] British private John Shaw wrote, "We came up with their advanced party, about seven miles from Camden, when the light troops and advanced guards on each side, necessarily engaged each other in the dark."[63] But Cornwallis "was unwilling to hazard in the dark, the advantages which their situation would afford him in the light. We then lay on our arms until daybreak, when both armies formed their lines, and approached within 100 yards of each other, and the Americans gave the first fire, which killed and wounded nearly one half of our number."[64]

The Americans formed their battle line before dawn. On the right of the Waxhaws road was General Mordecai Gist's 2nd Maryland brigade, which consisted of three regiments of the Maryland Line and the Delaware Regiment.[65] To the left of the road was Richard Caswell's 1,800 North Carolina militiamen and General Edward Stevens's 700 Virginians. The 1st Maryland Brigade was in reserve in the center under General William

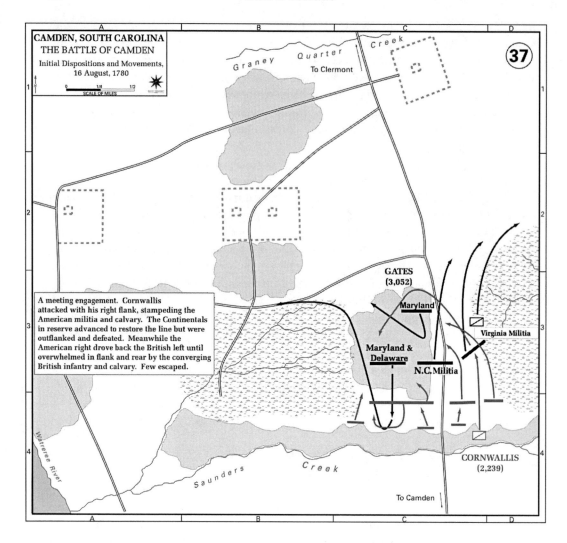

The Battle of Camden, August 16, 1780 (U.S. Military Academy).

Smallwood. Cornwallis had placed his seasoned British regulars on the right side, which meant they would be facing the militia, not the Maryland and Delaware Continentals, who were the battle-hardened veterans and the best the Americans had to offer. However, by this time many of the provincial units on the British left were also seasoned veterans. Garret Watts recalled that "the militia were in front and in a feeble condition at that time. They were fatigued. The weather was warm excessively. They been fed a short time previously on molasses entirely."[66]

For the time being, the Americans were positioned on the high ground, although it was not a very steep slope. The ground consisted of widely spaced pine trees with very little underbrush. Both flanks were anchored by wide swamps, which meant if the flanks held firm, they could not be turned. With artillery unable to operate outside of this confined area, the British had no choice but to go straight in. The British were facing uphill and had Saunders Creek about a mile in their rear; this was the only downside of their position, given their flanks rested on swamps.

Gates wrote, "At day Light the Enemy attacked, and drove in our Light Parties in Front, when I ordered our Left to advance and attack the Enemy—but to my Astonishment, the Left wing and North Carolina Militia gave Way. General Caswell and Myself ... did all in our Power to rally the broken Troops, but to no purpose."[67] The right side of the line, which consisted of de Kalb's Maryland and Delaware troops, held tight. But with the withdrawal of the North Carolina and Virginia militia units, the British now fell upon Smallwood's men, advancing to occupy the ground abandoned by the militia.

Meanwhile, a bitter struggle took place between de Kalb's men and Lord Rawdon's troops on the British left. Baron de Kalb fell in the melee, wounded multiple times. Finally, de Kalb's and Smallwood's troops broke as well, and the survivors scattered. Cornwallis remembered the moment exactly the same, recalling that "our line continued to advance in good order ... and, after an obstinate resistance for three quarters of an hour, threw the enemy into total confusion and forced them to give way in all quarters."[68]

Watts's account describes the poor performance of himself and his fellow soldiers: "The discharge and loud roar soon became general from one end of the line to the other. Amongst other things, I confess I was amongst the first that fled. The cause of that I cannot tell, except that everyone I saw was about to do the same. It was instantaneous. There was no effort to rally, no encouragement to fight. Officers and men joined in the flight."[69] Gates later wrote from Hillsborough, North Carolina, that "the militia had taken the Woods in all directions, and I concluded with General Caswell to retire towards Charlotte, I got there late in the night—but reflecting that there was neither Army, Ammunition, nor any prospect of collecting any Force at that place ... I proceeded with all Despatch hither."[70]

Cornwallis, meanwhile, had "ordered the cavalry to compleat the rout ... and ... continued the pursuit to Hanging Rock, 22 miles from the place where the action happened, during which many of the enemy were slain, a number of prisoners, near 150 waggons ... a considerable quantity of military stores, and all the baggage and camp equipage of the rebel army fell into our hands."[71]

General Gates, who had positioned himself in the center of the line, approximately 200 yards from the front, took off on his horse and never looked back. After reaching Charlotte, as he noted in his report, he then moved on to Hillsborough. Gates had ridden 180 miles from the battlefield. When he was in Charlotte, Colonel John Senf, Gates's chief engineer, wrote in his journal that "he [Gates] arrived that night in Charlotte but no view was left to assemble any forces there, and if it was possible, there was no ammunition, no arms, no provisions, and in the middle of a disaffected country."[72]

Partisan leader William Davie made the observation that "three fourths of this army were militia, these alone might have ben a match for the royal army if properly fought under such advantages as a country covered with woods morasses and broken grounds almost every where affords."[73] Davie further criticized Gates's generalship: "[H]e was entirely unacquainted with the character of the officers or the merits of the different corps which composed his army, and was ignorant of their numbers, having never received a return until after the orders of the 15th were issued, the regular troops wanted rest and refreshment. The whole of the militia wanted arrangement and the ordinary preparation for a battle was intirely neglected among them, in Rutherford's Brigade there was scarce a cartridge made up, and their arms were generally in bad order; the consequences of continual marching & exposure."[74]

Condemnation of Gates, however, was not universal. Thomas Pinckney, an aide-de-camp to Gates during the southern campaign, wrote a letter to William Johnson to defend Gates against accusations made by Johnson in his biography of General Greene. Pinckney delineated several areas where Gates was misunderstood about his intentions. For instance, "that on the movement of the night of 15th of August was not made with the intention of attacking the enemy, but for the purpose of occupying a strong position so near him as to confine his operations, to cut off his supplies of Provisions, from the upper parts of the Wateree & Pedee Rivers, & to harass him with detachment of light troops, & to oblige him whether to retreat or to come out & attack us upon our own ground, in a situation where the Militia which constituted our principal numerical force, might act to the best advantage."[75] It is important to note that Otho Williams knew nothing about this plan, and in his role it is hard to imagine that it escaped him and everyone else in Gates's circle.

Elsewhere in his letter, Pinckney appears to be creating explanations where none had existed. "After the breaking up of the Council of War on the 15th, Col. Williams presented the returns of the Army, from which it appeared that the number was considerably below that at which it had been estimated by the General ... adding however they are sufficient for our purpose." That purpose Gates did not explain it to him, but it certainly could not have been to attack a fortified post, well garrisoned.[76]

Later on in his letter, Pinckney exhibited pure rationalization of Gates's behavior. "Gen gates was not negligent on the subject of intelligence; that he took the means in his power to obtain it, & did all in that line that could be expected from an Officer without secret service money, a stranger in the Country, & who had been in command of the Army only 18 or 20 days."[77] According to Pinckney, Gates acted out of desperation by moving his army to Camden. He could have stayed where he was and starved, or moved to gain some relief. Gates chose to move.[78]

Gates's supporters contend that riding back to Charlotte would not have altered the military situation, and that to put his army back together again would require him to find a position in North Carolina behind the physical barriers of the rivers.[79] The mystery of why Gates placed militia against Cornwallis's regulars remains elusive. Why he did not place his best troops, the Delaware and Maryland Continentals, opposite Cornwallis's best, cannot be explained because the result was a rout, with Cornwallis sending in his cavalry to finish the deal.[80] Interestingly, Gates had not bothered to anticipate enemy cavalry action.

The Battle of Camden broke the morale of the people as well as the reputation of Gates. By leaving the scene of battle while part of the army was engaged, he opened himself up to critics, and they never let him forget it.[81] On October 5, Congress voted to conduct a court of inquiry regarding his actions at Camden. Luckily for Gates, Congress repealed the order on August 14, 1782, and Gates joined Washington's army at Newburgh, New York, as commander of the right wing, a stunning turn of events.[82]

After Camden, Lord Cornwallis ordered "that all the inhabitants of the province, who had submitted, and who had [then] taken part in this revolt, should be punished with the greatest rigor—that they should be imprisoned, and their whole property taken from them or destroyed." Additionally, he ordered "that every militia man, who had borne arms with the British, and afterwards joined the Americans, should be put to death."[83] In various locations, several of the inhabitants were hanged as a result of Cornwallis's order, and many men were forced out of necessity, mainly to save their property, to submit to the British and swallow their pride.[84] Even with the threat of severe punishment and the superiority of British forces in the backcountry, several of the most respectable citizens resisted the stranglehold of the enemy.[85]

The British victory at Camden should have meant an immediate springboard into North Carolina. According to Tarleton, "The immediate advance of the King's troops into North Carolina would ... have been productive of various and important advantages."[86] But circumstances would not allow it. Four days after the victory at Camden, Cornwallis wrote to Germain about the issues he was facing: "I was then at Camden but the corps with me being totally destitute of military stores, clothing, rum, salt and other articles necessary for troops in the operations of the field, and provisions of all kinds being deficient almost approaching to a famine in North Carolina, it was impossible for me to penetrate into that province before the harvest."[87] Tarleton admitted that "the number of sick in the hospital, the late addition of the wounded, the want of troops, and the deficiency of stores upon the frontier, operated with the present heat of the climate, and the scarcity of provisions in North Carolina."[88]

Cornwallis explained the objectives of his North Carolina campaign to Major James Wemyss, which was to raise a considerable number of men and then move to Salisbury to invite all loyalists to form into Provincial corps. They would then advance to Cross Creek so he would be in full communication with Charleston and receive all the equipment he would need by water.[89]

Cornwallis was having reservations about the situation in the backcountry. At Ninety Six, Lieutenant Colonel Balfour had "formed seven battalions of militia consisting of above four thousand men," but Cornwallis had concerns.[90] Cornwallis felt that "this militia can be of little use for distant military operations as they will not stir without a horse, and on that account your lordship will easily conceive the impossibility of keeping a number of them together without destroying the country."[91] His own experience informed him as well. "Many battalions were likewise formed by myself and other officers on the very extensive line from Broad River to Cheraws but they were in general either weak or not much to be relied on for their fidelity."[92] Cornwallis knew the situation was dire, and that there were not enough troops to garrison the entire territory to be held. At Ninety Six, the post was located in a vast hinterland of Whigs and Tories, and the only control the fort had over the region was the area in the fort's immediate vicinity. Uncertainty gripped the British.

As the retreating Americans made their way into Charlotte, Col. Williams noted that "no organization, nor order, had yet been attempted to be restored among the few troops that had arrived in Charlotte."[93] Charlotte was not an ideal place for retreat, as "the general idea was, that Charlotte, an open wooded village, without magazines of any sort—without a second cartridge per man—and without a second ration, was not tenable for an hour, against superior numbers, which might enter at every quarter."[94] The march out of Charlotte to Salisbury was reminiscent of scenes across the hinterlands of New Jersey after the fall of New York: "It consisted of the wretched remnant of the late southern army; a great number of distressed Whig families, and the whole tribe of Catawba Indians."[95] Williams remarked that "the nakedness of the Indians, and the number of their infants and aged persons, and the disorder of the whole line of march, conspired to render it a scene too picturesque and complicated for description. A just representation would exhibit an image of compound wretchedness—care, anxiety, pain, poverty, hurry, confusion, humiliation and dejection, would be characteristic traits in the mortifying picture."[96]

But Cornwallis had dealt the Americans a great reprieve, as Williams indicated in his parting shot. "His lordship [Cornwallis] certainly gave the world another instance in proof of the assertion, that it is not every general, upon whom fortune bestows her favors, who knows how to avail himself of all the advantages which are presented to him. Victory is not always attended ... with all the superiority it seems to bestow. The British army retired to Camden."[97] In this remarkable move, the British had failed to follow up and finish the job once and for all. When Howe allowed Washington to cross the Delaware at the end of 1776, he assumed one more push in the spring would end the Revolution for good. Cornwallis, who had doubts about the security of the backcountry and issues with the supplies of his own army, after a possibly fatal delay, decided to invade North Carolina.

At Camden, Cornwallis decided his strategy would include a three-pronged attack. In the east, his right wing would secure the coast and maintain supply lines to the main body of the army. The center, commanded by the general himself, would drive straight up through North Carolina. His left wing, commanded by Major Patrick Ferguson, would move through the upper part of South Carolina and across the North Carolina border with the loyalist militia and a few provincials. Ferguson's territory would also include the western frontier and mountainous region, where hopefully the enemy would be subdued and the loyalists would rally to Cornwallis's advancing army.

By the middle of September, Cornwallis's much-anticipated movement was underway. Cornwallis, with the main part of the army, crossed the Catawba on the 22nd, headed for Charlotte. Tarleton, because of the lack of forage in the Waxhaws, crossed the Wateree and moved up the east side of the river with the "body of the British dragoons, and the light and legion infantry."[98] After waiting several days for additional supplies and for Tarleton to recover from sickness, Cornwallis moved on to Charlotte. Colonel William Davie, commanding 150 men consisting of infantry and dragoons, said the town, "situated on rising ground[,] contains about twenty Houses built on two streets which cross each other at right angles in the intersection of which stands the Court-House."[99] As he entered the town, the enemy had drawn up in force by the courthouse, but were quickly dispersed.[100]

But Charlotte became a nightmare. "The town and environs abounded with inveterate enemies; the plantations in the neighborhood were small and uncultivated; the roads narrow, and crossed in every direction; the whole face of the country covered with close and thick woods."[101] Cornwallis had underestimated the ferocity of the inhabitants' response to their homes being occupied by British forces: "The people generally abandoned their habitations; some fled with such of their property as they could carry; others took the field, determined to dispute every foot of the ground, and some assembled in small parties, in their respective neighborhoods, determined to harass the enemy's foraging parties. His Lordship soon discovered that he was in an enemy's country, without provisions, without forage, without friends, without intelligence, ... his communication with Camden cut off and his dispatches intercepted."[102]

Tarleton noted as well "that the counties of Mecklenburg and Rohan [Rowan] were more hostile to England than any others in America. The vigilance and animosity of these surrounding districts checked the exertions of the well-affected and totally destroyed all communication between the King's troops and loyalists in other part of the province."[103]

Colonel Robert Gray, with the benefit of hindsight, criticized Cornwallis and his campaign because "had Lord Cornwallis had a sufficient army to have marched into North Carolina & to have established posts in his rear at convenient places to preserve his communication with South Carolina & to prevent the rebels from assembling in arms after he passed along, North Carolina would have fallen without a struggle, but the smallness of his numbers soon turned the tide against him."[104] Since he could not exert any control over the surrounding area, Cornwallis retreated from Charlotte on October 14. One account described the retreat as taking place "with great precipitation, leaving behind many of their Waggons, with valuable Baggage, behind them."[105]

The campaign had been a questionable military move. Cornwallis had acted prematurely and had rushed to secure his territory. By the time the invasion took place, the area east of the Wateree and Santee were in revolt, and the militia could not be relied on to maintain order. In addition, the situation at Charlotte had "been rendered very troublesome by the close attention paid them by Davidson, and Davie, who, with Colo. Morgan, are now hanging on and greatly distresses them; General Sumpter, with Colonels Campbell, Shelby and others, with upwards of Two Thousand Militia, keeping pace with them on the other side of the Catawba."[106]

Brigadier General Charles O'Hara, in a letter to the Duke of Grafton in the fall of 1780, was fearful of how the war in the south was being conducted. He was very prophetic when he wrote that "the New Mode adopted of pursuing the War in this Country by Arming American against American, I am afraid will prove a most dangerous experiment … for there can be no doubt if Lord Cornwallis receives the smallest check, our cause is irretrievable."[107]

That check came at Kings Mountain. Cornwallis's left wing was commanded by Major Patrick Ferguson, who would move through the upper part of South Carolina and across the North Carolina border. Ferguson, as Cornwallis reported, "with about eighty provincials and five or six hundred militia has made an incursion into the mountainous parts of Tryon County, where he has gained some advantages over the rebel militia and dispersed some parties who were said to be marching to join the insurgents."[108] His territory would also include the western frontier and the mountainous region where, hopefully, the enemy would be subdued and the loyalists would rally to Cornwallis's advancing army.

Patrick Ferguson was born in 1744, the second son of a wealthy and influential Scottish family. Ferguson enlisted in the army at the age of fifteen and by the age of thirty-five, the Scotsman already had twenty years' experience and had made quite a name for himself. His training and field experience came by way of the battlefields of Europe during the Seven Years' War, seeing action in Germany. Ferguson's military service was interrupted by illness in 1762, when he returned home and developed a keen interest in military science, especially the roles served by militia. His interest in the militia may have had some roots in the fact that his native Scotland had been forcibly disarmed by the English following the rebellion of 1745.

Prior to his service in the Americas, Ferguson had developed a new breech-loading rifle capable of rapid reloading and pinpoint accuracy over great distances. Ferguson perceived the need for this weapon to counter the long-range rifles used by the American frontiersmen. Even though it received the Crown's patent in 1776, it was abandoned after Ferguson was wounded in the elbow at Brandywine in 1777. After his recovery, Ferguson again took the field, learning to use his left hand in both the use of the sword and the writing of letters. Despite Ferguson's service and respect among his fellow soldiers, his relationship with Cornwallis and other officers was strained, likely a result of Ferguson's steadfast support of militia.

By September 7, Ferguson had pushed across the western North Carolina border, stopping at Gilbert Town. According to many accounts, Ferguson and his men terrorized Whig settlers in the countryside as they moved.[109] While at Gilbert Town, Ferguson sent a rider, a paroled Samuel Phillips into the mountains to strike fear into the hearts of residents who were clearly part of the rebel movement. A message was delivered to Col. Isaac Shelby, commander of the patriot militia of Sullivan County, North Carolina. The message was that "if they did not desist from their opposition to the British arms, he would march his army over the mountains, hang their leaders, and lay their country waste with fire and sword."[110] Ferguson backed up his words with deeds as he pursued a rebel party to the edges of the Blue Ridge Mountains before returning to Gilbert Town.[111] Isaac Shelby wasted little time and took off riding over forty miles to see John Sevier, the militia leader of Washington County, in what is termed the "overmountain region."[112] The two decided that forces would be rounded up, the mountains crossed to the east, and Ferguson defeated.[113]

The Over Mountain people were of Scots-Irish origin, with a little English, German and Welsh mixed in.[114] They were a hardy people who had moved down the west face of the Appalachian Mountains where life was hard. They had to contend with the Cherokee, whom they defeated, and the British, who knew they were on the wrong side of the Proclamation Line of 1763 but did nothing about it.[115] The Over Mountain people were hardened by years of a strenuous existence, and life could be short and violent. During the Revolution, the Over Mountain people lived in the area of what is now the northeastern corner of Tennessee along the Watauga, Nolachucky, and Holston Rivers.[116] No aspect of geography would stop them in their pursuit of Ferguson.

Among the loyalists he came across, Ferguson was correct in his assumptions that they had been hearing negative rhetoric about the British. Uzal Johnson, an American surgeon serving under Ferguson, commented on the people the militia were encountering. The inhabitants, he wrote, "have always been kept in ignorance, & told of the Cruelty of the English, one Poor Woman expressed great surprise at seeing our men so mild, she asked if there was not Heathens in our Army that eat Children, she had been told there was."[117] Ferguson offered amnesty to "those men that have been of the rebel side who remain at home and shew a disposition for peace and submission."[118] Ferguson offered a cash reward for "whoever by intelligence enables the King's troops or militia to strike a successful blow."[119]

Shelby and Sevier sent out a call for men from throughout the region, and they called for all forces to gather on September 25 at Sycamore Shoals, near what is today Elizabethton, Tennessee. They were joined by William Campbell of Virginia. These men were all experienced woodsmen, skilled in firearms, many of them in buckskin and supplied by knapsack, blanket, and long rifle. Some were on foot, others on horseback. Commanders were chosen on the basis of whose leadership would be followed.

On September 26, the Over Mountain men moved out, approximately 1000 strong, soon to be reinforced by 400 Virginians and 350 North Carolinians. Several days later the men would rendezvous at Cowpens, South Carolina, with other patriots intent on eliminating the threat of Ferguson for good. But by September 30, reports began to trickle in to Ferguson about the mustered Over Mountain men. In a letter to Cornwallis, he forwarded a report from a Captain James Dunlap, a member of the Queen's Rangers who was serving with Ferguson. Dunlap was a soldier both Cornwallis and Ferguson held in high regard,

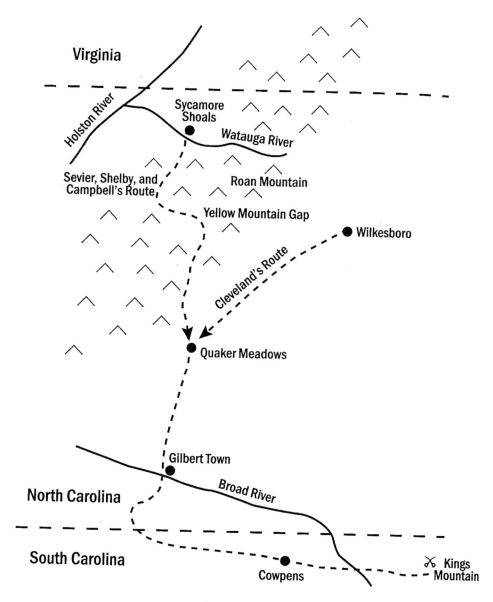

Line of March to Kings Mountain (from *The Revolutionary War in the Southern Back Country* by James K. Swisher, copyright 2008 James K. Swisher, used by permission of Pelican Publishing Company, Inc., www.pelicanpub.com).

so his report would carry weight. He reported that "McDowel and Shelvy were collecting men to return over the mountains. These men think, [fr]om what they themselves saw and heard, that their two partys will not fall short of 1,000 ... Do not make too light of all this, for advancing they certainly are, let their numbers be what they will."[120]

Ferguson, not certain where enemy forces were, or how many men were going to face him, fell back toward Cornwallis. By October 5, Ferguson realized that his force would not likely be able to withstand the combined forces of the Over Mountain men. He sent a request to Cornwallis for reinforcements. "I should hope for success against them myself;

but numbers compared that must be but doubtful. I am on my march towards you by a road leading from Cherokee Ford, north of King's Mountain. 3 or 400 good soldiers, part dragoons, would finish the business. *Something must be done soon.*"[121] What Ferguson did not know was that Cornwallis had a bad cold and Tarleton was laid up with a fever. No reinforcements were coming. Ferguson was now isolated. Rather than head to the safety of the main body of the army, Ferguson took refuge at a place called Kings Mountain on October 6.

Meanwhile, scouts had learned that Ferguson was near Charlotte around October 6, and decisions had to be made as to how to proceed. Out of the nearly 1800 men available for duty, the leaders chose the best 900 riflemen on the best mounts to confront the British.[122] After a tiring thirty-five-mile ride at night, on the morning of October 7, the men crossed the Broad River at Cherokee Ford, only a few miles west of Ferguson's position. Cornwallis wrote to Nisbet Balfour, commandant at Charleston, that he was "uneasy about Ferguson, and fear I must detach the Legion into Tryon County."[123] The following day, October 8, Cornwallis replied to Ferguson, suggesting that he retreat to the east side of the Catawba River until Cornwallis could arrange for reinforcements.[124] Unfortunately, the Over Mountain men had caught up with their quarry the day before.

Kings Mountain is part of a range that extends sixteen miles from north to south with several spurs spreading laterally in each direction.[125] The battlefield is about a mile and a half south of the North Carolina line and is a stony ridge, about one hundred feet above the ravines that surround it.[126] In October 1780, the top of the mountain was treeless, open ground, roughly 600 yards long and approximately 60 yards wide at the southwest end, widening to about 120 yards at the northeast corner. The dense tangle of woods that surround the hill today did not greet the combatants. Instead, hardwood trees such as oaks, hickories and chestnuts covered the slopes with massive trunks that could hide two men at a time, spread much further apart than on today's battlefield. The dense underbrush did not exist in 1780, and accounts from both sides indicate each side could easily see the other at long distances. Movement between the trees was facilitated by the distance between trees and the lack of underbrush. The hillsides were described as "gravelly, containing a few small bowlders."[127] One soldier noted that "the enemy was posted on a high, steep and rugged ridge, or spur of the mountain, very difficult of access, with a small stream of water running on each side."[128]

About a mile out from the base of the mountain, the patriot army dismounted from their horses and began the march to the base of the hill. They had been through hell on their journey. James Collins noted that "the pursuing army had not a single baggage waggon or any type of camp equipage; every one ate what he could get, and slept in his own blanket, sometimes eating raw turnips, and often resorting to a little parched corn."[129]

In his account, Collins reflected on what was at stake just a little way up the road. "The sky was overcast with clouds, and at times a light mist of rain falling; our provisions were scanty, and hungry men were apt to be fractious; each one felt his situation; the last stake was up and the severity of the game must be played; everything was at stake—life, liberty, prosperity, and even the fate of wife, children and friends, seemed to depend on the issue; death or victory was the only way to escape suffering."[130] Ensign Robert Campbell remembered that "they were fortunate enough to come on him [the enemy] undiscovered, and took his pickets, they not having it in their power to give an alarm."[131]

According to Colonel Isaac Shelby's account, at "about three o'clock the patriot force

Battle of Kings Mountain, October 7, 1780 (National Park Service, Kings Mountain National Military Park). The misspelling "King's" has long been common.

was led to the attack in four columns—Col. Campbell commanded the right centre column, Col Shelby the left centre, Col. Sevier the right flank column, and Col. Cleveland
the left flank. As they came to the foot of the mountain, the right centre and right flank
columns deployed to the right, and the left centre and left flank columns to the left, and
thus surrounding the mountain they marched up, commencing the action on all sides."[132]
Colonel William Hill recalled that "in the commencement of the action he [Ferguson]
ordered a charge on the Americans, but the ground was so rough ... that they were not
able to overtake the americans to injure them, in this way, & when they went a certain
distance they had orders to retreat to their camp, & then it was that the americans had
every advantage required."[133] Ensign Robert Campbell recalled that "the two armies being
full view, the center of the one nearly opposite the center of the other—the British main
guard posted nearly half way down the mountain—the commanding officer gave the word
of command to raise the Indian war-whoop and charge. In a moment, King's Mountain
resounded with their shouts, and on the first fire the guard retreated, leaving some of the
men to crimson the earth."[134]

Individual accounts of the battle noted the ferocity, confusion and intensity of the
combat. Col. William Campbell wrote: "Col. Shelby's regiment and mine began the attack, and sustained the whole fire of the enemy for about ten minutes, while the other
troops were forming around the height upon which the enemy was posted. The firing then
became general, as heavy as you can conceive for the number of men."[135] James Collins
recalled that "the shot of the enemy soon began to pass over us like hail; the first shock
was quickly over, and for my part, I was soon in a profuse sweat. My lot happened to be in
the centre, where the severest part of the battle was fought. We soon attempted to climb
the hill, but were fiercely charged upon and forced to fall back to our first position; we
tried a second time, but met the same fate; the fight then seemed to become more furious."[136] Charles Bowen "advanced without being sensible of his danger till within fifteen
or twenty paces of the enemy. [Bowen] slipped behind a tree, cocked his gun, and shot the
first man who hoisted the flag among the enemy and immediately turned his back to the
tree to reload his gun."[137] Leonard Hice wrote in his pension application: "I shot 3 rounds
before I was shot down. I then received a bullet through my left leg. The fourth bullet I
received in my right knee which shattered the bone of my right thigh and brought me to
the ground."[138]

Thomas Young wrote in his memoirs: "[W]e fought our way, from tree to tree, up
to the summit. I recollect I stood behind one tree, and fired until the bark was nearly all
knocked off, and my eyes pretty well filled with it."[139] With chaos all around, Young got
separated from his unit. "Before I was aware of it, I found myself apparently between
my regiment and the enemy, as I judged from seeing the paper which the Whigs wore in
their hats, and the pine twigs the tories wore in theirs, these being the badges of distinction."[140] Col. Shelby recalled years later that "they had taken that post at that place with
the confidence that no force could rout them.... They repelled us three times with charged
bayonets; but being determined to conquer or die, we came up a fourth time, and fairly
got possession of the top of the eminence."[141] William Campbell "gained the point of the
ridge, where my regiment fought, and drove them along the summit of it nearly to the
other end."[142]

Major Ferguson, trying to break out of this poor position, attempted to rally his men,
when according to loyalist Alexander Chesney, he "was at last recognized by his gallantry,

although wearing a hunting shirt, and fell pierced by seven balls at the moment he had killed the American Coll. Williams with his left hand (his right being useless)."[143] James Collins recalled the moment he saw Ferguson: "On examining the dead body of their great chief, it appeared that almost fifty rifles must have been leveled at him, at the same time; seven rifle balls had passed through his body, both of his arms were broken, and his hat and clothing were literally shot to pieces."[144]

The fall of Ferguson did not mean the end to the killing. Colonel Shelby remembered that "it was some time before a complete cessation of the firing, on our part could be effected. Our men, who had scattered in the battle, were continually coming up, and continued to fire, without comprehending in the heat of the moment, what had happened; and some, who had heard that at Buford's defeat the British had refused quarters to many who asked it, were willing to follow that bad example."[145] Alexander Chesney "had just rallied the troops a second time by Ferguson's orders when Captain DePeyster succeeded to command and after gave up and sent out a flag of truce, but as the Americans resumed firing, afterwards ours renewed under the supposition that they would not give quarter. And dreadful havoc took place until the flag was sent out a second time when the work of destruction ceased. The Americans surrounded us with double line, and we grounded arms, with the loss of one third of our numbers."[146]

Finally, it was over. One hundred and fifty-seven loyalists were killed and 163 so badly wounded they could not be moved at all. Almost 700 were taken prisoner. The Americans had twenty-eight killed and sixty-two wounded. Unfortunately, for those taken prisoner, their ordeal was not over. Chesney left behind his observations on the night after the battle.

> We passed the night on the spot where we surrendered amidst the dead and groans of the dying who had not surgical aid or water to quench their thirst[.] Early next morning [October 8, 1780] we marched at a rapid pace towards Gilbert's town between double lines of Americans; the officers in the rear and obliged to carry two muskets each which was my fate although wounded and stripped of my shoes and silver buckles in an inclement season without covering or provisions until Monday night when an ear of Indian corn was served to each; at Gilbert's town a mock trial held and 24 sentenced to death of whom 10 suffered before the approach of Tarleton's force.[147]

This escalation of violence brought the wrath of Col. Arthur Campbell. In his general orders, he stated, "I must request the officers of all ranks in the army to endeavor to restrain the disorderly manner of slaughtering and disturbing the prisoners. If it cannot be prevented by moderate measures, such effectual punishment shall be executed upon delinquents as will put a stop to it."l put a stop to it."[148]

By November 1, reports were trickling into New York from patriot sources about Ferguson's defeat. Brigadier General Charles O'Hara mentioned some of these rumors in a letter to the Duke of Grafton. "If this unfortunate stroke should prove true to the extent related by the Rebels, I am afraid it may be productive of the most fatal consequences to Lord Cornwallis."[149] O'Hara's prediction proved to be accurate. In a twist of irony, Ferguson's foray near the Over Mountain area, intended to fortify loyalist militia, did just the opposite. With the rebel militia's unexpected victory, they surged in confidence and saw increases in numbers of their own militia.

Kings Mountain was that first, important step in the revival of the revolutionary cause in the South. It was the first military success after many defeats and, more notably, it was a militia victory. Col. Arthur Campbell summed it up succinctly: "It was Ferguson's defeat that was the first link in a grand chain of causes, which finally drew down ruin on the British interests in the Southern States, and finally terminated the war of the Revolution."[150] Sir Henry Clinton later lamented that the American victory "unhappily proved the first link in a chain of evils that followed each other in regular succession until they at last ended in the total loss of America."[151]

Not surprisingly, blame came in from various camps, and sometimes praise for Ferguson's attempts to hold off the Americans. Colonel Robert Gray noted that "the rebels despairing of being able to effect anything against his Lordship, resolved to make a grand effort against Major Ferguson, who, although he knew his danger & was ordered to join the army, yet after retreating 60 miles he loitered away two days most unaccountably at King's Mountain & thereby gave time to the rebel Militia under the command of Gen. Williams to come up with him, the rebels were greatly superior to him in number."[152] Yet Gray recognized Ferguson's talents, lamenting that "the want of a man of his genius was soon severely felt & if ever another is found to supply his place he will go great lengths turning the scale of the war in our favor."[153]

Others were not so generous. Col. William Hill, in his memoirs, acknowledged that "Col. Ferguson was a brave military character ... brought to his own ruin by chosing this spot of ground on which he had to fight under every disadvantage."[154] Hill added that there were "a great number of fallen & standing trees so that the Americans could attack his camp on all quarters, & their shot went over the americans without effect."[155] Loyalist Alexander Chesney admitted that "Kings Mountain from its height would have enabled us to oppose a superior force with advantage, had it not been covered with wood which sheltered the Americans and enabled them to fight in the favorite manner."[156]

The rebels were now in control of their destiny for the time being. Loyalist elements in the south had lost their momentum, and Cornwallis was obliged to retreat into South Carolina and forego an invasion of North Carolina. If it seemed that events could not get worse for the British, in December they were about to face a new general of the tattered American army who would change the face of the contest. Cornwallis would rue the day when Washington's principal lieutenant, Nathanael Greene, took control of events in the south.

PART II
_____

Winning Hearts and Minds

4

Greene Takes Command

With Ferguson's demise at Kings Mountain, Cornwallis moved to Winnsborough, South Carolina, where "its spacious plantations yielded a tolerable post; its centrical situation between the Broad river and the Wateree afforded protection to Ninety Six and Camden; and its vicinity to the Dutch forks, and a rich country in the rear, promised abundant supplies of flour, forage, and cattle."[1] But the situation with the British army remained perilous.

On Cornwallis's eastern flank, Francis Marion was on the move. Cornwallis informed his boss: "Col. Marion had so wrought on the minds of the People, partly by the terror of his threats & cruelty of his punishments, and partly by the Promise of Plunder, that there was scarce an Inhabitant between the Santee and Pedee that was not in arms against us. Some parties had even crossed the Santee, and carried the terror to the Gates of Charles-town."[2] Tarleton noted Marion's unique tactics by remarking that "he collected his adherents at the shortest notice … and after making incursions into the friendly districts, or threatening communications, to avoid pursuit, disbanded his followers. The alarms occasioned by these insurrections frequently retarded supplies on their way to the army; and a late report of Marion's strength delayed the junction of recruits, who arrived from New York for the corps in the country."[3]

The disaster at Kings Mountain had opened Cornwallis up to criticism, and the failure to make gains in the early part of the southern campaign had changed the way the war was fought. Cornwallis was forced to use regular troops not only to fight the American partisans, but also to retain British posts in the interior, while his numbers began to diminish and casualties began to mount.[4] Cornwallis was effecting a shift in the war in the South, by protecting gains he had made with regular troops instead of using loyalists.[5] Colonel Robert Gray noted that "all the country on Lord Cornwallis' rear was laid open to all the incursions of the enemy."[6]

Gray also had unkind words for the inhabitants of Charleston, who "were amusing themselves with the aspect of the war in the different quarters of the globe, [while] the unfortunate loyalist on the frontier found the fury of the whole war let loose upon him. He was no longer safe to sleep in his house. He hid himself in the swamps."[7]

Colonel Rawdon, who had commanded Cornwallis's left wing at Camden, was frustrated by the inability to bring the enemy to action because "the enemy are mostly mounted militia, not to be overtaken by our infantry nor to be safely pursued in this strong country by our cavalry; our fear is that instead of meeting us they would slip by us into this province, were we to proceed far from it, and might again stimulate the disaffected to serious insurrection."[8]

Henry Clinton was critical on several fronts. He felt that Cornwallis "was certainly too apt to risk detachments without proper support, which is the more to be wondered at, as Lexington, Bennington, Danbury, and Trenton were recent instances which His Lordship could not have forgot."[9] After Ferguson's debacle at Kings Mountain, Clinton was rankled about the retreat from Charlotte:

> When Lord Cornwallis first heard of this misfortune and the effect it was likely to have on South Carolina, he suddenly abandoned the post at Charlottetown and returned with his whole force to that province. But the precipitancy with which this retrograde movement was made contributed ... to increase the despondency of the Kings's friends, especially in North Carolina, where the loyalists whom His Lordship's presence had encouraged to show themselves, being exposed to persecution and ruin by his retreat, threw away after all their confidence of support from the King's army.[10]

Meanwhile, George Washington had finally succeeded in getting Nathanael Greene named as commander-in-chief of the southern theatre on October 14, 1780. Greene's reputation as Washington's principal lieutenant in the northern campaigns lent legitimacy to the choice. As early as 1777, Washington had recognized Greene's skills in a letter to John Hancock: "This Gentleman is so much in my confidence—so intimately acquainted with my ideas—with our strength, and our weaknesses—with everything respecting the Army."[11] More importantly, he added, "from the rank he holds as an able & good Officer in the estimations of all who know him, he deserves the greatest respect, and much regard is due his Opinions in the line of his profession."[12] Colonel Henry Lee, Greene's able cavalry commander, noted in his memoirs that "so manifold and important were his services, that he became a very highly trusted counselor of the commander-in-chief; respected for his sincerity, prized for his disinterestedness, and valued for his wisdom. It followed, of course, when calamity thickened, and the means of resistance grew thin, that Greene should be summoned."[13]

Greene's rise to his current station defied the background in which he grew up. As a middle-class Quaker from Kent County, Rhode Island, Greene led an early life that consisted of hard work and very little schooling, and with most of the population Quaker or Baptist, a simple life was the order of the day. His father selected him to be the resident manager of the Coventry Iron Works, which had been established around 1741 because of the growth of the grist mill and forge business in Potowomut, Warwick, Rhode Island.[14] The new property, located on the south branch of the Pawtuxet River, made large ship anchors and chains that were carted to Apponaug, and then made their way to Newport, the principal market for naval stores.[15]

On his frequent trips to Newport on family business, Greene began to be more inquisitive about the world around him and began to acquire volumes on a variety of subjects, such as history, government, philosophy, law, religion, math, and science.[16] His favorites were those books that contained military treatises and tactics. His lack of formal schooling led him to express his frustration to his friend Samuel Ward: "I lament the want of a liberal education; I feel the mist [of] Ignorance to surround me, for my own part I was Educated a Quaker ... and that of itself is a sufficient Obstacle to cramp the best of Geniuses."[17] Greene was tutored in Latin and geometry, and family members all related that Greene read whenever he could, even while operating the grist mill. His father disapproved of many of the books he read. Greene also sought out other men who were far better educated than himself, like his friend Samuel Ward, James Varnum, and his good friend Thomas Arnold.[18]

Greene's first military experience was with the Kentish Guards in Rhode Island, one of many militia companies that formed all over New England as a result of the Boston Tea Party and the Intolerable Acts. He was rejected as an officer, but after much protest, he served in the ranks.[19] After Lexington and Concord, Rhode Island voted for the creation of an Army of Observation with Greene as the commander, holding the rank of brigadier general.[20] Greene's rise had been meteoric and by 1776, he became a major general in the Continental Army. As a result of his participation in military affairs, though, his membership in the Society of Friends was terminated.

One interesting piece of Greene's personality was that he appeared to be more concerned with the needs of disabled soldiers and their families than most of his contemporaries, including Washington. Greene used his friendship with John Adams to urge Congress to act. "If the Congress was to fix a certain support upon every Officer and Soldier that got maim'd in the service or upon the families of those that were kild it would have as happy an influence towards engageing people in the service and inspire those engaged with as much courage as any measure that can be fixt upon."[21] Adams responded affirmatively, agreeing that "the policy of making Provision for the unfortunate Officer, or Soldier, is extremely just," but deferring action until the current Revolution was resolved.[22]

Greene had learned some hard lessons early on in the war. The debacle in front of Fort Washington was indeed the worst. Washington's decision to hold out was surely swayed by Greene and others. Greene was subjected to withering criticism of his actions, but never tried to shift the blame off himself. At the time, Greene's lack of military experience helped created one of the biggest disasters of the early Revolutionary War.[23] Greene wrote his friend Henry Knox, and the despair can be heard in his letter. "I feel mad, vext, sick and sorry," he wrote.[24] Greene's redemption came on December 25, when the successful attack on Trenton erased all memory of the Fort Washington debacle. Greene performed brilliantly. His division had blocked any escape of the Hessians to the north and had moved to the center of the town to confront the enemy.[25] On January 2, 1777, as Cornwallis headed to Trenton to trap Washington, Greene's division slowed the British approach so Washington would have time to withdraw the army along back roads toward Princeton, in order that they would be able to engage the British garrison there.[26]

Greene was approximately five feet ten inches tall, broad at the shoulder and chest, with strong arms, and he had blue eyes with a high forehead and a rosy complexion.[27] At the time of his tenure as commander of the Southern Department, cavalry legend Henry Lee described him as follows: "This illustrious man had now reached his thirty-eighth year. In person he was rather corpulent, and above the common size. His complexion was fair and florid; his countenance serene and mild, indicating a goodness which seemed to shade and soften the fire and greatness of his expression. His health was delicate, but preserved by temperance and exercise."[28] Lee was generous with his praise, describing the general as "capable of doing much with little" and "not discouraged by this unfavorable prospect."[29] He was able to "inspire confidence, to rekindle courage, to decide hesitation, and infuse a spirit of exalted patriotism in the citizens of the State."[30]

At the same time, Greene had some severe critics, and most of those criticisms were actually caused by his own actions. In 1777, for example, Greene kept an ear to the ground over matters of politics between the army and Congress. When Greene heard a report that Rhode Island was recruiting men for militia units and not the Continental army, he could not hold back his impetuousness and wrote an angry letter to Governor Cooke, lecturing him on the need for the country to be steered by national interests and not local ones. Unfortunately for Greene, this report turned out to be false.[31] On May 29, 1777, Greene sent a scathing letter to John Adams after hearing rumors that General Philip Schuyler of New York was on the verge of being selected for president of Congress while still holding his commission in the army.[32] Again, the letter was based on rumor, not facts.

During the winter of 1777–78, following the losses at Brandywine and Germantown and the fall of the capital in Philadelphia, one of Greene's harshest critics was Thomas Mifflin, the former aide to Washington and member of the Continental Congress. Mifflin thought Greene incompetent and Washington indecisive, and maintained both were responsible for the loss of Philadelphia.[33] Dr. Benjamin Rush, a physician in Philadelphia and one of the signers of the Declaration of Independence, accused Greene as being "a sychophant to the General, speculative, without enterprise."[34] Greene had managed to damage his friendship with John Adams and alienated himself from others in Congress.

Working his way up, Greene was heroic in the field, but late in the Valley Forge disaster, Washington appointed him Quartermaster General in 1778. It was one of the most thankless and difficult jobs in the entire Continental Army, but Greene threw himself into his work. With the spring campaign season close at hand, Greene had surpassed all expectations, finding supplies and hiring wagon teams to move a prodigious amount of material. Washington was so pleased with Greene's efforts that he wrote Congress in August reporting to Henry Laurens that "by his conduct and industry [the Quartermaster Department] has undergone a very happy change, and such as enabled us, with great facility, to make a sudden move with the whole Army and baggage from Valley Forge in pursuit of the Enemy [to Monmouth, New Jersey] and to perform a march to this place [White Plains, New York]."[35]

This is where Greene's ascendancy hit a snag. He encountered many problems in his new venture. Greene's purchasing agents worked on commission, and combined with the continuing fall of the value of the Continental dollar, the short supply of goods, and inflation, the expenditures of his department had quadrupled since 1776.[36] Congress launched an investigation into the finances of the department, and by September, nothing could be bought on credit. Congress suggested that the army turn to the states for help, which turned out to be a worthless endeavor. Greene had had enough. He wanted to resign, but Congress ignored his plea. Greene had constantly been concerned about a lack of resources to do his job properly, and when Congress reorganized the department, Greene felt he could not operate under the new plan. Congress was drastically reducing personnel, and salaries were to replace commissions.[37] Greene despised the interference in his department. He resigned on July 26, 1780, and Congress looked poorly on the timing of Greene's resignation.

His view of Congress was as dim as their view of him. "Nothing is viewed in Congress respecting the Staff departments but through the dark medium of prejudice. The business was so difficult and the prejudice so great that I determined to be quit of it at any rate."[38] Some delegates in Congress were tired of Greene's insolence and his disrespect for the body itself, and events had progressed so poorly that there was talk of removing him from the army completely.[39] Washington had expressed his concern over the situation, but Greene had survived this drama nonetheless.

Greene had reached depths he never thought were possible, but several weeks after the Benedict Arnold debacle and the hanging of the spy John Andre, Greene had attained command of the entire southern army. As he read the words from Washington in a letter, his spirits must have soared as the long nightmare of the quartermaster general affair was over. "As Congress have been pleased to leave the Officer to command on this occasion to my choice, it is my wish to appoint you."[40] It must have been more satisfying when Greene learned that a congressional delegation of three southern states concurred with Washington's appointment. Greene responded to his appointment in humble fashion, writing Washington, "I am fully sensible of the honor you do me and will endeavor to manifest my gratitude by a conduct that will not disgrace the appointment…. I only lament that my abilities are not more competent to the duties that will be required of me…. But as far as zeal and attention can supply the defect, I flatter myself my Country will have little cause to complain."[41]

In a letter to his lovely wife, Catharine, his thoughts turned to home and family: "I had been pleasing my self with the agreeable prospect of spending the winter here with you…. But alas, before we can have [the] happiness of meeting, I am ordered away to another quarter. How unfriendly is war to domestic happiness."[42] But he also noted in his letter to her that this appointment was "so foreign to my wishes that I am distressed exceedingly."[43]

Those "wishes" were not foreign to Greene, and the circumstances around his appointment were not simply a matter of Washington's giving him the job. Greene had written Washington in 1779 that he "should be happy to obtain" the southern command if "General Lincoln's Leg is likely to render him incapable."[44] Greene also had an ally in Congress to whom he floated the idea in early October 1780. John Mathews of South Carolina was a genuine supporter of Washington and was as impatient as Greene was about the sluggishness of Congress. He and Greene had become friends while serving on a committee together, and his letter to Mathews contradicts what he wrote to his wife later when the post was thrust upon him.[45] "But if you find it necessary to appoint another officer to that command, and I think I can be useful in that quarter, my endeavors will not be wanting to protect the people and serve my country," wrote Greene.[46]

On October 6, interestingly, Samuel Huntington, president of the Continental Congress, wrote Washington that he should choose the successor to Horatio Gates after the Camden disaster. On the same day, Mathews informed Washington, on behalf of three southern states, that Greene should be appointed to command.[47] Washington also had numerous reasons why Greene should be appointed command of the southern army. He had experience in battle and had demonstrated the proper temperament to lead, had learned from his mistakes, had developed as a sound tactician and strategist, and as quartermaster general had gained valuable experience supplying an army.[48]

The transfer of command from Gates to Greene was very civil. Gates thanked the troops for their perseverance in the wake of major privations and wished them well in their future endeavors and ultimately, victory.[49] Greene, in his orders of December 5, 1780, "returns his Thanks to the Hon'ble Major General Gates for the polite Manner in which he had introduced him to his command, and for the good wishes, for the Success of the Southern Army."[50]

Torn between his wife and his country, Greene set to work before assuming command on December 2. In a letter to Brigadier General Edward Stevens written in Salisbury, North Carolina, the day before, Greene urged Stevens to begin exploring the Yadkin River. In order to properly supply the army, Greene wanted "to go up the Yadkin as high as Hughes Creek to explore carefully the River, the depth of Water, the Current and the

Rocks, and every other obstruction that will impede the Business of Transportation."[51] With great attention to detail, Greene wanted "to construct Boats of a peculiar kind for this Service, that will carry Forty or Fifty Barrels and yet draw little more than a common Canoe half loaded."[52]

Greene was also taking into consideration the state of the road network, directing Stevens to have a subordinate "ride across the Country from that place [Hughes Creek] thro' the Town of Bethania to the upper Saura Town, and report the Distance and Condition of the Roads. I also wish the officer to make enquiry respecting the Transportation that may be had from the Yadkin to the Catawba River, and whether the Transportation cannot be performed with Batteaus down that River."[53] On December 8, Greene sent his Polish engineer, Thaddeus Kosciuszko, to explore the Catawba. In a single canoe, with his guide Captain William Thompson, they set out into the wilderness to survey the western North Carolina rivers, which would be of great importance to Greene's army.[54] Greene had immediately brought into play his experience as quartermaster general.

Greene appointed Col. Edward Carrington Quartermaster General and instructed him "to repair to Richmond without Loss of Time and fix with the Quarter Master for the State the Rout thro' Virginia for the Stores coming from the Northward."[55] Greene also addressed the need for axes, horseshoes, and a "half a Ton of Boat nails for constructing Batteaus."[56] With an ominous foreboding, Greene told Carrington, "Without Tools, we can do nothing and none are to be got in this country, not even a common felling Axe."[57] Carrington was not an experienced officer for this type of work, but had served as an artillery commander of the southern army. He had an aptitude for logistics and had been asked by General Gates to produce and transport military supplies throughout the state of Virginia, which he successfully did.[58] Carrington was also tasked with organizing a supply delivery system that depended on Taylor's Ferry on the Roanoke River as the key link between Richmond and Greene's army, with transportation by wagon being the biggest logistical problem of all to solve.[59]

As a former quartermaster general himself, Greene recognized the importance of a supply department to the functioning of an army. Regarding the exploration of the Dan River, Carrington informed Greene in a letter of December 6 that he had "found much difficulty in getting the necessary hands to pole him up. The people are backward in lending such aid to the service, as I am convinced they might with but little inconvenience part with, and I have been reduced to the necessity of giving the Capt [Anthony Singleton, 1st regiment of Artillery] a press Warrant for impressing Negroes for the purpose."[60] He reassured Greene that navigation should be no problem, and that he should not have difficulty finding and building the necessary boats.[61]

After a careful study of the North Carolina topography, Greene established two main magazines at Salisbury and Oliphant's Mill on the Catawba River and "several small ones upon the north side of the Pedee as high up towards the narrows as possible that the position of this army may cover them."[62] The legislature approved the plan, but with a lack of timely implementation by locals and the British invasion of North Carolina in 1781, the plan was never implemented.[63] Nonetheless, Greene chose his campsites well, next to mills almost all the time, and as a result, Greene was able to access grain, water and open space for his men.[64] Greene had not forgotten the maxims of war from his reading of Frederick the Great, in which "the first rule is to place magazines and fortified places behind the localities where you are assembling the army."[65]

Greene, as well as Gates before him, faced major shortages of soldiers, food, clothing and myriad other military necessities that had been exacerbated by the surrender of Charleston.[66] Greene wrote Gov. Thomas Jefferson on the 6th appealing for supplies and revealing the hard truths about the southern army: "I find the troops under his command [Gates] in a most wretched Condition, destitute of every thing necessary either for the Comfort or Convenience of Soldiers.... Your troops may literally be said to be naked, and I shall be obliged to send a considerable Number of them away into some secure place and warm Quarters until they can be furnished with Cloathing."[67] Greene minced no words with the governor, adding, "It will answer no good purpose to send men here in such a Condition, for they are nothing but added Weight upon the Army, and altogether incapable of aiding its operations."[68] On December 19, the Virginia Assembly authorized Jefferson to impress clothing and blankets for the troops if they could not be purchased.

Greene reiterated many of his views on the prosecution of the war to Governor Abner Nash of North Carolina, as well as on the procurement of supplies and support from the state government. But one theme emerged as important as the supply of his army: the support of the populace, with the understanding that their liberties were the first priority and their property was of secondary significance. "It is natural for People who are affected w'th the Calamities of War, to wish to make a great Effort to remove the Evil, but ill judged Exertions only serve to fix the Chains so much the faster. I may not always agree w'th the People respecting the manner of conducting the War, but they may be assured I have their true Interest at heart."[69] Greene knew that the countryside held one of the keys to overall success in the south, and much of his strategy would be predicated on winning the hearts and minds of the people. He would have to be cautious. To Henry Knox, he wrote, "Every Thing here depends upon opinion, and it is equally dangerous to go forward as to stand still for if you lose the Confidence of the People you lose all Support and if you rush into Danger you hazard everything."[70]

As Greene grasped the details of his command, he wrote Gates, asking for information that Greene lacked in order to fully harness the scope of his responsibilities, such as "what bills you have drawn, on what States and to what amount, in whose favor, and for what purpose ... [and] names and places of abode of all the persons you have commissioned to make purchases for this army ... a report respecting the Arms and Ammunition, or refer me to the person who has superintendence of them." He also asked for any maps Gates may have at his disposal.[71] Gates appears to have provided the information Greene was seeking, although the list of bills Gates provided has not been found.[72]

As the arduous task of commander-in-chief of a theatre in which Charles Lee, Benjamin Lincoln, and Horatio Gates had failed, Greene needed to rely on his experience under Washington in the northern campaigns to provide the leadership necessary for a climactic victory over the British. As the remnants of Washington's army retreated across New Jersey after the fall of New York in an attempt to cross the Delaware ahead of the British, Greene had placed food and fodder along the way. The provisions preserved the army long enough to prevent its demise before the all-important assault on Trenton and the resurrection of America's fortunes.[73] Probably more importantly, Greene had learned the advantages of a well-organized withdrawal in front of a superior force. This strategy was used in both theatres of action, and the ability to withdraw from a superior force and to strike and harass the enemy on numerous occasions made it clear the British would have to defeat the entire elusive American army in order to win the war.[74]

Greene realized that fighting the British would require a mobile force with incredible speed of movement, while sieges without the necessary firepower would accomplish nothing.[75] He was also going to have to adapt to a completely different set of circumstances in this theatre, as the war in the South was vastly different from the one he had seen in the North. Manufactured goods in this primarily rural region were hard to come by, and everything for the army had to be funneled down from the North.[76] A poor road network, a reduced number of men available for duty in South Carolina because of a large slave population, and the siding of many communities in North Carolina with the Tories presented Greene with multiple challenges.[77]

Greene's approach to command was much more suited for the contest that was about to take place. Unlike Gates, Greene made the partisan bands of Francis Marion, Thomas Sumter, and Andrew Pickens an integral part of his strategy.[78] Depending on circumstances, Greene would divide his forces, and at times unite them, but never put them into a position of being torn to pieces in a set battle with Cornwallis.[79] Greene had acknowledged the role that Marion had played thus far and that his reputation preceded him, informing him that "we must endeavor to keep up a Partizan War and preserve the Tide of Sentiment among the people as much as possible in our Favour. Spies are the Eyes of an Army, and without them a general is always groping in the dark and can neither secure himself nor annoy his Enemy."[80] But Greene's overall attitude toward the militia was negative. He could not enforce army-style discipline with the militia, as he feared the loss of support would be detrimental to his military goals. Since they were not under his direct control, it took a great deal of political finesse to get them to act in concert with Continental troops.[81] But, as Greene knew, their main role was to keep a watchful eye on Tory actions, protect lines of communication and supply, deny the enemy the ability to forage in the countryside, and gain intelligence about enemy movements.[82]

Now Greene needed to get down to the business of war. He was faced with a deplorable situation no commander wanted to face. His command consisted of 2,307 men, of whom 1,482 were fit for duty. There were ninety cavalry and sixty artillerists, and only 949 were Continentals. The rest were militia. Only 800 men were properly clothed and fed.[83] The American army had originally been ordered to the Yadkin River fords in southwestern North Carolina, where food supplies were adequate for the army, and where it had the ability to march on Charleston in the event of the arrival of a French fleet there. The state of the countryside was so bad, the army was again forced to move, this time to Charlotte, where conditions were no better.[84]

Greene nonetheless began to instill discipline in his troops. Orders were obeyed and there were consequences if they were not. Soldiers were not allowed to leave camp and return when they wanted. One man was executed for such an offense in front of the entire army. The troops, he wrote to Joseph Reed, had "lost all their discipline, and so addicted to plundering, that they were a terror to the inhabitants."[85] Since the country had been stripped clean, Greene knew that food supplies were too scarce for the army to survive together. Kosciuszko was given the task of finding a location suitable for Greene, which he did on the Pee Dee River near Cheraw Hill, just south of the border between the Carolinas.[86] It was here that Greene would make a momentous decision that would affect the entire conduct of the war in the South.

Greene decided to split his army in the face of a larger and more formidable force than his own, a break with conventional military tactics. Defying the ancient tenet "that he who divides his force will be beaten in detail," Greene split his forces because the area around Charlotte could not support an army. With a command of 320 light infantry from the Maryland and Delaware Continental lines, a detachment of 200 Virginia militiamen, and eighty of Lieutenant Colonel William Washington's Regiment of Light Dragoons (cavalrymen), Greene instructed Daniel Morgan to proceed to the west side of the Catawba River. He was "to annoy the enemy in that quarter, collect the provisions and forage out of the way of the enemy, which you will have formed into a number of small magazeines in the rear of the position you make think proper to take."[87]

With an eye to the allegiance of the populace, Greene advised Morgan to "prevent plundering as much as possible, and be carefull of your provisions and forage as may be, giving receipts for whatever you take to all such as are friends to the independence of America."[88] In the event of a British show of force towards the Pee Dee, Greene advised Morgan "to move in such direction as to enable you to join me if necessary, or to fall upon the flank or into the rear of the enemy as occasion may require."[89] Greene saw that by separating his army into two parts, it was easier to subsist off the land, and it was draining supplies from the very area Cornwallis was trying to draw his supplies. Even though Greene was outnumbered, he was relying on the superior mobility of his forces as compared to the bulkier British army.[90]

Interestingly, Greene did not call a council of war before he made his decision. As a member of Washington's inner circle, he had seen the wrong decision made too often, and as a matter of course, would seek out opinions informally from his officers, then make the decisions for the next course of action.[91] Greene's dividing of his forces prior to operations at Cowpens demonstrated a thorough understanding of supplying his army, and also had the purposeful effect of depriving the British of forage in the same area.[92] An independent detachment for Morgan, thought Greene, would restore confidence on the patriot movement as well, and make Cornwallis's western flank susceptible to American advances with the addition of militia.[93] Cornwallis was in a bind. If he did not divide his army and attacked Greene with a single force, he would still have to think about Morgan at his rear, but a move against Morgan would precipitate a move against Camden and Charleston by Greene.[94] Cornwallis also had to be concerned about the safety of Ninety Six, and if he felt that was threatened, a second invasion of North Carolina seemed unlikely.[95]

Morgan left Charlotte on December 21 with approximately 600 men, and by the 24th had crossed the Broad River. Hopefully, he would be joined by William Davidson's militia. By Christmas Day, they were in camp at Grindall's Ford on the left bank of the Pacolet River.[96]

General Daniel Morgan was a tall, sinewy Virginia frontiersman, who had a volatile temper; he was thin-skinned and had a deep yearning for glory on the battlefield.[97] His experience thus far would prove to be immeasurable for Greene. Morgan was with General Edward Braddock as a teamster on the ill-fated expedition in 1755 to drive the French from British territory. When the war broke out, he assembled a company of Virginia riflemen and joined the fight in Boston in 1775. He took part in the attack on Quebec with Benedict Arnold; he was captured and then exchanged. Morgan made a name for himself at Saratoga, but later was overlooked by Washington for command of a "light infantry unit" that went to General Anthony Wayne.[98]

Gates asked Morgan to join the army, but Morgan held back to see if Congress would give him a promotion. The disaster at Camden changed his mind, and Morgan joined

Gates in September, was put in command of a corps of light infantry, and was promoted to general on October 13. Early on, Morgan recognized the value of light infantry. The war was fought over long distances on varied terrain that would challenge a standard army. Light infantry could also strike quickly for maximum advantage, as he did during the Saratoga campaign.[99] Now Morgan was on the left flank of Cornwallis in the South Carolina backcountry.

After Morgan dispatched a small Tory raiding party on the 28th at a place called Hammond's Store, Cornwallis realized that the British strongholds of Ninety Six and Winnsboro were open to attack. He promptly dispatched Tarleton to Ninety Six, while Major General Alexander Leslie moved towards Camden, and Cornwallis himself moved with the main body up from Winnsboro to the areas between the Broad and Pee Dee Rivers.[100] When Tarleton realized Ninety-Six was not threatened, he moved directly against Morgan. "Lieutenant-colonel Tarleton assured Earl Cornwallis that he would endeavor to pass the Pacolet, purposefully to force general Morgan to retreat towards Broad river, and requested his lordship to proceed up the eastern bank without delay, because such a movement might perhaps admit of cooperation, and would undoubtedly stop the retreat of the Americans."[101]

As Tarleton moved against Morgan, Greene was immersed in the issues that bedeviled the southern army. He spent much of his time trying to subdue local fighting between Whigs and Tories who "have almost laid Waste the Country & so corrupted the Principles of the People that they think of nothing but plundering one another."[102] Greene was unsure how he was going to bring the area under control and stop the chaos that was erupting between rival factions, but he would "endeavor to treat all with Civility."[103] General Leslie arrived at Charleston and intended to move on to meet with Cornwallis at Camden. He reported to Gen. Robert Howe that the American army was in no shape to move against either British force. "What the Enemy may attempt I know not, but it is certain, we have it not in our Power to attempt any Thing at all, or least nothing but some little Partizan strokes."[104]

Much of Greene's time was spent dealing with his lack of resources. Greene realized the vastness of the Southern Department, coupled with the dearth of available resources for supplying his army, was causing the cost of the war to be too high. Corresponding with Gen. Ezekiel Cornell of Rhode Island, he expressed concern that "the great expence of employing the Militia in a Country so extensive as this, where the Inhabitants live so distant from one another; and where the Staff departments are so badly regulated, would ruin any Nation on Earth. You may as well attempt to bail the sea dry as to think of arming and equipping the whole Militia of this Country; and the manner of going to war all on horse back will lay waste a whole Country."[105] Greene felt that limiting the quality rather than the quantity of soldiers would be the difference maker, and that the army's ideal size was "not to exceed six or seven thousand Men. A greater number than this, cannot be well supported in this Country nor can the enemy move with a force that will render a larger army necessary."[106]

Greene also wanted to use the lack of supplies in the area as a geographical advantage against the British. He told Colonel John Marshel that "removal of all the provisions from that Country will be the most effectual barrier against the enemy."[107] Greene wanted all livestock removed from the area around the newly reinforced Cornwallis, and for sentries to be posted on the roads to watch for any British movement. Greene also suggested the use of women to be sent into Camden as spies.[108]

By the end of 1780, events of the last month had changed the military landscape. Cornwallis was on his heels, Francis Marion and Henry Lee were harassing his rear, Greene was on the Pee Dee and Morgan was to the west.[109] Cornwallis wrote to Clinton shortly after the new year with his own set of problems: "The difficulties I have had to struggle with have not been occasioned by the opposite army (they always keep at a considerable distance, and retire on our approach) but [by] the constant incursions of refugees, North Carolinians, and back country men, and the perpetual risings in the different parts of the province. The invariable successes of all these parties against our militia keep the whole country in continual alarm, and render the assistance of regular troops everywhere necessary."[110] This was a failure of a key component of the British strategy in the South.

Outside of America, the end of the year found the British under great stress as well. Spain and France combined in warfare against Britain, and both their fleets threatened its West Indies possessions. Spain was pressing its siege of Gibraltar. Denmark and Sweden, in conjunction with Russia, struck at British commerce by declaring that neutral powers may carry goods anywhere in the world not subject to search and seizure.[111] Britain had declared war against Holland in early December after discovering the relationship between Holland and the United States and its pursuit of a commercial treaty.[112] The British struck immediately at Dutch colonies and commerce.

Tarleton remained optimistic about the operations in South Carolina. He felt that "the superiority of his [Cornwallis's] force, when compared with General Greene's, gave every reasonable assurance, that with proper care the latter might be destroyed, or driven over the Roanoke."[113] On the second of January, Tarleton began moving from Brierley's Ferry southeast of Winnsborough across the Broad River.[114] British movements were directly relayed to Morgan, and Andrew Pickens began his movement west to act as a screen between Morgan and Tarleton, while Morgan secured river crossings and an escape route, along with strengthening his flanks.[115] As Tarleton pursued Morgan, his scouts informed him that Morgan was being reinforced, so Tarleton requested another unit, the 7th Fusiliers, which Cornwallis agreed to, and Tarleton continued his march northwest.[116]

Moving out by January 7, Cornwallis encountered heavy rains and made only 10 miles, but Greene's intelligence informed him of his northern movement, convincing him that the invasion of North Carolina was underway.[117] As Cornwallis moved slowly forward, General Leslie was also slowed on his advance because of the swamps along the Pee Dee.[118] On January 14, Morgan moved his troops north toward the Broad River. This was a brilliant maneuver, for moving further north stripped the land of provisions and drew Tarleton further away from his support, and moved Morgan's men toward supplies as he moved northwest toward Cowpens.[119]

By the 15th, Tarleton had crossed the Pacolet. A long countermarch to avoid militia guarding the Pacolet fords had put Tarleton within six miles of Morgan, but at a cost: Tarleton's men had lost needed sleep and added miles to weary legs.[120] On the night of the 15th, "a party of determined loyalists made an American colonel prisoner ... and conducted him to the British camp. The examination of the militia colonel, and other accounts soon after wards received, evinced the propriety of hanging upon General Morgan's rear, to impede the junction of reinforcements, said to be approaching, and likewise to prevent his passing the Broad river without the knowledge of the light troops, who could perplex his design, and call in the assistance of the main army if necessity required."[121]

Morgan had been evading Tarleton for several days before he reached the grounds of the Cowpens on the 16th, anxiously awaiting militia reinforcements. Tarleton had been pressing his troops hard, and the rapid pursuit and lack of rest by the British would play an integral part in this affair.[122] Tarleton, impatient to strike the Americans, determined to catch them south of the Broad River. With the British seventeen miles from the river crossing, Tarleton woke his men at 2:00 a.m. to catch the Americans, and were directed to follow the route taken by them. "The ground which the Americans had passed being broken, and much intersected by creeks and ravines, the march of the British troops during the darkness was exceedingly slow, on account of the time employed in examining the front and flanks as they proceeded."[123]

As Tarleton pushed his men hard, Morgan made his dispositions and fed his men. Dennis Trammell declared in his pension statement that the Cowpens was within two and a half miles of his residence, and that General Morgan had called upon him "to assist in selecting the battle ground … with the company under his command together with General Morgan and his life guard and Aide camp…. After the battle ground was chosen, this applicant remembers the impression of Genl Morgan which was as follows … 'Captain here is Morgan's grave or victory.'"[124]

According to Major Joseph McJunkin, "the Cols. Brandon and Roebuck, with some others, had the special charge of watching Tarleton's movements from the time he reached the valley of the Pacolet. They sat on their horses as he approached and passed that stream and counted his men and sent their report to headquarters. They watched his camp on the night of the 16th until he began his march to give battle. Morgan appears to have had the most exact information of everything necessary."[125]

According to Major Thomas Young, the Americans "arrived at the field of the Cowpens about sundown, and were then told we should meet the enemy. The news was received with great joy by the army."[126] Morgan went among the men that night, building their morale and their confidence in his leadership. Major Young "was more convinced of General Morgan's qualifications to command militia than I had ever been before. He went among the volunteers, helped them fix their swords, joked with them about their sweethearts, and told them to keep in good spirits, and the day would be ours."[127] Tarleton, meanwhile, continued to push on, and captured several members of an American patrol, thereby learning that the main body was at Cowpens. Daylight had yet to occur by the time Tarleton arrived at the lower end of the fields at Cowpens. But the Americans were already in position.

The geography of the battlefield is essential to understanding how the terrain affected the outcome of the battle. The modern-day visitor to the field would see a landscape similar to 1781 but certainly not the same. Two hundred years of agriculture and roads that used to run through the park have altered the field, but have not changed it so much that interpretation is not possible. All accounts of the battle describe a partially open field, with areas that had thicker tree cover than others.[128] James Kelly described the field as "part in the woods & part an old field."[129] When entering the battlefield from the south, the field would have sloped slightly downward from left to right. The field itself was generally flat, and the only part of the field that had any elevation was a ridge in the rear, with an eminence that would have hidden a man on horseback.[130]

Tarleton described the terrain as woods that were "open and free from swamps; that the part of Broad river, just above where King's creek joined the stream, was about six miles distant from the enemy's left flank, and that the river, by making a curve to the westward, ran parallel to the rear."[131] Before the battle, one British officer recalled that

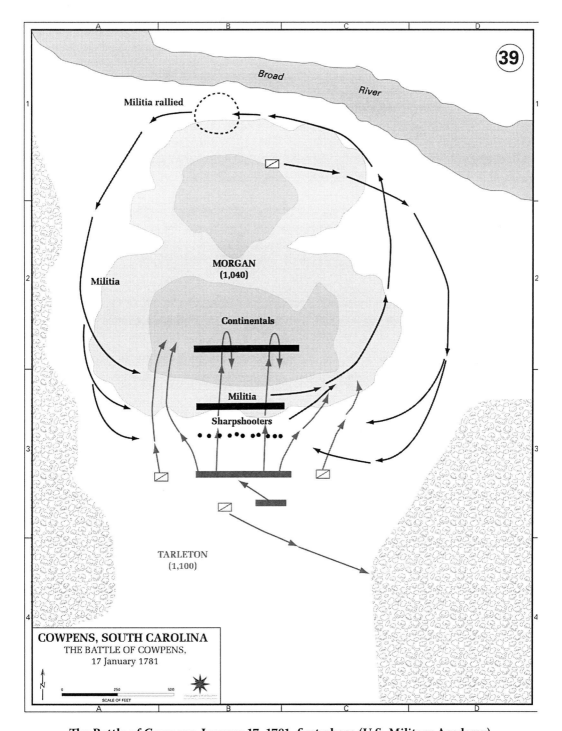

The following labels appear on the map:

39

Broad River

Militia rallied

MORGAN
(1,040)

Militia

Continentals

Militia

Sharpshooters

TARLETON
(1,100)

COWPENS, SOUTH CAROLINA
THE BATTLE OF COWPENS,
17 January 1781

0   250   500
SCALE OF FEET

The Battle of Cowpens, January 17, 1781, first phase (U.S. Military Academy)

"the ground he [Americans] occupied does not appear to have been well chosen: it was an open wood and consequently liable to be penetrated by the British cavalry: Both flanks were exposed; and the river, at no great distance, ran parallel to his rear. In such a situation he gave a manifest advantage to the enemy with a superior body of cavalry; and in case of defeat, the destruction of his whole detachment was inevitable."[132]

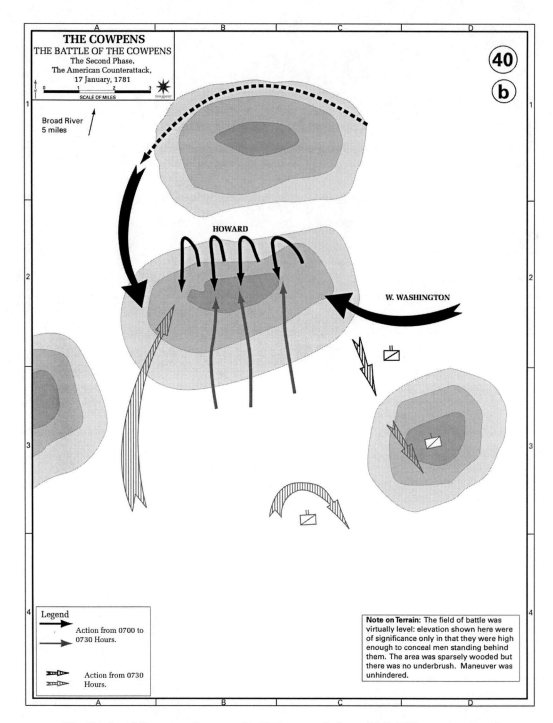

The Battle of Cowpens, January 17, 1781, second phase (U.S. Military Academy).

An important point should be made about the woods. They were clear of under-brush, and it was said that a rider on a horse could ride through the woods unimpeded. The ground Morgan had selected was also described as "gently ascending for about three hundred and fifty yards."[133] The ground of both flanks was swampy, and rivercane, a native bamboo, flanked both sides of the field with an impenetrable thicket that funneled British troops advancing down Green River Road into what amounted to a head-on assault into militia and Continental troops.

General Morgan's plan was to create a defense in depth. He posted three battle lines. The first line of defense was a group of skirmishers, about 120 in number, and loosely placed across the front and about three miles behind the videttes that were posted to announce the arrival of Tarleton.[134] The skirmish line was located in an area with partial sapling growth, but most of the field was open.[135] The skirmishers were ordered to hold their fire until the enemy came within fifty yards and then fall back slowly to the next line.[136] They were instructed to "mark the epaulette men" as the British approached.[137] The second militia line, commanded by Pickens, consisted of about 250 militiamen and were set at the first rise in the open terrain, extending about 300 yards in total distance.[138] The line was not long enough to cover the space between swamps on either flank, but when the skirmishers fell back, they would be able to fill the gaps.[139]

Andrew Pickens was of Scots-Irish descent and was a farmer and justice of the peace as the Revolution broke out. Soon, however, he took part in several actions at Ninety Six and Kettle Creek. After the surrender of Charleston, he went home on parole, but after his plantation was plundered, he gave notice his parole was invalid and took the field again. Considered grim with little sense of humor, the austere Presbyterian was lean, of medium height and robust. Henry Lee recalled that "this gentleman ... distinguished himself and corps in the progress of the war by the patience and cheerfulness with which every privation was borne, and the gallantry with which every danger was confronted."[140] He usually ranged between Ninety Six and Augusta.

The third line was drawn up on the crest of the rise with 600 men from the Maryland regulars, Virginia militia, a company of Virginia state troops, a detachment of North Carolina state troops, and about twenty-five Burke County militiamen.[141] Covering the rear was the cavalry of Lieutenant Colonel William Washington with approximately 125 men. Washington was told to cover Pickens as he retired from his line after delivering "two deliberate charges."[142] Morgan's dispositions were unorthodox. He had placed his most unreliable units in front, knowing that they would flee, but would return to the next line forming behind them.[143] The area occupied by cavalry screened them from British fire, but on horseback they could still view the field. It also provided a rallying point for militia.[144]

The morning of January 17 was cold by all accounts. Major Thomas Young recollected that "the men were slapping their hands together to keep warm—an exertion not long necessary."[145] The Americans were standing still in soggy ground, compounding the fact that they spent the night in even colder conditions, while Tarleton's men had been on the move all night.[146] Morgan had set his tactics based on topography, but also in anticipation of Tarleton's tendency for a frontal assault. If the British had made any attempt to envelop the flank, Morgan would have been heavily criticized for poor leadership and management of the battle.[147] According to Morgan, "An hour before daylight one of my scouts returned and informed me that Lieut. Col. Tarleton had advanced within five miles of our camp. On this information, I hastened to form as good a disposition as circumstances would admit, and from the alacrity of the troops, we were soon prepared to receive them."[148]

From the outset, Morgan instilled confidence in his troops. One soldier noted, "General Morgan boldly stood on his defence, and drew up his troops with great judgement."[149] Henry Wells wrote that "at the outset we were much alarmed by the Superiority of the

Enemy in numbers, but the powerful & trumpet like voice of our Commander drove fear from every bosom, and gave new energies to every arm."[150]

Tarleton appeared on the field around seven o'clock and his assault was formed about 400 yards from the American skirmishers. The light infantry was on the right, the infantry of Tarleton's Legion was in the center, and the 7th Royal Fusiliers on the left. Troops of light dragoons flanked the foot, and the reserve consisted of the 71st Highlanders and the cavalry of Tarleton's Legion. All told, his force consisted of about 1,100 men.

The first British mistake was made immediately, as the ever-aggressive Tarleton moved his men forward before everyone was in position. His 7th Regiment had not formed as he began his advance. Charles Stedman recalled: "Tarleton, relying on the valour of his troops, impatient of delay, and too confident of success, led on in person the first line to the attack, even before it was fully formed, and whilst major Newmarsh, who commanded the seventh regiment, was posting his officers: neither had the reserve yet reached the ground which it was to occupy."[151]

The British advanced rapidly. "The first line of the Americans being composed of militia, did not long withstand the charge of the British regulars: it gave way in all quarters."[152] As the skirmishers retreated in good order, they moved into line with Pickens's militia. Seeing this retreat, the British troops moved forward at quickstep, raising a great shout as they advanced. Tarleton, impetuous and moving with his usual aggressiveness, had not allowed the 7th Regiment to catch up, possibly fearing that the Americans would have time to ready themselves.[153]

As the British came within range of the militia line, the militia delivered a deadly fire, picking off officers and forcing the British line to forfeit their momentum, if only briefly.[154] Joseph McJunkin recalled in his memoirs: "John Savage ... darted a few paces in front, laid his rifle against a sapling, a blue gas streamed above his head, the sharp crack of a rifle broke the solemn stillness of the occasion and a horse without a rider wheeled from the front of the advancing column. In a few moments the fire is general."[155] The fire was devastating, and the British suffered catastrophic losses. Four British Legion companies suffered over 90 percent casualties in either killed or captured.[156] After firing twice, the militia retreated in good order through the main line and reformed behind the left flank. The British had reached the main line, physically exhausted, hungry, and now without many of their officers.

Awaiting the British line was Lieutenant Colonel John Eager Howard, commanding the Continentals and the Virginians. Howard was born to a wealthy Maryland planter, was well-educated, and began the war as a captain in the 2nd Maryland Brigade of the "Flying Camp" in 1776 and fought at White Plains. After his term of service ended, he became a major in the 4th Maryland Regiment; he and his troops performed admirably at Germantown in 1777. He was promoted to lieutenant colonel in the Fifth Regiment in 1778, and then transferred to the Second Regiment the following year. At Camden, he furthered his reputation, and was always known to be in the thickest of the fighting. Howard was known to be reserved and quiet, but on the battlefield he could be fierce. After today, Howard would receive a silver medal from Congress for his actions on this battlefield.

The British redressed their lines and moved forward. Tarleton, always sensing an opportunity, seized on the retreat of the militia and sent the 17th Light Dragoons against the American left in a flanking maneuver. Many sought safety near the crest of the rise where Washington's cavalry was posted. John Roberts remembered that "we gave way and retreated for our horses, Tarleton's cavalry pursued us … just as we got to our horses, they overtook us and began to make a few hacks at some, however, without doing much injury."[157]

Morgan saw the dragoons moving forward and unleashed Washington's cavalry to stem the tide. "In a few moments, Col. Washington's cavalry was among them, like a whirlwind, and the poor fellows began to keel from their horses, without being able to remount. The shock was so sudden and violent, they could not stand it, and immediately betook themselves to flight."[158] Morgan recalled that Washington "pushed forward, and charged with such firmness," and he was surprised at the lack of impetus from Tarleton's troops.[159]

On the American right, another possible envelopment was taking place. The arrival of the 71st Highlanders enabled the British to extend beyond Howard's right. Howard, sensing the danger of the current position of the British, ordered his right flank to reform to face the British. When Howard ordered the Virginians to reform, others in the line misinterpreted his order as a retreat, and the entire line began to retreat. Sensing a victory was at hand, the British surged forward. But Morgan ordered the Continentals to face about and fire at close range. Morgan wrote that "we retired in good order about 50 Paces, formed, advanced on the Enemy & gave them a fortunate Volley which threw them into Disorder."[160] Colonel Howard "gave orders for the Line to charge Bayonets, which was done with such Address that they fled with the utmost Precipitation, leaving the Field Pieces in our Possession."[161]

The raw recruits of the 7th Regiment fell back, and the Highlanders, still moving forward as a mob, were finally repulsed. Washington's cavalry hit the left and right of the 71st, and Pickens's militia reformed and pushed forward to the right flank of the Highlanders. According to Charles Stedman, "an order, it is said, was dispatched to the cavalry to charge the enemy when in confusion; but if such an order was delivered, it was not obeyed; and the infantry, enfeebled by their fatiguing march in the morning, through swamps and broken grounds, and by their subsequent exertions in the actions, were unable to come up with the flying enemy."[162] British troops found themselves surrounded, and Morgan had perfectly executed a double envelopment. In less an hour of intense fighting, the battle was over.

Stedman noted that "the whole loss of the British troops, in this unfortunate affair, amounted to at least six hundred men; and of them near one half was either killed or wounded. The loss of the Americans, according to their report of it, was so small as scarcely to deserve credit. It amounted to twelve killed and sixty wounded."[163] Tarleton admitted that "all attempts to restore order, recollection, or courage, proved fruitless. Above two hundred dragoons forsook their leader, and left the field of battle."[164] Tarleton himself was pursued for twenty-four miles from the battlefield, but ultimately escaped. Morgan reported to Greene: "The enemy's loss was 10 commissioned officers and over 100 rank and file killed and 200 wounded, twenty-nine commissioned officers and about 500 privates, prisoners which fell into our hands, with two pieces of artillery, two standards, 800 muskets, one travelling forge, thirty-five baggage wagons, seventy negroes and upwards of 100 dragoon horses, with all their musick."[165]

Condemnation of Tarleton was swift and harsh, and came from both sides. William Moultrie exclaimed that "there is no doubt but Colonel Tarleton was a brave man, and a good soldier, but in this affair he displayed neither generalship nor courage, but galloped off with his two hundred and fifty horse, when pursued by about seventy continental cavalry, and forty-five horse, and left his infantry to be made prisoners of."[166] Loyalist Alexander Chesney said that Tarleton "behaved bravely but imprudently the consequence was his force disperced in all directions."[167]

Charles Stedman recalled that "every disaster that befell Cornwallis, after Tarleton's most shameful defeat at the Cowpens, may most justly be attributed to the imprudence and unsoldierly conduct of that officer in the action. It was asked, why he did not consult majors M'Arthur and Newmarsh, officers of experience and reputation, who had been in service before Tarleton was born?"[168] Stedman felt that Tarleton's "talents ... never exceeded that of a partisan captain of light dragoons, daring in skirmishes," but it is the consequences of the defeat which were the most impactful.[169] "The loss of the light troops, at all times necessary to an army, but on a march through a woody and thinly settled country, almost indispensible, was not to be repaired."[170] Tarleton had lost 90 percent of his force, and a fourth of Cornwallis's army.[171]

Henry Wells recalled in his pension statement that many of the men went into winter quarters near the Cowpens until spring, and that "the British were driven out of the neighborhood, and the Tories were so much under, that they were afraid to make a show of opposition."[172] A week after the Battle of Cowpens, Governor Sir James Wright of Georgia wrote to Lord George Germain, concerned about the security of the southern provinces. He wrote that nothing has "quelled the spirit of rebellion and they [rebels] have retaliated fully. I cannot think this province [Georgia] and South Carolina in a state of security, and if Lord Cornwallis penetrates far into North Carolina I shall expect a rebel army will come in behind him and throw us into the utmost confusion and danger, for this province is still left in a defenceless state."[173]

5

The Long Retreat

With Morgan detached to the west, Greene wasted no time and went straight to work, dealing with the innumerable issues that faced the army. By early January 1781, Greene had not heard from Morgan, but that did not matter. Greene was looking forward now. Greene wrote to Gov. Abner Nash, having heard that Cornwallis had been reinforced by General Leslie, and very concerned with what this would mean for his army, "should the enemy advance with their collective force."[1] He lamented that "the little force which I have in the field, is better calculated to excite the pity of its friends, than alarm the fears of its enemies."[2] Greene had also recommended the appointment of Col. William Davie as commissary general of the department, so that supplies could be gathered and distributed more efficiently.[3]

But the issue of how the war was being conducted bothered Greene. He wrote Sumter a letter in early January, while Sumter was recovering from a wound sustained at Blackstock's Plantation in November. Sumter would not take the field again until February. Greene was frustrated about the inability to raise what he considered to be a real army that could contend with the British in the field. As long as these hit-and-run strikes continued, it would remain unwinnable, Greene said. The perceived conduct of the militia bothered Greene as well, as they were more bound to their terms of service and the availability of plunder than to the cause of liberty. Bluntly, he thought these "shoals of useless militia" did more harm than good.[4]

Frustrations for the commander were rising. When Greene's baggage had arrived, it had come without his tent. He vented to Colonel John Cox, "When I left the northern world I expected to meet difficulties in this, but they are multiplied beyond my apprehension. There is but barely the shadow of government remaining in this country.... When I say here I mean North Carolina, for in South Carolina and Georgia, there is not the shadow of it remaining."[5] To Alexander Hamilton, he complained about the diversity of the people and how the lack of order had contributed to the chaos around him: "The inhabitants are from all quarters of the globe; and as various in their opinions[,] projects and schemes, as their manners and habits are from their early education."[6]

Greene had received and sent several letters specifically regarding acquisition of supplies for his army. He was mostly concerned with salt, for the preservation of what little food he had, as well as clothes for his overexposed army. He was beginning to meet with some success thanks to loyal merchants in the South, but many were unwilling to proceed without the promise of protection from both the British and the bands of Whig and Tory militia that were laying waste to the countryside.[7]

Cornwallis had heard about the change in command among the rebels, but seems to have been less optimistic than before. After Kings Mountain, he had learned that the southern theatre could be a cruel and unpredictable place and was no longer sure of a swift victory. In a long letter to Clinton on December 3, 1780, Cornwallis related that he was "informed that Green [*sic*] is expected in few days to relieve Gates.... After everything that has happened, I will not presume to make your Excellency any sanguine promises."[8] He promised Clinton he would keep him informed, "and it is from events alone that any future plan can be proposed."[9]

Cornwallis also shared his observations of the cruel conditions in the South, especially the treatment of prisoners. He juxtaposed the fair treatment of rebel prisoners with the cruel treatment of British prisoners. "Far different was the treatment of the unhappy men who were taken with Major Ferguson. I will not hurt your Excellency's feelings by attempting to describe the shocking tortures and inhuman murders which are committed by the enemy, not only on those who have taken part with us, but on many who refuse to join them ... but I am very sure that unless some steps are taken to check it, the war in this quarter will become truly savage."[10] Clinton's reply indicated a serious fear of losing the South following Ferguson's defeat, which he first heard of through rebel accounts.

Due to the fear of the rebels' gaining in power, Clinton had dispatched General Benedict Arnold into the Chesapeake. Clinton admitted that "it remains to be proved whether we have friends in North Carolina—I am sure we had three years ago. That experiment now will, however, be fairly tried. If it succeeds and we hold the entrance of the Chesapeak, I think the rebels will never attempt either of those provinces."[11]

Later in the month, Cornwallis reported the arrival of Gen. Leslie on December 14 with no significant losses, a seemingly rare successful boat journey to the South. Despite the numbers, Cornwallis was not thrilled, describing the troops as "exclusive of the Guards and Regiment of Bose [Hessians], exceedingly bad."[12] He also complained that "the want of specie in this province puts us under the greatest difficulties ... but the sum actually in the province is so inadequate to the necessary demands that we scarcely have been able to pay the subsistence of the troops."[13]

The month at Wynnesborough had proved to be most difficult. Although Gen. Leslie had joined Cornwallis and the British held numerical superiority over the Americans, moving a large army presented its own set of difficulties. In the winter, rivers and creeks were rain-swollen, and fording—made necessary by the lack of bridges—became impossible. In summer, the extreme heat and humidity made any rapid movements virtually nonexistent.

The news about Cowpens filtered in to both camps and created promise for one army and impending trouble for another. Greene discussed his advantageous position in a letter, while noting Cornwallis was in a less favorable one. "It makes the most of my inferior force, for it compels my adversary to divide his, and hold him in doubt as to his own line of conduct. He cannot leave Morgan behind to come at me, or his posts of Ninety-Six and Augusta be exposed. And he cannot chase Morgan far, or prosecute his views upon Virginia, while I am here with the whole country open before me."[14] Despite this advantage, the British held an advantage of their own. The geography below the falls where Greene was currently situated was significantly more difficult to traverse than that above the falls, and Greene intended to move his army in that direction once the situation presented itself.[15]

On the morning of January 18, Tarleton rode into camp at Turkey Creek with the terrible news. With Tarleton's defeat, almost 1,000 British and loyalist soldiers were prisoners of war in North Carolina.[16] The loss of Cornwallis's light troops had considerably crippled the army, and that was only the beginning of issues both in the Carolinas and abroad. In Britain, war weariness had set in. The economy was in poor shape due to increased taxation and the debt created by this war that was now in its sixth year.[17] The cost of war was becoming unsustainable.

The same day Cornwallis was reunited with Tarleton, Major General Alexander Leslie arrived with 1,200 reinforcements from Charleston, swelling Cornwallis's numbers to approximately 2,500 men. Fortunately for Cornwallis, he had not detached to Tarleton his most important battle units: the 33rd Foot, the Royal Welsh Fusiliers (23rd Foot), and the 2nd Battalion of Fraser's Highlanders (71st Foot).[18] Leslie brought with him the German unit, the von Bose Regiment, a British brigade, and a regiment of North Carolina Volunteers. But Cornwallis had wasted much time, and Morgan was already on the move.

After the Battle of Cowpens, Morgan had wasted little time, and headed north across the Broad River with his nearly 600 prisoners. Morgan knew that he needed to be out of range of Cornwallis's numerically superior army, and he knew that he had to make contact with Greene. By the time Cornwallis was on the move, Morgan was at Gilbert Town, twenty miles north of Cowpens. Cornwallis was determined to catch Greene or Morgan (possibly both), and "hoped by rapid marches to get between General Greene and Virginia and by that means force him to fight without receiving reinforcement."[19] Greene needed to avoid being destroyed with his army separated into two wings, and needed to escape the grasp of Cornwallis if he were to remain in the field.[20] Reinforcements were essential.

Cornwallis began his march after Morgan on the morning of January 19. Almost immediately, he ran into problems. The first problem was that Cornwallis misjudged the degree of flooding that occurred in the rivers above the forks. He was aware that the large number of fords for crossing made any particular one less apt to be defended, but the potential for flooding was much higher. The second problem was the conditions of the road networks in winter. Benjamin J. Lossing, who traveled these roads long after the war, noted the severity, commenting that "no one can form an idea of the character of the roads in winter … without passing over them. Until I had done so, I could not appreciate the difficulties experienced by the two armies … particularly in the transportation of baggage wagons or of artillery."[21] Compounding matters, Cornwallis took the wrong road and lost two days in his pursuit of Morgan. Discovering his error, Cornwallis struggled through swollen streams and virtually impassable roads. The loss of his light troops from Cowpens had hampered Cornwallis's ability to provide intelligence and to harass the enemy.[22]

Morgan, meanwhile, had moved his prisoners northward, and crossed the Catawba River at Sherrald's Ford. Even though Cornwallis had picked up Morgan's trail two days after he had set out, Morgan was able to keep the swollen river between him and his pursuers. Even Tarleton gave the Americans credit: "But the celerity made use of by the Americans … enabled them to evade his lordship's army and reach the Catawba. In the mean time, General Greene appointed the eastern bank of that river for the place of rendezvous of the militia, and to effect a junction, if possible, of the continentals. In order to complete his plan, he prepared to dispute the passage of the British, with General Morgan's division and the militia, till the other corps of continentals could, by forced marches, reach the upper parts of North Carolina."[23] Morgan had reported to Greene on the 23rd that Cornwallis was in pursuit, but was several days behind him due to "bad intelligence."[24]

Greene had initially wanted to draw Cornwallis away from Morgan by attacking

Ninety Six, but had to change his mind due to the expiring enlistments of Stevens's Virginia militia. With the loss of troops, Greene decided to reunite with Morgan against Cornwallis's invasion of North Carolina. To prepare for all eventualities, Greene ordered all prisoners and supplies to Virginia and the assembly of boats on the Dan River in case of a retreat.[25] Greene instructed Brigadier General Isaac Huger of the South Carolina militia to move Greene's army to Salisbury for a junction with Morgan. Then on January 28, Greene set off on a 125-mile ride across enemy country to take control of Morgan's detachment in Cornwallis's front.[26]

On January 25, Cornwallis arrived at Ramsour's Mill, only to discover that Morgan had already passed through two days before and was now about 20 miles east on the opposite bank of the Catawba River.[27] The rains were constant and the river was rising, and finally Morgan could rest his men. Cornwallis had taken three days and covered only thirty miles.[28] Brigadier General Charles O'Hara had observed that North Carolina was "almost a continued thick Forrest, cut with numberless Broad, Deep and rapid Waters and it was evident that the movements of the Army, would be attended with many difficulties."[29]

Cornwallis, understanding the nature of the terrain and weather and the necessity of catching Morgan and Greene, made a fateful decision that would haunt him the rest of the campaign. Cornwallis destroyed most of his wagon train and attempted to turn his army into the light troops that he had lost at Cowpens. "I employed a halt of two days in collecting some flour and in destroying superfluous baggage and all my wagons except those loaded with hospital stores, salt, ammunition and four reserved empty in readiness for sick and wounded."[30] Cornwallis was to push on, his men unable to cover themselves with tents, and with only the food they could carry.[31]

O'Hara correctly stated the British situation in North Carolina: "Without Baggage, necessaries, or Provisions of any sort for Officer or Soldier, in the most barren, inhospitable unhealthy part of North America, opposed to the most savage, inveterate perfidious cruel Enemy, with zeal and Bayonets only, it was resolved to follow Greene's army to the end of the World."[32] Charles Stedman remembered "the hardships suffered by the British troops, for want of their tents and usual baggage, in this long and rapid pursuit, through a wild and unsettled country, were uncommonly great; yet such was their ardor in the service, that they submitted to them without a murmur."[33]

Greene had finally reached Morgan on January 30, and was hastily making preparations and keeping up with his voluminous correspondence. He updated Col. William Campbell and noted that "the enemy are pushing into the country and are now as high up the Catawba as [Sherrarld's] ford; and seem determined … to push the Continental troops out of the State. To prevent so great a misfortune, I could wish you would bring to our assistance 1000 good Volunteers to serve one month, after they arrive at Headquarters. Such a force … will enable us to push the Enemy in turn."[34] Greene was eager to supplement his forces because when he learned that Cornwallis had burned most of his wagons in order to become light infantry, he felt that the larger British force was able to move more rapidly than the Americans.[35]

General William L. Davidson put out a call for militia, but that raised only 300 men, and he did not expect to get many more than that.[36] Greene was unhappy with the lack of militia turnout for General Davidson's summons. He tried to shine a light on the seriousness of the situation. To the officers commanding the militia in the Salisbury district of North Carolina, he wrote, "The inattention to his call and the backwardness of the people is unaccountable."[37] Greene reminded them of the good fortune the Americans had shared recently at Cowpens and at Georgetown. "If after these advantages you neglect to take the field and suffer the enemy to over run the Country, you will deserve the miseries ever inseparable from slavery."[38] This call to arms appears to have been largely unsuccessful, and several copies were intercepted by the British, including by Tarleton himself.

On January 31, Greene called a rare council of war at Beattie's Ford with Morgan, Davidson, and Colonel Washington. Captain Joseph Graham, a North Carolina militiaman, was present also. Sitting on a log a short distance from camp, they discussed their upcoming plans. According to Captain Graham, "the British vanguard of about four or five hundred men, appeared on the opposite hill beyond the river. Shortly after their arrival, some principal officer, with a numerous staff, thought to be Lord Cornwallis, passed in front of them at different stations, halting and apparently viewing us with spy-glasses."[39] It did not take Greene long to come to the obvious conclusion. Davidson's 800 militiamen and Morgan's men would be unable to defend the numerous fords, so they would dispute Cornwallis's crossing long enough so that the Continentals would get a head start toward Salisbury and allow Huger's men to rendezvous there coming from the Great Pee Dee. The Catawba was falling and would be fordable in the next several days.[40]

Greene regarded Salisbury as a key to the retreat, for it was a major supply depot for the southern army and would be a necessary stop on this long retreat.[41] So Greene headed toward Salisbury on the main road, while Morgan and Washington took a different route, looking to eventually link up with Col. John Eager Howard.

Meanwhile, Cornwallis was on the move. In the early morning hours of February 1, Cornwallis began his march to the Catawba to force a crossing at daybreak. Davidson had predicted that Cornwallis would not contest a crossing at Sherrald's or Beattie's Ford, but four miles south at a place known as Cowan's Ford. The river at this point was no more than 500 yards wide, but had steep banks and was heavily wooded.[42] Davidson had deployed 250 militia to cover two crossings, a wagon ford and a horse crossing.[43] As night fell on the 31st, a young man by the name of Robert Henry remembered that "a man across the river hooted like an owl and was answered. A man went to a canoe some distance off and brought word from him that all was silent in the British camp. The guard all lay down with their guns in their arms, and were all sound asleep at day-break, except Joel Jetton, who discovered the noise of horses in deep water."[44]

Quickly, word spread of horses splashing in the water. Robert Henry noted that "by the time I was ready to fire, the rest of the guard had fired."[45] Approximately 1,200 British and Hessian soldiers had approached the ford so quietly that the rebels had no idea they were so close. The current was swift, there was a heavy mist, but nonetheless, the British began the crossing. Sergeant Roger Lamb reported that "Lord Cornwallis, according to his usual manner, dashed first into the river, mounted on a very fine spirited horse, the brigade of guards followed, two three pounders next, the Royal Welch fuzileers after them."[46] Under fire from the shoreline, the British were facing more than just the enemy firing down on them. Henry recorded that "the water at the Ford was fully waist-band deep, and in many places much deeper, with a very heavy pressing current, and when a man was killed or wounded, the current immediately floated him away, so that none of them that were killed or wounded were ever brought to the shore; and none but those slightly wounded reached the bank."[47]

Major General Leslie's and General O'Hara's horses dumped their riders into the swift current. Both men survived and were fortunate. Other infantrymen were drowned. The British advanced without firing "as our cartouch boxes were all tied at the back of our necks. This urged us on with great rapidity, till we gained the opposite shore, where we were obliged to scramble up a very high hill under a heavy fire."[48] General Davidson heard the firing and hurried his men to the riverbank. By the time Davidson had reached the scene, the British were out of the water, loading their muskets and firing as they went.[49] Davidson had ridden from the upper horse crossing to the wagon ford and was attempting to form his men. "The enemy was advancing slowly in line, and only firing scatteringly, when General Davidson was pierced by a ball and fell dead from his horse," recalled Graham.[50] Without their leader, many militiamen scattered and fled.

The number of British dead from this operation is disputed. While Cornwallis stated that he lost four killed and thirty-six wounded, other witnesses offered their own appraisals of the cost of the British crossing. "That a great number of British dead were found on Thompson's fish-dam, and in his trap, and numbers lodged on brush, and drifted to the banks: that the river stunk with dead carcasses; that the British could not have lost less than one hundred men on that occasion," stated Robert Henry.[51] According to Henry, this was "the report of every person who lived at or near the river between Cowan's Ford and Tuckaseage Ford."[52] American losses as well could not be verified, although they had lost fewer than the British.

The British immediately reorganized upon crossing at Cowan's Ford. After all the fords were abandoned, and all units had reunited, Cornwallis made camp on the night of February 1 about six miles from Beattie's Ford.[53] Before setting out from the ford, Cornwallis dispatched Tarleton with his dragoons to find Greene. Instead, Tarleton found some of Davidson's militia who had not fallen back to Salisbury as Greene had ordered. He found them at a place called Torrence's Tavern or Tarrant's Tavern on the road to Salisbury. After a skirmish, which remains controversial because it was alleged the militiamen were drunk, Tarleton claimed he "attacked them instantly, and totally routed them, with little loss on his own side, and on their's, between forty and fifty killed, wounded or prisoners."[54] Charles Stedman contradicts Tarleton's account of the number killed, reporting that "a British officer, who rode over the ground not long after the action, relates, that he did not see ten dead bodies of the provincials on the whole."[55]

Even with the Americans in full pursuit, the British were faced with other obstacles than just swollen rivers and poor roads. Cornwallis's army, who desperately needed the support of the populace, had alienated them instead. The behavior of the British soldiers was deplorable. They had destroyed civilian property, burned the home of a local Whig, and torched Torrence's Tavern.[56] Refugees and wagonloads of their possessions flooded the roads, along with farm animals of every kind, in the face of the advancing British army. The winter rains added to the misery of the scene.

Cornwallis tried to stem the tide of British destruction, with an entry in a British orderly book stating: "Lord Cornwallis is highly displeas'd that Several Houses was set on fire during the march this day, A Disgrace to the Army; & that he will punish with the Utmost Severity any person or persons who shall be found Guilty of Committing so disgracefull an Outrage."[57] Four days later, officers were on notice: "Any Officer who looks on with Indifference & does not do his Utmost to prevent the Shameful Marauding Which has of late prevail'd in the Army Will be Consider'd in a more Criminal light than the persons who commit those Scandalous Crimes."[58]

As Greene retreated further and further across North Carolina, he was creating an opportunity for his own army. He was pulling Cornwallis deeper and deeper into the hinterlands away from his base of supply.[59] Greene had written Isaac Huger on February 1 and reported that Cornwallis had crossed the river and their destination was to be Salisbury, and they should be there in a day or two because he did not have the ability to slow him down. He recommended that Huger advance along the east side of the Yadkin, secure the provisions and baggage in the area, and reroute all supplies to Guilford.[60]

Not having yet received Greene's letter about Cornwallis's crossing, Huger also wrote Greene on the 1st informing him that the army was in motion, but that he lacked sufficient meal for the troops. He also told Greene that the supplies that the army had available would have to be moved by land, since "the river is so rapid that it is impossible for boats to stem it, and this difficulty will create delay in crossing the Pedee."[61]

Greene was feeling the pressure of Cornwallis's advance, and the lack of necessary troops was creating worry. Major Ichabod Burnet wrote to Henry Lee discussing this very topic. "If you knew the anxiety of General Greene, who is now exposing himself to collect the militia, which he expects only to accomplish by having a superiority of horse. Indeed our army cannot keep the field one moment after they cross the Yadkin, unless we have a superiority of cavalry."[62] At this point, Greene was focusing on collecting cavalry to challenge those under Tarleton. Currently, Greene had only William Washington's dragoons on hand, numbering only 60 men. Tarleton reportedly had 250 dragoons and the militia under him.[63]

Greene had been warned of Cornwallis's crossing of the Catawba and in the early morning hours of February 2, he set off for Salisbury. He spent only enough time there to coordinate the evacuation of supplies. He also ordered Captain Joseph Marbury to the Moravian towns in order to move the large quantities of stores that had been placed in them. Greene believed it was "most probable that the destruction of public Stores will be one of their first objects."[64] Since the stores were of the utmost importance, "Marbury will be held 'harmless' for 'any steps' he has to take in this business."[65]

Greene and Morgan crossed the Yadkin at Trading Ford on February 3 in the early morning hours. The weather made it all the worse, with Lieutenant Thomas Anderson noting that "it having rained incessantly all night, which rendered the roads almost inaccessible."[66] The British had indeed marched for Salisbury, and halted there to forage for food and supplies, and to free some prisoners held in the jail. But every minute wasted put distance between Cornwallis and Greene. Cornwallis had redoubled his efforts to catch Morgan. He lightened his baggage even further and even mounted more of his infantry. But as the British column approached the Yadkin, disappointment once again visited the British. Morgan and Greene had already crossed except for a few wagons from his rear guard.[67] On the eastern bank of the river, all the boats were tied up safely out of British hands. The British had marched twenty miles in pouring rain and trudged through muddy roads, but once again, instead of continuing the pursuit, they rested. Greene did not.

Since Huger had not been able to rendezvous at the Yadkin, Greene advised him in a letter of February 5 to march to Guilford Courthouse. "It is not improbable from Lord Cornwallises pushing disposition, and the contempt he has for our army, we may precipitate him into some capital misfortune. I wish to be prepar'd, either for attacking, or for receiving one."[68] Greene knew the odds were stacked against him, but all was not lost yet. "If Lord Cornwallis knows his true interest he will pursue our army. If he can disperse that, he compleats the reduction of the State: and without that he will do nothing to the effect."[69]

Morgan would arrive at Guilford Courthouse on February 6, while Greene stayed back watching Cornwallis. Even with Cornwallis on the other bank, Greene coolly dispatched some important letters. He wrote the commanding officer of the Guilford Militia, explaining the situation, and ordered him to assemble the local militia and gather as many supplies as he could.[70] Similarly, Greene wrote to the officer commanding the militia behind Cornwallis, requesting information as to their numbers and supplies, and he wanted to know if they had a way around the British so they could join the main southern army.[71]

With Trading Ford impassable, Cornwallis sent Tarleton upriver to find a place to cross, which he did at a place called Shallow Ford. It was twenty-five miles north of Trading Ford, but in road miles it turned out to be forty. Again, the rain soaked them and the red clay roads made travel extremely slow, at about one mile per hour.[72] The British passed through several Moravian communities along the way, including Bethania, Bethabara, and Salem, commandeering food and supplies after the area had already been plundered by Whig militias. The Moravians took a dim view of the British requisitions after a while. "Just now the question is not who are friends of the land, but who are friends of the king."[73]

Finally, on February 7, the missing pieces of the southern army came together at Guilford Courthouse. Huger's troops finally marched into camp, as well as Henry Lee and his Legion. Huger's men were in deplorable condition, many destitute of shoes and clothed in rags. Lee's men were the only ones who could have been described as adequately outfitted. Through long marches and heavy rains, Huger had not lost a man.

On the afternoon of February 9, Greene called together a council of war to discuss the military situation. The Americans were in difficult straits, with only 1,426 men who were regular infantry, along with 600 militiamen, many of whom were badly equipped.[74] The enemy was estimated to be 2,500–3,000 men, and with a bad supply situation, the council unanimously voted that the army "ought to avoid a general Action at all Events, and that the Army ought to retreat immediately over the Roanoke River."[75] Greene also appointed Andrew Pickens to command the militia in the rear of the enemy to replace the fallen General Davidson.[76]

But soon, Greene would be losing one of his key soldiers, Daniel Morgan. Since Cowpens, Morgan had been suffering from sciatica, rheumatism, and other painful ailments, made all the worse by the cold and the long march and campaigning in general. Morgan wrote to Greene on February 6, "I am much indisposed with pains, and to add to my misfortunes, am violently attacked with the piles, so that I can scarcely sit upon my horse."[77] On February 10, he could take it no more. He climbed into a carriage for the ride to Virginia and home. Greene had granted a leave of absence to Morgan, leaving the door open to a return to the fight. It was an incredible loss, as Morgan had made himself an indispensable part of Greene's army.

But one of the more crucial decisions Greene made was to appoint Colonel Otho Holland Williams as the commander of a light corps of 700 men that would have gone to Morgan had he been able to stay. This corps would be used to harass Cornwallis's army and lure him away from the main body so it could reach the Dan River unmolested. Williams would be reinforced by a unit of infantry and horse from Henry Lee, William Washington's horsemen from the 1st and 3rd Continental Light Dragoons, a 280-man detachment of Virginia, Maryland, and Delaware light infantry under Lt. Col. John Eager Howard, as well as 60 Virginia riflemen.[78]

Greene had sent out many letters during the period of February 9–11 to ensure what valuable supplies he had were moved into Virginia so that Cornwallis could not seize or destroy them. He told Steuben that no militia had made it to the rendezvous point following Cornwallis's crossing of the Catawba, and he had little information on the numbers of militia available in South Carolina behind enemy lines.[79] Greene also updated Governor Nash on the decision of the council to retreat. He told Nash to do all he could to protect public stores in the area. He also took the opportunity to take a swipe at the militia: "I think it an endless task to attempt to arm and equip all your Militia. Such a waste of arms and ammunition as I have seen in different parts of this State, is enough to exhaust all the Arsenals of Europe. Nor ought arms in my opinion to be put into the hands of doubt[ful] characters: for you may depend upon it such will never be useful in the hour of diffi[cul]ty."[80]

Cornwallis, meanwhile, had finally crossed the Yadkin on February 9 and the following day entered Salem. He was now within a day's march of Guilford Courthouse, about twenty-five miles to the east. Cornwallis had learned through his spies that Greene would try to ford the Dan River on the upper part of the river just north of Guilford Courthouse and would avoid the lower parts of the river because of the lack of boats and the depth of the river.[81] With his location at Salem, Cornwallis was equidistant from the upper fords as Greene, and concluded that "not having time to collect the North Carolina militia and having no reinforcement from Virginia, I concluded that he would do everything in his power to avoid an action on the south side of the Dan; and, it being my interest to force him to fight."[82] If Greene were caught, Virginia lay open to Cornwallis and the course of the war would be in jeopardy for the Americans.[83] Cornwallis, continuing to lack proper intelligence on the movements of Greene's army, headed east attempting to get between Huger's division and Greene, not realizing that they had already united.[84]

On February 10, 1781, the race to the Dan River began. Greene had planned to withdraw his army to the safety of the north side of the Dan by using the two ferries northeast of Guilford Courthouse, Irwin's Ferry near present-day Turbeville, Virginia, and Boyd's Ferry, four miles to the east. Col. Edward Carrington had reported to Greene that he had six boats ready at the crossings, and Greene had further urged Carrington to assemble anything that could float in order to get the men across.[85] It must be remembered that the Dan River had been stripped of boats before the retreat even started. Greene would head to the two lower ferries, while Williams would make a move to the upper fords, attempting to draw Cornwallis away from the main body. Kosciuszko was preparing fortifications to cover the crossing at the Dan.[86]

Greene had begun his march towards Boyd's Ferry, about 70 miles northeast of Guilford Courthouse, on February 10, while Williams headed northwest toward Bruce's Cross Roads to make contact with the British and draw the British away from the main body of the army.

The common soldier endured incredible hardships since beginning the retreat back at Cowpens. William Seymour noted in his journal that he had made "a march of two hundred and fifty miles from the time we left our encampment at Pacolet River."[87] He also noted that he "marched for the most part both day and night, the main army of the British being so close in our rear, so that we had not scarce time to cook our victuals, their whole attention being on our light troops."[88] Greene's men battled rain and snow, traversing roads thick with mud by day and frozen by night. They marched 19 hours a day, briefly halting for one daily meal and a few hours of sleep. Many marched without shoes over the frozen terrain, blood staining the ground every step of the way. Often, they were without meat and flour and crossed a barren landscape with little hope of food. With the little protection they had from the elements, they still had to ford creeks, and their clothes remained wet until they were able to dry them by a fire at night.[89] It had been one of the most remarkable feats of endurance and devotion ever displayed by American troops in war, but the pressure was on and Cornwallis was pushing relentlessly forward.

Col. Williams was demonstrating his abilities in his rear-guard action. Lee's Legion was dangerously close to Cornwallis. On February 11, Williams wrote Greene that the British were within 6 to 8 miles of his position, and the whole British army was on the move.[90] Williams was in sight of Cornwallis's advanced forces each day, and skirmishing was constant day and night.[91] Lee recalled that "the duty, severe in the day, became more so at night; for numerous patroles and strong piquets were necessarily furnished by the light troops, not only for their own safety, but to prevent the enemy from placing himself, by a circuitous march, between Williams and Greene."[92] These were tense days. Williams wrote Greene on the 13th warning him that Cornwallis was rapidly approaching and that the enemy was not more than ten miles behind him. Williams was concerned that Greene would not reach the next crossing in time and was prepared to lay in wait for the enemy so as to buy Greene enough time to cross the Dan.[93]

On February 13, William's rear guard skirmished with the British advance and decided to end his feint. He turned his forces away from Dix's Ferry and the upstream fords and began the final push northeast for the lower fords and Greene's main body. Cornwallis already knew the Americans were headed for the lower fords, and the chase took on a greater intensity. According to Lee, "Cornwallis … urged his march with redoubled zeal, confident of overtaking his adversary before he could reach the Dan."[94] Cornwallis and Williams were at a forced march for the duration.

At nightfall on the 13th, the British had finally stopped to rest, and the Americans did as well, but not for long. The British advance was closing on the American pickets and Williams continued on with the torrid pace. "About midnight our troops were put in motion, in consequence of the enemy's advance on our piquets, which the British general had been induced to order from knowing that he was within forty miles of the Dan, and that all his hope depended on the exertions of the following day," wrote Lee.[95] Lee also noted that "the roads continued deep and broken, and were rendered worse by being incrusted with frost: nevertheless, the march was pushed with great expedition."[96] At two o'clock on February 14, a note from Greene arrived with important news: "The greater part of our wagons are over, and the troops are crossing."[97] Later that day, at 5:30 p.m., another note arrived from Greene: "½ past 5 o'clock. All our troops are over and the stage is clear…. I am ready to receive you and give you a hearty welcome."[98]

Greene had decided to cross the river at Irwin's Ferry when Williams arrived. The infantry and Washington's dragoons arrived in the early evening. Lee's Legion crossed at Boyd's Ferry with the men in boats and the horses swimming the swollen river at about 9:00 p.m. The most spectacular retreat of the American Revolution was over, and Nathanael Greene had once against bested his opponent.

George Washington may have saved the Revolution in 1776 with the crossing of the Delaware, but Greene's retreat may exceed Washington's retreat across New Jersey in terms of its overall importance in the war. This retreat seriously weakened Cornwallis's ability to wage war. Greene brought Cornwallis over 200 miles from his supply base into a barren wasteland. And once again, it was another river that could not be crossed. Greene's army was established in the breastworks on the north bank of the river and on the hill where Ferry Street runs today, and there was nothing Cornwallis could do about it. "In the evening lord Cornwallis had received the unwelcome news of Greene's safe passage over the Dan; and now relinquishing his expectation of annihilating a second army, and despairing of striking the light corps, so long in his view and always safe, he gave repose to his vainly wearied troops."[99]

Sometime in the early morning hours of February 15, a group of British officers led by Cornwallis rode out from Boyd's Tavern toward the Dan River. Cornwallis did not record anything about learning of Greene's crossing, but when he observed the scene of his failure, he must have had a bitter sense of frustration and bewilderment. He had driven his army hard, but Greene had driven his harder. Greene had saved his army from a major engagement with the British they could not have survived. It was a momentous occasion and it has been underrated in the historical record. Greene's leadership and his devotion to the cause, as well as the men who struggled through this brutal retreat, should be recognized justly, much like the men who crossed the icy Delaware on a cold Christmas night several years earlier.

After the crossing, several men reflected on what had happened. Major Ichabod Burnet, Greene's aide, wrote that the army had been "hard pushed [and] obliged to march from twenty to thirty miles a day," but now they were "safe over the river and … laughing at the enemy who are on the opposite bank."[100] Tarleton, rarely complimentary to the Americans, reluctantly acknowledged that "every measure of the Americans, during their march from the Catawba to Virginia, was judiciously designed and vigorously executed."[101] Cornwallis wrote to Germain that despite the best efforts of the British, bad roads, weather and intelligence allowed Greene's army to slip away.[102]

Otho Williams, after a brilliantly led retreat with the light troops, admitted to his brother that "the enemy have driven us out of the Carolinas are now on the opposite side of the River. The Inferiority of our force obliges the General to retire and we have no flattering expectations."[103] Williams was correct. Greene's army was safe for the time being, but it had been heavily depleted and exhausted. In addition, many of the militia had deserted, and the North Carolina militia had failed to link up with Greene due to the speed of Cornwallis' movement.[104]

Henry Lee reflected for several pages in his memoirs regarding this crossing. He praised Greene and Carrington, whose efforts were surely monumental, but his praise for the common soldier and his ordeal tells of the difficulties that had to be surmounted. "The difficulty of the retreat from South Carolina with an inferior army … presented in themselves impediments great and difficult. When we add the comfortless condition of our clothing, the rigor of the season, the inclemency of the weather, our short stock of ammunition, and shorter stocks of provisions … we have abundant cause to honor the soldier whose mental resources smoothed every difficulty, and ultimately made a good retreat of two hundred and thirty miles … without the loss of troops or stores."[105] Lee even went as far as praising his British counterparts, for their "bearing incessant toil, courting danger, and submitting to privation of necessary food with alacrity; exhibiting … unquestionable evidence of fidelity, zeal and courage."[106]

Clockwise from top left: Nathanael Greene (1742–1786) by Charles Wilson Peale, from life, 1783 (Independence National Historical Park). Charles Cornwallis, c. 1803 (University of South Carolina). Horatio Gates (1728/9–1806) by Charles Wilson Peale, from life, 1782 (Independence National Historical Park). Sir Henry Clinton, commander in chief of British Forces in North America, engraving, c. 1800 (New York Historical Society). Daniel Morgan (1736–1802) by Charles Wilson Peale, from life, c. 1794 (courtesy Independence National Historical Park).

Top, left: Francis Marion, ca. 1780 (University of South Carolina). *Above:* Henry Lee (1756–1818) by Charles Wilson Peale, from life, c. 1782 (Independence National Historical Park). *Left:* Benjamin Lincoln, c. 1864 (University of South Carolina).

Regardless of the success of the American retreat, North and South Carolina had been left in mostly British hands. Loyalists were emboldened. The partisan bands of Sumter, Pickens and Marion were the only American forces left in these states, and they did not have the manpower or reach to combat British occupation. They could create havoc against foraging parties and interrupt supply lines, but they were no match for British regulars.[107] However, it appeared that Cornwallis would not be crossing the river.

Greene, active as ever, wrote to the North Carolina legislature on the 15th, providing an

The death of Major Patrick Ferguson at the Battle of Kings Mountain, October 7, 1780 (University of South Carolina).

update on his condition, and again requested more troops be sent. He emphasized that he could not win the war without more men. "The Legislature may rest assured that nothing on my part shall be wanting to repel the Enemy; but I can effect nothing, unless I am largely reinforced."[108] He also believed that Cornwallis planned to march on Hillsborough and Halifax, and he planned to follow them as soon as they did so. Should Cornwallis make that move, Greene urged that all useable supplies and horses be moved out of his way so he would not be able to supply himself en route.[109] Greene had discussed the importance of these places with Steuben, noting that he wanted "to prevent the enemy from taking post there; as it is one of the richest counties and will give them possession of the greatest part of the Store of the State, and break up the only Manufactures established in N. Carolina."[110] Greene sent Kosciuszko to Halifax to determine whether the

William Washington (1752–1810), by Charles Wilson Peale, from life, 1781–1782 (Independence National Historical Park).

Clockwise from top left: **Andrew Pickens, early 1800s (University of South Carolina). Lord Rawdon, c. 1791 (University of South Carolina). Thomas Sumter, c. 1795 (University of South Carolina). John Eager Howard (1752–1827) by Charles Wilson Peale, from life, c. 1781–1784 (courtesy Independence National Historical Park).**

city was in a defendable position, and Col. Nicholas Long and Gen. Richard Caswell would assist however possible.

Greene had set up camp at Halifax Courthouse by the 16th, and would now be forced to wait for Cornwallis's next move. Greene had sent out numerous letters requesting more men, estimating he would require about 4000 men to "check the enemy."[111] He also received a letter from Jefferson, who had ordered 700 riflemen and 400 militia to join Greene.[112] Washington confirmed with Greene that he had spoken to Jefferson about sending more men, and he also took time to congratulate Greene on his recent success avoiding the British army. "I am most wonderfully Elated at your Successes since you took command of the Southern Army. Lett not the loss of a little ground now discourage you. We have Country enough to Manoeuvre in and a proper opportunity may teach his Lordship to Advance with more prudence at a future day."[113] Washington also advised caution, urging Greene to carefully consider every move, knowing that a mistake could prove fatal to his army and his cause.[114]

Despite all Greene's efforts in procuring more men under arms, it was not happening as fast as he wanted it to. On the 18th, Greene wrote to Steuben pleading him to accelerate the mustering of 500 men promised on the 3rd of February.[115] Unbeknownst to Greene, Steuben had penned a letter the day before explaining that a lack of clothing for the troops was going to delay their being sent until at least the 25th of February.[116] Greene also reminded Steuben about the importance of preventing a rendezvous between Cornwallis and General Benedict Arnold. "Indeed your whole attention ought to be directed to that quarter until Lord Cornwallis's movements are further explained."[117] However, Greene would be somewhat rewarded for all his hard work. He was able to acquire horses from Virginia farms and plantations, with Jefferson's approval, and he was able to obtain some clothing for his men.[118] New militiamen reported for duty, several hundred led by General Edward Stevens, at Greene's Halifax Courthouse headquarters. But reinforcements intended for the patriot army were moved elsewhere by state governments, denying Greene what he wanted.[119]

Cornwallis's actions would soon be apparent. At about 4 p.m. the afternoon of the 18th, Colonel Henry Lee reported that he had indirect information leading him to believe Cornwallis would depart in the direction of Hillsborough. Greene would be re-crossing the river back into North Carolina.

6

Regaining the Initiative: The Path to Guilford Courthouse

Colonel Otho Williams wrote to his brother from the north side of the Dan on February 21 describing the heroic aspects of the retreat, but the most important piece of information was that "Lord Cornwallis … did not attempt to pass the Dan River but faced about on the morning of the 19th instant and marched towards Hillsborough."[1]

Indeed, Cornwallis had set off for Hillsborough, some fifty miles south of the Dan. "My force being ill suited to enter by that quarter so powerfull a province as Virginia, and North Carolina being in the utmost confusion, after giving the troops a halt of one day, I proceeded by easy marches to Hillsborough, where I erected the King's standard and invited by proclamation all loyal subjects," Cornwallis wrote to Germain.[2] Cornwallis's situation south of the Dan had been perilous. His nearest supply base was back in Camden, and no supplies were moving towards the Dan. He had not set up any magazines, so his food supply was low, and he had no medical facilities for the sick and wounded. Reinforcements were not coming, and he had no knowledge of the political climate of the country in which he was moving.[3]

Cornwallis admitted to Lord Rawdon that he "tried by a most rapid march to strike a blow either at Greene or Morgan before they got over the Dan, but could not affect it. The enemy, however, was too hurried to be able to raise any militia in this province. The fatigue of our troops and the hardships which they suffered were excessive."[4] Cornwallis knew that Greene would be reinforced, and requested of Rawdon that he send "the three regiments expected from Ireland to be sent to me as soon as possible by way of Cape Fear, with orders to proceed without loss of time to Cross Creek."[5] Cornwallis's men were "in the greatest want of shoes and other necessaries."[6]

Once he arrived in Hillsborough, Cornwallis's time there was rapidly becoming a problem. Charles Stedman recounted that he "was obliged to go from house to house, throughout the town, to take provisions from the inhabitants, many of whom were greatly distressed by this measure, which could be justified only by extreme necessity."[7] To compound issues, a British orderly book, in an entry dated February 22, indicated concerns with the behavior of the soldiers. One entry noted that "with great concern that Lord Cornwallis hears every day reports of Soldiers being taken by the Enemy, in consequence of their Straggling out of Camp in search of Whiskey."[8] Soldiers were on notice that "he will render himself unserviceable to it during the whole War, & of passing some Years in a Lonesome prison Subject to the bitter Insults of the Rebels, for the Chance of a momentary Gratification of his Appetite."[9] Even with these threats, the soldiery changed their habits very little if at all.

On February 20, when Cornwallis raised the royal standard, it was met with bitter disappointment. Charles O'Hara described the scene: "The novelty of a Camp in the back Woods of America ... brought several People to stare at us, their curiosity once satisfied, they returned to their Homes; I am certain that in our March of near a Thousand Miles, almost in as many directions, thro' every part of North Carolina, tho every means possible was taken to persuade our Friends as they are called ... we never had with us at any one time One Hundred men in Arms."[10] Charles Stedman had ruminated on the decline of loyalists in the region, at once more numerous than in any other colonies, "but the misfortunes consequent on premature risings had considerably thinned them. Some had suffered, others had left the country and joined the king's troops to the southward, and those who remained were become cautious from the recollection of past miscarriages."[11]

Tarleton clearly had a sense of Greene's designs by re-crossing the river. He knew Greene would not offer battle "without manifest superiority and advantage; but to keep alive the courage of the party, to depress that of the loyalists, to wait for the additional assistance which he expected, and to harass the foragers and detachments of the British."[12]

The grand movement of the army back into North Carolina began on February 19, when Greene dispatched Pickens and Lee under the overall command of Col. Otho Williams to follow Cornwallis, cut off communications with the countryside, and keep the Tories tempered down.[13] Pickens had already anticipated this order, and had marched north with 700 men. However, many of Pickens's men hailed from South Carolina and Georgia, and they were uninterested in marching further north than Guilford Courthouse.

One officer, Pickens wrote Greene, was terrorizing loyalists with his band of men. The men, though "very brave, are bent chiefly to plunder and no doubt but at times Friends as well as foes suffer."[14] At such an important time, this was an unneeded distraction. But it was not the only one. Greene had also been plagued by desertions from the North Carolina militia, and all but eighty had left.[15]

Greene wrote to General Caswell on the 20th informing him that the British were en route to Hillsborough and that the light troops were already crossing the Dan, with the rest to follow that night and in the morning. Greene instructed him to destroy bridges and fell the trees along Cornwallis's route to impede his progress.[16]

Finally, on February 23, the main body of Greene's army was over the river, headed for an eventual collision with Cornwallis. Lewis Morris, Jr., of the Continental Army, in a letter to his father, General Lewis Morris, indicated how high the stakes were at this moment. "The army was evidently the object of the enemy, and while we can keep that together the country can never be conquered—disperse it, and the people are subjugated."[17] That same day, Lee wrote Greene that he had joined Gen. Pickens, and that "we shall exert ourselves to alarm the enemy by night, & harass them by day."[18]

But beginning on the 23rd, a series of events helped to change the course of the campaign. Cornwallis had ordered Tarleton, with 200 horse, 150 men of the 33rd Foot and 100 Jaegers to move west of the Haw River to cover loyalist militia as they assembled and made their way to the army's camp.[19] Pickens and Lee were soon informed by scouts of this movement, and it was not long before they learned it was Tarleton himself, not a foraging party, as was their initial thought. As Lee wrote in his memoirs, "guides became unnecessary now; for the British detachment had plundered all the houses on the road ... to be the property of patriots, and symbols of devastation marked their steps."[20]

For two days, Pickens and Lee followed Tarleton until they made contact with the loyalist volunteers on the 25th. A loyalist militia unit under Col. John Pyle consisting of nearly 400 Tories had accidently fallen in with Lee's green-coated dragoons, mistaking them for Tarleton's men, and allowed them to pass on the road. The events of this action have been disputed, but what can be discerned is that once Lee's horsemen had flanked the Tories, someone in the loyalist ranks opened fire when it was recognized that this was not Tarleton. Ninety Tories were hacked to death with sabers. The rest were injured and escaped. All in all, two to three hundred men were either killed, wounded, or captured. Pyle lost his life and the reverberations of this action had a devastating effect on the British campaign. A large force of Tories, the first to join Cornwallis since Greene's retreat into Virginia, and under the supposed protection of Tarleton, had failed to join the main army.[21] It helped to perpetuate the hopeless cycle of retaliation in the Carolina backcountry and prevented any further hope of Tory militia flocking to Cornwallis's standard. In a letter to Greene, Andrew Pickens acknowledged that this action "has knocked up Toryism altogether in this part."[22] Charles Stedman noted: "Humanity shudders at the recital of so foul a massacre: But cold and unfeeling policy avows it as the most effectual means of intimidating the friends of royal government."[23]

The pressure on the British did not let up. Only hours after Pyle's Defeat, another American unit was aiming for Tarleton as well. Under the command of Colonels William Preston and Hugh Crockett, 300 Virginia riflemen were closing in on Tarleton when a deserter gave Tarleton news of the impending attack, forcing Tarleton to leave his camp, crossing the Haw River at High Rock Ford. Interestingly, Tarleton claimed he was preparing to attack the Americans when he received word from Cornwallis to return to the main body.[24]

By the 24th, Greene was 18 miles from Hillsborough, and there was a flurry of letters that indicated more bad news for an army that wanted to confront Cornwallis on the field of battle. Greene was desperate for the reinforcements being led by William Campbell. He described his situation as critical and said he wanted to attack, but without Campbell's reinforcements the army was "too weak to attempt any thing."[25] Greene received a letter from General Robert Lawson, stationed in Prince Edward, Virginia, that a lack of firearms was preventing adequate numbers of militia from being mustered.[26] He received a similar letter from Col. Francis Lock, camped in North Carolina, complaining that his men were "entirely without lead, unable to produce a second ball for their muskets."[27] Furthermore, the Marquis de Malmedy wrote to Major Ichabod Burnet, Greene's adjutant, informing him that Cornwallis's arrival in Hillsborough had "entirely disconcerted" the militia and was hindering his efforts to organize his troops. In addition, he intended to act as a partisan under Greene's command since he could not find General Caswell. With only forty men under his command, he intended to carry out small raids against the British.[28]

Greene's return over the Dan also prompted Cornwallis to change his position. "On the 26th the royal standard marched by the left, passed through Hillsborough, and pointed their course toward the Haw. The fruitlessness of the country, and the protections of a body of the King's friends, supposed to reside in that district, were the reasons for this movement."[29] Cornwallis took up position on Alamance Creek on February 27.[30] Cornwallis noted in a letter to Germain that his "situation for the former few days had been amongst timid friends and adjoining to inveterate rebels," further troubling him.[31]

Meanwhile, Greene changed position constantly, operating between Troublesome Creek and Reedy Fork.[32] When Greene discovered that Cornwallis was south of his main body, he ordered Williams to screen the army, and Williams ordered Pickens and Lee to join him along with the Virginia riflemen they met after Pyle's Defeat.[33] Williams continued to excel in the field. He was responsible for many of the small engagements that took place with militia units, foraging parties, and detachments of the British army that were essentially delaying actions, and which protected Greene's force and the supply route that ran from Virginia through Hillsborough.[34] Cornwallis was troubled, for Pickens and Lee were constantly hovering, and his foraging parties were under constant pressure. Cornwallis was having difficulty sending out a detachment for fear of weakening the main body of the army.[35]

Even though Cornwallis was having his problems, Greene's issues with his army remained difficult as well. Greene was informed by Col. William Campbell that he had only sixty men with him instead of the 1,000 Greene had expected. It was a major setback. Campbell said he was "vex'd, asham'd, and affronted," but there was nothing else he could do.[36] Greene also poured out his frustrations to Governor Abner Nash. Greene had faced nothing but uncertainty since crossing back over the Dan, and he could not make any decisive moves to roll back British forces. Again, he addressed his continued disgust of trying "to prosecute a War under the disadvantages of depending on Militia and short enlistments. Every moment hazards the reputation of any Man who depends on them."[37] He pressed Nash for regular troops for "the desertions which prevail in the Militia will … dwindle my force into a body too weak to act offencively."[38] Greene was looking to make a decisive move against Cornwallis, but could not. He had partial successes against Tories, but that was not going to win a war. His efforts would be in vain if he was to try to "save a Country under such circumstances."[39]

The flurry of activity that had marked the last several days, and actually since the re-crossing of the Dan, reached a high point on March 6. Cornwallis decided to "beat up the American posts at Reedy Fork, in order to compel them to a greater distance, or perhaps allure Greene, who lay in the direction of Guildford Court-House, to a general engagement."[40] Cornwallis was in desperate straits. He began having trouble with desertions, and plundering had reached new heights.[41] Charles O'Hara lamented that the army is "so completely worn out, by the excessive Fatigues of the Campaign in a march of above a Thousand Miles, most of them barefoot, naked and for days together living upon Carrion, which they had often not time to dress, and three or four ounces of unground Indian Corn has totally distroy'd this army."[42] Cornwallis had to try something.

According to Otho Williams, Cornwallis had "Decamped early in the morning and had taken a rout leading to my left. We were instantly in motion. They had approach'd within two miles of our position, and their intention was manifestly to Surprize us."[43] Cornwallis had indeed marched north toward the Haw River, led by Lieutenant Colonel James Webster's brigade and Tarleton's Legion. Williams was south of the Haw and the rest of Greene's army was north of the river, and if Cornwallis could get in behind Williams, it would pose a major threat to the American army. Luckily for Williams, one of his patrols made visual contact in the early morning hours with the British advance, and he quickly began the race to Weitzel's Mill on Reedy Fork Creek. The two armies were moving in the same direction on parallel roads, and Williams attempted to harass the British as he conducted his retreat.[44] At times, Williams's rear guard was on the flanks of the British as he sped forward.[45]

Williams reached Reedy Fork first, with the British very close behind. He posted

Pickens's South Carolina and Georgia militia as well as Col. Preston's and Col. Campbell's Virginia riflemen south of the ford to provide covering fire for the Continentals as they crossed.[46] Once the Continentals had crossed, they provided cover for the retreating militiamen and riflemen. Once everyone was across, "the enemy pursued some distance but receiving several severe checks from small covering parties and being cow'd by our Cavalry He [Cornwallis] thot proper to halt."[47]

Cornwallis had been foiled again, but Greene's army had suffered from this engagement as well. Although Williams had described casualties as "inconsiderable," many of the militiamen had bristled about having to be deployed to cover the Continentals in the crossing and decided they had had enough and decided to go home, mostly because "they were to made a sacrifice by the Regular Officers to screen their own troops."[48] They had also lost their horses. Greene had decided that the army's large number of horses was threatening its ability to subsist, and almost 1,000 horses were released from the army.[49] Pickens had written Greene that the "plan of dismounting them [militia] ... has proved a bone of contention for them."[50] With few choices, Greene decided to send Pickens back to South Carolina with the men and to put him under Sumter, and continue harassing British posts in the interior of that state.[51]

On March 10, Greene finally found the luck he so desperately sought. While Cornwallis camped in the forks of the Deep River near the Quaker meetinghouse at New Garden, determining his opponent's next move, Greene began to receive reinforcements. "On the 11th of this month," he wrote to Joseph Reed, "I formed a junction, at the High Rock Ford, with a considerable body of Virginia and North Carolina militia, and with a Virginia regiment of eighteen months' men. Our force being now much more considerable than it had been and upon a more permanent footing, I took the determination of giving the enemy battle without loss of time and the necessary dispositions accordingly[.]"[52] Greene had received over 1,000 North Carolina militia under the command of General John Butler and General Thomas Eaton, as well as several hundred Virginia militia under the command of General Robert Lawson.[53] In addition, 400 Virginia Continentals had arrived under Lt. Col. Richard Campbell with several companies of light dragoons from North Carolina and Virginia.[54] Greene's army now had nearly 4,400 men.

Greene also reorganized his forces. Greene wrote to Henry Lee reporting that he had dissolved the light infantry into a new formation more conducive to attacking the enemy. To replace the functions of the light infantry, Greene organized "two parties of observation," one commanded by Henry Lee and the other by Col. Washington. Both parties will "give the enemy all the annoyance in your power."[55] Otho Williams would now command the Maryland Continental brigade and serve as Greene's adjutant general.[56]

On the 14th, Cornwallis learned from his scouts that Greene had settled at Guilford Courthouse. Now twelve miles away, Cornwallis began moving his army towards the prey that had consumed him for so long. Greene, not to be outdone by his adversary, sensed that Cornwallis would be on the move, but did not have any prior warning as to the advance of the British army. Nonetheless, Greene ordered Lee to take position on the New Garden Road to the west of the army, while Col. Washington was "to post himself about two miles on our front upon the Main Salisbury Road."[57] Lee, later in the evening, detached Lt. James Heard "with a party of dragoons to place himself near the British camp, and to report from time to time such occurrences as might happen."[58] At 2 a.m., Lee received word that Cornwallis was advancing and informed Greene, who began preparing for battle.

The British had actually begun their march around 5:30 a.m. and "had proceeded seven miles on the great Salisbury road to Guildford, when the light troops drove in a picket of the enemy."[59] Tarleton was leading the British advance with nearly 300 men of the British Legion, accompanied by one hundred British Guards Light Infantry and eighty-four Ansbach jaegers.[60] Lee, who had ridden out to meet Heard, decided to retreat to a place that he felt suitable to engage Tarleton's cavalry. Lee retreated to a position on New Garden Road, "in a long lane, with very high curved fences on each side of the road."[61] When Tarleton ordered a charge, it had only a limited effect on the Americans because of the confining nature of the lane. Lee then ordered a charge, and "the dragoons came instantly to the right about ... [and] rushed upon the foe."[62] Tarleton quickly saw the futility of the action and withdrew. He knew his infantry was too far away to provide any support.

Tarleton and his men fled the engagement with the Americans on to a road through the woods that branched southeast from the Great Salisbury Road. Then he turned right to reach the New Garden Meeting House, where the main body of the British army was now advancing.[63] Lee, however, followed the main road with his main goal to "place his horse between Tarleton and Cornwallis."[64] However, Lee found that when he arrived at the meetinghouse, "the British guards had just reached it; and displaying in a moment, gave the American cavalry a close and general fire."[65] The skirmish around the meetinghouse became more general as more troops arrived and became engaged.

Lee was feeling the squeeze, and had his cavalry maintain a holding action while his infantry retreated back down the Salisbury Road to a place called "Cross Roads."[66] Lee, who knew "from the appearance of the guards, that Cornwallis was not far in the rear, drew off his infantry; and covering them from any attempt of the British horse, retired toward the American army. General Greene, being immediately advised of what had passed, prepared for battle; not doubting, that the long avoided, now wished for, hour was at hand."[67] Lee had given Greene an extra two hours to prepare by virtue of his delaying action.

Cornwallis was anxious for battle. Since Cowpens, he had undertaken a long and fruitless pursuit of Greene's army. At every turn, he was hindered by difficult terrain, flooded rivers, and an absence of reliable intelligence. The countryside, having been picked clean by the Americans and British alike, was devoid of usable forage for the hungry armies. Cornwallis was looking for that all-decisive battle that had eluded him all winter, the opportunity to crush Greene and finally to convince those loyalists who had remained hesitant to join, and that government under British rule was still possible. He wrote, "I was determined to fight the rebel army if it approached me, being convinced that it would be impossible to succeed in that great object of our arduous campaign, the calling forth the numerous loyalists of North Carolina, whilst a doubt remained on their minds of the superiority of our arms."[68]

But Greene had a numerical advantage, and had already studied the terrain weeks earlier. Cornwallis would be approaching across an open field, and then the British would be forced to push down the main road that was bordered by dense woods on both sides before reaching an open field. William Davie described the terrain as "covered with woods, deep ravines, and broken ground, well calculated to favor the action of militia and equally unfavorable to the action of Cavalry...."[69] The courthouse was perched on high ground on top of a steep slope that came up from a ravine.[70]

In formulating his tactics for the engagement, Greene did not have to look far back in time. Thus, Greene's deployment of his soldiers reflected the brilliant strategy used by Morgan at Cowpens—he deployed his troops in three distinct lines. The first line was composed of about 1000 North Carolina militia, "advantageously posted under cover of a rail fence, along the margin of woods."[71] Most of the militia were raw and lacked battle experience, but what they did have was the accurate shot necessary to knock the British off balance. They were to fire two shots and head for the rear.

The second line was located about 350 yards behind the first, although accounts vary of the actual distance, consisting of 1200 Virginia militia commanded by Generals Edward Stevens and Robert Lawson. The second line had slightly more battle experience, yet contained many untried men. This position was different from the first because these men were atop a gently sloping ridge and oak trees provided cover from the British juggernaut.[72]

The third line was approximately 300 yards (according to Greene, but more like 400 yards) behind the second line and consisted of Continental soldiers from Maryland, Virginia, and Delaware, approximately 1,400 strong. "The Army was drawn up upon a large Hill of ground surrounded by other Hills, the greater part of which was covered with Timber and thick under brush," according to Greene.[73] This was the best position on the field, with a commanding view of the valley that sloped in front of it and the Reedy Fork Road about a hundred yards in the rear should a retreat be necessary.

William Washington, with his cavalry and a detachment of light infantry composed of Continental troops and a regiment of riflemen, secured the right flank, while Henry Lee with his Legion, a detachment of light infantry and a corps of riflemen under Col. William Campbell, secured the left flank.[74] Greene's position was strong, but he also had a major disadvantage. The distance between the lines left little chance for support during the battle. The North Carolina militia were particularly exposed, with the Continentals a half mile behind them and out of sight.[75]

Sometime after noon, Cornwallis deployed his men, spreading out on both sides of the road leading toward the woods. Cornwallis described what was in front of him: "Immediately between the head of the column and the enemy's line was a considerable plantation, one large field of which was on our left of the road, and two others with a wood of two hundred yards broad between them on our right of it…. The woods on our right and left were reported to be impracticable for cannon, but as that on our right appeared to be most open, I resolved to attack the left wing of the enemy, and whilst my disposition was making for that purpose, I ordered Lieutenant Macleod to bring forward the guns and cannonade their center."[76] The British right consisted of the Regiment of Bose and the 71st Regiment led by Major General Leslie, supported by the 1st Battalion of Guards. On the left, Lieutenant Colonel Webster led the 23rd and 33rd Regiments, supported by the Grenadiers and the 2nd Battalion of Guards commanded by Brigadier General O'Hara. The Jaegers and the light infantry of the Guards were on the left of the guns, and the cavalry was in the road, ready to react on a moment's notice.

As the British advanced through the fields, the North Carolina militiamen were posted behind a split-rail fence, which, according to some sources, offered little protection. William Davie described their cover as "too insignificant to inspire any confidence…."[77] Also controversial was the overall performance of the first line. It is generally thought that the militiamen opened at long range, within one hundred and forty yards, and the first British volleys forced them to flight, some before firing one shot. Royal Welsh sergeant

Roger Lamb contradicts that account from his own observations. He claimed that the British began moving across the fields, and "when arrived within forty yards of the enemy's line ... a general pause took place; both parties surveyed each other for the moment with the most anxious suspense" before Webster moved his men forward.[78] Lamb records that "they rushed forward amidst the enemy's fire; dreadful was the havoc on both sides."[79] Lee differed with Lamb's account and wrote in his memoirs: "To our infinite distress and mortification, the North Carolina militia took to flight, a few only of Eaton's brigade excepted.... Every effort was made by the generals Butler and Eaton, assisted by colonel Davie, commissary general, with many of the officers of every grade, to stop this unaccountable panic."[80] Nonetheless, Leslie's need to call up support shows he was taking casualties.

Had the militia stood and fought, perhaps the British right could have been broken. Instead, Cornwallis reported: "Major General Leslie, after being obliged by the great extent of the enemy's line to bring up the 1st battalion of Guards to the right of the Regiment of Bose, soon defeated everything before him."[81] The flanks of the American line began a fighting withdrawal, and as they withdrew, the British units in pursuit of them began to separate from the main body. Lee, for instance, had orders to withdraw and support the second line after the first one gave way, and the thick woods made it difficult to orient himself to the battlefield. Lee moved southeast, and in doing so, failed to connect with the second line. Large units of redcoats and Hessians had split off and pursued Lee in a separate battle, and this clearly had serious consequences for the battle plans of both sides. Regardless, the British continued moving forward toward the second line.

The attack proceeded up the road, where it hit the second line of Virginia militia located in the cover of trees. Here, resistance stiffened, and the Americans were able to inflict heavy casualties. The second line sat astride the New Garden Road with a strong position on the high ground. As Cornwallis remarked, "The excessive thickness of the woods rendered our bayonets of little use, and enabled the broken enemy to make frequent stands with an irregular fire, which occasioned some loss and to several of the corps great delay."[82] The Americans were able to fire behind the thick trees, combining with the undergrowth to made it impossible for the British to maintain their lines.

The British assault degenerated into a cluster of smaller engagements, with groups of British and Hessians exchanging fire with other smaller American units. Col. Otho Williams recalled the intensity of the fighting on the second line near the road. "The Virginia Brigades of militia ... gave the enemy so warm a reception, and continued their opposition with such firmness ... during which time the roar of musquetry and cracking of rifles were almost perpetual and as heavy as any I ever heard."[83] Stevens's brigade put up a greater resistance than Lawson's brigade, but finally gave way to the Guards and the Grenadiers.[84] Major St. George Tucker of the Virginia militia, after finding the British in their rear, wrote to his wife Fanny that "this threw the militia into such confusion that, without attending in the least to their officers who endeavored to halt them and make them face about and engage the enemy, Holcombe's regiment and ours instantly broke off without firing a single gun and dispersed like a flock of sheep frightened by dogs."[85] Tucker did praise many of his comrades for their fortitude in battle. "But it is not a little to the honor of those who rallied that they fired away fifteen or eighteen rounds—and some twenty rounds—a man, after being put into such disorder."[86] Because of the resistance put up by the Virginians, the British advance toward the third American line was disjointed, some units "having been impeded by some deep ravines."[87]

Greene and his third line had been poised on the high ground near the courthouse waiting for the action to reach them. Even though the British had moved through the first two lines, Greene's position took advantage of the fact that the enemy had to climb out of the valley before confronting his Maryland and Delaware Continentals. Cornwallis was moving forward, and his units were tiring. They had marched since daybreak and had been engaged continuously since arriving on the field. When the British Guards under Webster finally emerged from the valley and got within thirty or forty yards, some of the fiercest fighting of the day ensued.

Lieutenant Colonel John Eager Howard described Greene's position. "The First [Maryland] regiment under Gunby was formed in a hollow, in the wood, and to the right [west] of the cleared ground about the Courthouse. The Virginia Brigade under Genl. Huger were to our right. The second [Maryland] regiment was at some distance to the left of the first, in the cleared ground, with its left flank thrown back as to form a line almost at right angles [to the] 1st regt."[88] The 33rd Regiment arrived first on the field and immediately attacked into the left center of the Continental line, Otho Williams's troops. They were met with massive infantry and artillery firepower, and were driven back immediately in complete disorder. Webster regrouped his men on an eminence, awaiting the rest of the British troops. The 2nd Guards Battalion came on next, to Webster's right, with a bayonet attack, intent on dislodging the 2nd Maryland. They fell upon Col. Benjamin Ford's inexperienced Marylanders, who broke and fled, and captured two of Captain Anthony Singleton's artillery field pieces in the process.

As the breakthrough was about to materialize, Col. Gunby was informed by John Eager Howard that the First Maryland was needed to prevent a wholesale destruction of the American line. Howard immediately "rode to Gunby and gave him the information. He did not hesitate to order the regiment to face about."[89] It eventually devolved into hand-to-hand combat and bayonets. Greene, fearful of further sacrifice, "thought it most advisable to order a retreat."[90] At about the same time Greene ordered the retreat, the American left flank got some much-needed help when Lieut. Col. Washington streamed in from the right, and slashed away, inflicting many casualties, and the British were "driven back into the field … with the loss of the six-pounders that had been taken."[91]

As Cornwallis rode into the clearing below the fighting and saw what was happening, he was forced to take immediate action. He ordered Lieutenant John McLeod of the Royal artillery to fire grapeshot toward Washington's dragoons, who were pursuing the retreating Guards after their repulse by the 1st Maryland. Cornwallis noted that "the enemy's cavalry was soon repulsed by a well directed fire from two three-pounders…."[92] When the British regrouped and began to outflank Greene's line, Greene began his exit from the field. Col. John Green's Virginia regiment, of Huger's brigade, began to cover the retreat.[93]

Cornwallis ordered the "23rd and 71st Regiments with part of the cavalry … to pursue," but eventually called it off because the troops were "excessively fatigued … and our wounded, dispersed over an extensive space of country, required immediate attention."[94] Cornwallis explained later to Germain that he was unable to follow up with his victory because of the large number of wounded and the lack of provisions in a blighted landscape, and because the enemy did not end their retreat until they reached the Ironworks on Troublesome Creek some eighteen miles from the battlefield.[95]

Cornwallis's army of 1,900 forced Greene to retreat from the battlefield, but he suffered casualties of nearly twenty-five percent in the process. Even though he had been forced from the field, the day belonged to Greene. His army had suffered seventy-nine killed and 184 wounded, a six percent casualty rate.[96] Most of the militia had left the field and gone home. Though historians often fault Cornwallis for winning a Pyrrhic victory, biographers Franklin and Mary Wickwire argue he was the only British commander who could have achieved any type of victory at Guilford. Regardless of such speculation, Cornwallis lost a significant number of regulars, including many officers. This setback left the earl's army in a critical situation. In effect, Cornwallis could no longer field an army.

Post-battle observations describe the horrors of the field and its effect on British fortunes. Charles Stedman, reflecting on the battle, wrote, "A Victory achieved under such disadvantages of numbers and ground, was of the most honourable kind, and placed the bravery of the troops beyond all praise; but the expense at which it was obtained rendered it of no utility. Before the provincials finally retreated, more than one third of all British troops engaged had fallen."[97] Stedman also took time to praise Greene and his actions. "The American general had chosen his ground, which was strong and commanding, and advantageous; he had time not only to make his disposition, but to send away his baggage, and every encumbrance."[98]

Charles O'Hara noted that "we remained on the very ground on which it was fought cover'd with Dead, with Dying and with Hundreds of Wounded, Rebels, as well as our own—A Violent and constant Rain that lasted above Forty Hours made it equally impracticable to remove or administer the smallest comfort to many of the wounded."[99] A Hessian account of the aftermath draws a bleak picture of the conditions of Cornwallis's men. One soldier wrote that "we had won but we had no foodstuffs, no shoes on our feet, and no shirts on our bodies."[100] Aspirations for a successful conclusion of the war were fading. "Here we stood. There was no hope of help from our army because we were 700 English miles from it, in the middle of North Carolina. Our army in New York could not know where we were. They considered us to be lost."[101]

While British fortunes were waning, Greene was optimistic and issuing orders. The day after the battle he requested "the officers will take every precaution to secure their Arms & Ammunition & make every preparation for another field day."[102] Clearly, Greene was expecting the action to continue after the fighting on the 15th. Despite his losses, Greene reported to Samuel Huntington, President of the Continental Congress, the men were ready for another day in the field. "The firmness of the Officers and Soldiers during the whole campaign has been almost unparalleled. Amidst innumerable difficulties they have discovered a degree of magnanimity and fortitude that will forever add a lustre to their military reputation."[103]

Despite having been forced from the field, Greene sensed an opportunity for victory and was scrambling to gather enough forces for one more offensive. In a letter to Lee on the 19th, Greene stated he was unsure which way the British would move next. Greene, however, would move towards "the headwaters of the Rocky River" in the morning and wanted Lee to remain in pursuit of the enemy so as to provide the "earliest intelligence."[104]

Cornwallis had weighed the possibility of following up the blow at Guilford Courthouse and then made a fateful decision. "With a third of my army sick and wounded, which I was obliged to carry in wagons or on horseback, the remainder without shoes and worn down by fatigue, I thought it was time to look for some place of rest and refitment. I therefore by easy marches (taking care to pass through all the settlements that had been described to me as most friendly) proceeded to Cross Creek."[105]

But Greene was not going to make this retreat an easy one for his enemy. Even though the British began to move too rapidly for Greene, considering his lack of supplies, Greene wrote General Lillington to seize public stores along the Cape Fear River in order to prevent a union of British forces from Wilmington with Cornwallis at Cross Creek.[106] Receiving supplies from Wilmington was not to be. Charles O'Hara explained that "our advanced Guard were fired upon when we enter'd Cross Creek, and both Shores of the Cape Fear River proved so very hostile, as to render the Navigation for us totally impracticable."[107] Cornwallis found to his "great mortification and contrary to all former accounts, that it was impossible to procure any considerable quantity of provisions, and there was not four days' forage within twenty miles."[108]

To complicate matters further for Cornwallis, he received a letter from Major Craig from Wilmington about another serious matter. He told Cornwallis that "on the west side of the river Marion is to be guarded against. He is between us and the Pedee and, by the last information I could get of him … was three or four hundred strong. One of his haunts is the White Marsh within twenty miles of the river. Plunder being his object, he must be well watched."[109] With Cross Creek untenable, Charles O'Hara wrote, "Cornwallis was obliged to fall back upon Wilmington where we arrived the 12th of this month [April], and have remained ever since, endeavoring to recruit and repair, our very Shatter'd, exhausted, ragged troops."[110] They actually arrived in Wilmington on April 7.

Cornwallis, even in retreat, continued to ravage the countryside. A planter by the name of William Dickson wrote his cousin in Ireland and described the effects of the army on the civilians in its path. "Horses, cattle and sheep, and every kind of stock were driven off from every plantation, corn and forage taken for the supply of the army and no compensation given, houses plundered and robbed, chests, trunks, etc. and every kind of household furniture taken away. The outrages were committed mostly by a train of loyal refugees … whose business it was to follow the camps and under the protection of the army enrich themselves on the plunder…."[111]

Once in Wilmington, Cornwallis was "employed in disposing of the sick and wounded, and in procuring supplies of all kinds to put the troops into a proper state to take the field."[112] Charles Stedman wrote that Cornwallis "was apprehensive lest General Greene should return to South Carolina. Accordingly, several messengers were dispatched to lord Rawdon at Camden, to prepare him for such an event; but unfortunately neither the messengers nor their dispatches ever reached the place of their destination."[113] With resupply being the obvious immediate objective, Cornwallis was faced with the critical decision on where to go from here, a decision that could make or break the entire British southern strategy.

Troop returns taken on April 15 list 1,829 rank and file present and fit for duty, a number with which Cornwallis was uncomfortable attempting another march through the hostile Carolinas.[114] "The immense extent of this country," Cornwallis wrote to Germain, "cut with numberless rivers and creeks, and the total want of internal navigation, which renders it impossible for our army to remain long in the heart of the country, will make it very difficult to reduce this province to obedience by a direct attack on it."[115] Coming off the exhausting and constantly frustrating winter campaign through North Carolina, it is not surprising that Cornwallis would not be eager to lead another campaign through that territory. O'Hara believed that the British strategy in the Carolinas was doomed from the start, based on flawed intelligence in a hostile environment.[116]

But Cornwallis's attention had turned to the North in Virginia. He had received news

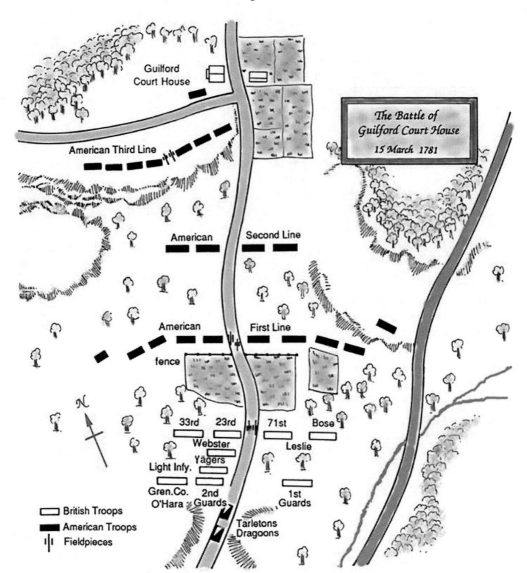

The following labels appear on the map:

Guilford Court House

The Battle of
Guilford Court House
15 March 1781

American Third Line

American   Second Line

American   First Line

fence

N

33rd   23rd   71st   Bose

Webster   Leslie

Yagers

Light Infy.

Gren.Co.   2nd   1st
O'Hara   Guards   Guards

Tarletons
Dragoons

British Troops
American Troops
Fieldpieces

The Battle of Guilford Court House (Wikimedia Commons, CC-By-2.5, map by Richard Harvey).

in Wilmington that Clinton had sent Major General William Phillips to the Chesapeake with approximately 2,000 troops. A major decision had to be made. Cornwallis could return to South Carolina, or he could join with General Phillips in Virginia to subdue that province and prevent the movement of men and supplies south. Washington did not decide to move his own army south until much later.

On April 10th, Cornwallis wrote a revealing letter to Phillips. He was candid about the disdain he had for the loyalists, as "the idea of our friends rising in any number and to any purpose totally failed."[117] He was exasperated from "marching about the country in quest of adventures," and if the plan was to go on the offensive, Cornwallis wrote that "we must abandon New York, and bring our whole force into Virginia; we then have a stake to fight for, and a successful battle may give us America."[118] If the plan was defensive, Cornwallis added, "let us quit the Carolinas (which cannot be held defensively while Virginia can be so easily armed against us)."[119] Without any input from Clinton, Cornwallis was prepared to rendezvous with Phillips by land and abandon the loyalists after a most difficult campaign that took him far from any base of support.

Relations between Cornwallis and Clinton had significantly soured, which can be seen in their correspondence. Cornwallis's April 10 letter to Clinton lacks the formal respect usually displayed in such letters. He complained of "impatiently looking out for the expected reinforcement from Europe," as well as being "very anxious to receive your Excellency's commands, being as yet totally in the dark as to the intended operations of the summer."[120] That tone is not present in Cornwallis's frequent correspondence with Germain, Clinton's superior in England. In a private letter to Germain, Cornwallis described himself as "engaged in a most difficult service, where I have as many cares and as much responsibility as usually fall to the share of a Commander in Chief...."[121] Cornwallis clearly felt that he was being neglected by his superior, and doubtless his correspondence with Germain, behind Clinton's back, would exacerbate the later conflict between the two.

Tarleton, in his memoirs, felt that "an instant movement from Cross Creek towards Camden would have been an advisable measure," adding that "it may be deemed unfortunate that so eligible a plan was not carried into execution."[122] Tarleton grudgingly gave credit to American efforts because they "not only deranged all the designs of Earl Cornwallis at Wilmington, but threatened severe consequences to the British forces in South Carolina. Lord Rawdon ... had now an unexpected and more formidable enemy to contend with."[123]

Cornwallis, in a letter to Germain on April 23, presented his argument for not reinforcing Camden. He felt that "the want of forage and subsistence on the greater part of the road, and the difficulty of passing the Pedee when opposed by an enemy render it utterly impossible for me to give immediate assistance." He feared that "this might enable General Greene to hem me in among the rivers and, by cutting off our subsistence, render our arms useless."[124] Cornwallis then informed Germain of his fateful decision. "I have ... resolved to take advantage of General Greene's having left the back part of Virginia open, and march immediately into that province to attempt a junction with General Phillips."[125]

Tarleton lamented the move into Virginia. In many ways, it can be argued that Tarleton was better suited than his superior to carry out the sort of savage war that the Revolution had become in the south. Cornwallis's training on European battlefields left him constantly desiring that one major engagement against his enemy, which had marked the most recent campaign. Tarleton, on the other hand, was built for the raids and brutal small engagements that characterized backcountry warfare and made him infamous among his enemies.

While Cornwallis was tending to his broken army, Greene was making his own strategic decision that was to change the course of the war in the South. In a letter to George Washington on March 29, Greene laid out his plan. "If the enemy falls down towards Wilmington they will be in a position where it would be impossible for us to injure them if we had a force. In this critical and distressing situation I am determined to carry the War immediately into South Carolina. The enemy will be obliged to follow us or give up their posts in that State."[126] Greene's concept was unique and violated traditional military policy by leaving an enemy army unchallenged in his rear. But war was not always traditional; Greene had proved that, and would still continue to do so. Guilford Courthouse had become his most famous engagement of the war.

7

Greene Invades South Carolina

After the action at Guilford Courthouse, Greene reflected privately to Samuel Huntington, the president of the Continental Congress, about his inability to press forward with the war without men and supplies and the problems associated with a temporary army. He wrote, "On Monday all the Virginia Militia return home, and once more I shall be left with a handful of Men exposed to a superior force, and be obliged to seek security in a flight." He lamented that "the greatest advantages are often lost by the Troops disbanding at the most critical moment."[1]

Those feelings did not stop Greene from preparing to move. Greene wrote Sumter that same day and told him that he anticipated that Cornwallis would fall down to Cross Creek and probably Wilmington. Given the circumstances, Greene announced to Sumter that he will "push directly into South Carolina. This will oblige the enemy to give up their prospects in this State, or their posts in South Carolina; and if our Army can be subsisted there we can fight them upon as good terms with your aid as we can here. I beg you will therefore give orders the Genls [Andrew] Pickens and Merion [Francis Marion] to collect all the militia they can to co-operate with us."[2] Greene was emphatic with Sumter about collecting as many provisions as possible, "for on this our whole operations will depend." He concluded by telling him to "inform me of your prospects, and the probable force I may expect to co-operate with us."[3]

Greene had followed Cornwallis no further than Ramsey's Mill on the Deep River, and on April 6, he began his movement toward South Carolina. Cornwallis was now seventy-five miles below Cross Creek and within fifteen miles of Wilmington.[4] When Greene decided to invade South Carolina, Cornwallis would never be able to challenge him. Lord Rawdon was 150 miles away in Camden and separated from Cornwallis by large rivers. Should Cornwallis head to the interior, he could easily be trapped by Greene.[5] Although Greene's move into South Carolina drew him further away from his supply base, he was counting on provisioning his troops with captured stores in South Carolina.[6]

Cornwallis took note of Greene's movement to the interior. "My situation is distressing. Greene took the advantage of my being obliged to come to this place, and has marched into South Carolina," he wrote to General Phillips.[7] Cornwallis also expressed concern for the safety of Lord Rawdon's post in Camden and was very prophetic with his comments. "Mountaineers and militia have poured into the back part of that province; and I much fear that Lord Rawdon's posts will be so distant from each other, and his troops so scattered, as to put him into the greatest danger of being beaten in detail."[8]

Of all the British posts in South Carolina, Camden was the strongest, held by Lord Rawdon with about nine hundred men. Taking Camden would mean a break in the British line of forts and the destruction of a significant portion of the British army.[9] As Greene moved toward Camden, he described the conditions of the Carolinas to Samuel Huntington as "totally exhausted; and the little produce that remains lies so remote, and the means of transportation so difficult to command, that it is next to an impossibility to collect it."[10] Greene also thought that most of the inhabitants appeared to be in the King's interest and that the militia "can do little more than keep Tories in subjection, and in many places not that."[11] William Seymour, of the Delaware Regiment, had a similar observation, describing the region as "a poor barren part of the country" where "the inhabitants are chiefly of a Scotch extraction … and are much disaffected, being great enemies to their country."[12]

As Greene approached Camden, and orders were sent out to subordinates, Thomas Sumter became a thorn in the side of Greene. Sumter had written Greene on April 7 promising that "nothing in the Summit of my Power Shall be Neglected that may in the least tend to further your operations against the enemy."[13] But Greene would hear nothing further from Sumter. On the 14th, Greene wrote him asking him "to cut off, or interrupt the communication between Camden and the other posts of the enemy, keeping it in your power to cooperate with or *join* this army."[14] By the 19th, Greene was still in the dark as to the whereabouts of Sumter, imploring to know "how you have disposed of yourself, so as to cooperate with our army on any particular emergency."[15] On the 22nd, Greene wrote to Henry Lee, "General Sumter I have not heard of but imagine he must be on the Congarees a little above you. I wish I could learn where he is and inform me."[16] Greene wrote Sumter again on the 23rd, eagerly awaiting his dispositions, but it was not until the 25th that Greene finally heard from him, and the news was frustrating: "My movements are very slow."[17] Greene now knew Sumter would be no help.

To make matters worse, Sumter informed Greene that "Gen. [Andrew] Pickens joined me today. He has none of his Brigade with him."[18] Partisan support of the army was going to be essential for Greene as he began his task of retaking South Carolina, and Sumter was not cooperating. Greene had demonstrated incredible patience thus far, but that would soon be tested.

Camden was built "upon a plane covered on two sides by the River Wateree and Pine Tree Creek , the other two sides by a chain of strong Redoubts all nearly of the same size, and independent of each other."[19] Greene described the country as "extremely difficult to operate in, being much cut to pieces by Deep Creeks and impassable Morasses; and many parts are covered with such heavy timber and thick under brush as exposes an army, and particularly to frequent surprises."[20] Greene had hoped to surprise the garrison, but circumstances prevented such an approach. Greene was moving through hostile country and even foraging parties needed protection.[21] As Greene moved toward Camden, he began to flesh out his plan. Sumter would protect the western flank from reinforcement from Ninety Six or Augusta, and Lee would join forces with Marion to prevent any reinforcement from the south.[22] Greene would invest Camden.

Greene assessed the situation in front of Camden, and after positioning himself six hundred yards north of the Camden fort at Logtown, decided that the works were too strong for an assault. He fell back about a mile to Hobkirk's Hill, hoping to draw Rawdon out to attack him.[23] Hobkirk's Hill was a narrow ridge of no significant elevation, covered by a thick growth of forest through which ran the Waxhaws road.[24] The approach to the American camp was concealed by the woods and the topography of the landscape, and it was only when the British came within range of the pickets that Greene got warning of their approach.[25] Davie, however, contends that "the village and the enemys works were visible from our camp ... and they were discovered ... as they issued from the lines of their own on that side."[26] Greene had a total force of about 1,500 men with him, including two regiments of Virginia and Maryland Continentals, 250 North Carolina militia, William Washington's cavalry, Kirkwood's light infantry, and forty artillerymen.[27]

Rawdon, with his force of 900 men, had other factors to consider besides Greene, who lay in front of him. Francis Marion and Henry Lee had moved against Fort Watson, a key British post on the Santee just below where it merged with the Congaree. It was a vital communications link to Charleston, and Lee and Marion had successfully taken it on April 23, creating a gap in the British defenses in South Carolina. Rawdon was expecting the commander of the fort, Colonel John Watson, to come to his aid. Lee and Marion had ensured that would not happen.

Greene had hoped Sumter would provide reinforcements, but that would fail to materialize as well. But Rawdon had received another piece of bad news from Lieutenant Colonel Nisbet Balfour, the British commandant in Charleston. Balfour informed Rawdon that Cornwallis was making a move into Virginia and that Rawdon must abandon Camden and retreat below the line of the Santee River.[28] Rawdon thought this move unwieldy due to the vast American presence between him and the coast.[29] Greene's force was not large enough to envelop Rawdon and force a surrender, so Greene's only option was to get him out into the open and decisively beat him in battle.[30]

Rawdon, however, made the first move. According to John Eager Howard, "one of our drummers deserted and informed Lord Rawdon of our situation and that we had no artillery, which was the case, for the artillery came up afterwards."[31] On the morning of April 25, Charles Stedman recounted, "he [Rawdon] marched out with all his force he could muster, and making a circuit, and keeping close to the edge of a swamp, under cover of the woods, happily gained the left flank of the enemy undiscovered."[32] Greene's pickets were driven in on the left, and Captain Robert Kirkwood advanced to support the retreating pickets.[33]

As Kirkwood was engaged, Greene ordered his men into line of battle. To the east of the Waxhaws road were the 1st and 2nd Maryland Continentals, led by Colonel John Gunby and Colonel Benjamin Ford respectively, and in overall command was Colonel Williams. On the west side of the road, General Huger commanded the 4th Virginia led by Lieutenant Colonel Richard Campbell and the 5th Virginia by Lieutenant Colonel Samuel Hawes. The artillery had finally arrived and was placed in the center, and in reserve were 250 North Carolina militia and William Washington's cavalry.[34]

Rawdon, even though his approach was with stealth, presented a narrow front to his enemy. Rawdon had the 63rd Regiment on the right supported by the Loyalist Volunteers of Ireland, the King's American Regiment on the left, and the New York Volunteers in the center. In reserve were the South Carolina Provincial Regiment and the New York Dragoons. Charles Stedman recalled that "the enemy, although apparently surprised, and at first in some confusion, formed with great expedition, and met the attack with resolution and bravery."[35]

Greene recognized Rawdon's narrow front and immediately ordered the artillery to open with grapeshot. As Greene recounted in his report to Samuel Huntington, "Lieut Col Ford with the 2d Maryland Regiment had orders to advance and flank them on the left, Lieut Col Campbell had orders to do the like upon the right. Col Gunby with the first Maryland Regiment, and Lieut Col Haws [sic] with the second Virginia Regiment had

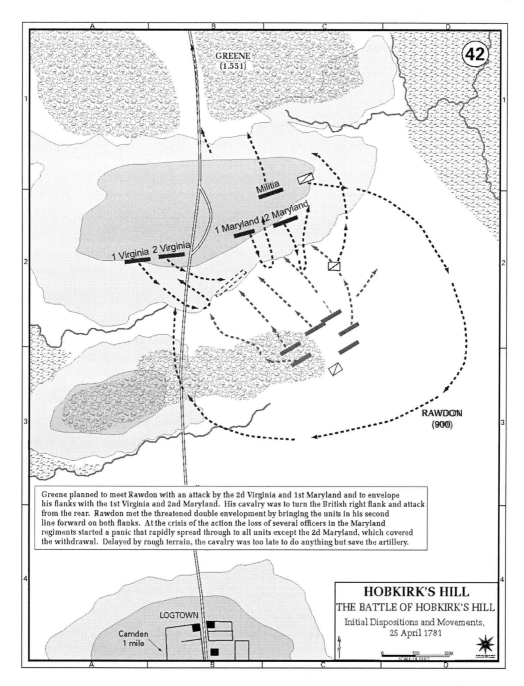

Battle of Hobkirk's Hill, April 25, 1781 (U.S. Military Academy).

orders to advance down the hill and charge them in front. Lieut Col Washington had orders to turn the Enemies flank and charge them in the rear."[36] Greene had decided on a double envelopment. Rawdon reacted quickly and began ordering regiments up from the rear to fill in gaps in the line in order to overlap the American force in his front.[37] The British advance was halted and began to give way throughout their line.

But then, disaster struck for Greene. The normally reliable and battle-tested First Maryland Regiment became confused. Several companies on the left were lagging behind the others, and Colonel Gunby ordered the rest of the regiment to halt in order to reestablish the broken line. As Greene recalled, Gunby "gave an order for the rest of the Regiment then advancing to take a new position in the rear, where the two companies were rallying. This impressed the whole Regiment with an Idea of a retreat, and communicated itself to the 2d Regiment which immediately followed the first on their retiring. Both were rallied, but it was too late, the Enemy had gained the Hill, and obliged the Artillery to retire."[38] Samuel Hawes's Fifth Virginia was the only unit to remain steady and the only saving grace in the American line. But with his formations in total disarray, Greene was forced to retreat, using Hawes's men to cover his movement from the field.[39]

The clash at Hobkirk's Hill exposed some problems from the American perspective. First, with a slight advantage in troop strength, Greene may have been better off not going on the offensive, something he was normally reluctant to do. The preservation of his army was paramount to success in the southern theatre, and staying on the defensive and receiving Rawdon's attack may have been a better tactic.[40] His artillery was up and he held the high ground, but the surprise on his flank began the unfortunate chain of events.

Secondly, Washington's dragoons failed to fully engage in the day's fighting. Although Greene spoke favorably of Washington's actions during the battle, a long detour around dense underbrush left him far behind the enemy's battle line. If Washington had engaged Rawdon while he was trying to extend his front, the outcome might have been different.[41] Instead, he was dealing with noncombatants, stragglers, and the wounded.[42]

Greene also failed to comment on the lack of reinforcements. Sumter had stymied him by not following his orders, and after numerous letters, Greene finally cut him loose. In a restrained manner, conscious of appearances and the necessity of a united front with his subordinates and the public at large, Greene left Sumter "at liberty to prosecute your original plan."[43] Also, various states had not reinforced Greene. In a letter to Joseph Reed, Greene's normal restraint failed to present itself. "When I made this last Movement I expected 2000 Virginia Militia to operate with us, and 1000 men with Sumter but both have failed me; and I am in the greatest distress."[44] He knew that if he had these reinforcements, he would have crushed Rawdon.

The final issue with the battle was Greene's blame of Gunby's actions for the loss. This was Greene at his worst, and there was no excuse for it. Greene was unrelenting, blaming Gunby to everyone with whom he communicated. To Joseph Reed, he stated, "Gunby was the sole cause of the defeat, and I found him much more blameable afterwards than I represented in my public letters."[45] Gunby, trying to protect his reputation, failed to recover it in his lifetime. Greene had found a scapegoat, possibly had tried to protect other subordinates around him whose services he would desperately need in the future, and failed to take responsibility where it lay—with himself. Greene had obviously not remembered how, as Washington's subordinate, he had lost Fort Washington during the battle of New York and owned up to it. Greene refused to take responsibility for Hobkirk's Hill, and ruined the reputation of a subordinate in the process. Long after the battle, it was said by Greene's officers that Greene blamed Sumter for the loss at Hobkirk's Hill for not making a junction with him in front of Camden. Even though there is no hint in Greene's letters to Sumter, William Davie claimed that Greene told him: "Sumter refuses to obey my orders, and carries off with him all the active force of this unhappy State on rambling, predatory excursions, unconnected with the operations of the army."[46]

On the evening of the 25th, Rawdon wrote Cornwallis a brief letter explaining his rationale as to why he gave battle instead of retreating behind the Santee line, contrary to orders. Rawdon explained that "hearing that Lee, Sumter, and Marion were coming to Greene, and the South Carolina Regiment having got safe to me from Ninety-Six, I thought it best to risque an action."[47] The next day Rawdon gave a more detailed explanation of his actions. He explained to Cornwallis that Greene's army was not as numerous as he thought, because the "efforts of the enemy to examine our works, and in particular to destroy our mill," had resulted in intelligence gained from prisoners. Rawdon "did not think that the disparity of numbers was such as should justify a bare defence."[48]

Although Greene had lost at Hobkirk's Hill, it was a hollow victory for the British. Charles Stedman, whose pen was very active during this time period, noted that "American partisans were more than ever active in making predatory incursions into various part of the province, and interrupting the communication between Camden and Charlestown."[49] But Stedman's comments also reflected what was happening elsewhere in the province. He also noted "a very general spirit of revolt ... particularly in the district of Ninety-Six ... and on the north-east of that tract of country which lies between the two great rivers Pedee and Santee."[50] More importantly to the British cause in the Carolinas, Stedman believed that many of the inhabitants of Charleston, "although awed and restrained by the presence of the garrison, gave signs of disaffection."[51]

The next day, April 26, Greene marched his defeated army up to the plantation of Colonel Henry Rugeley, about four miles from Camden. Recovering very quickly from the loss, Greene wrote Marion and began issuing orders to cut off British resupply of Camden.[52] As Greene tried to ascertain the direction of Cornwallis's next movement, he gave the order for Lee to join the army immediately.

He also asked Marion to give an accounting of his numbers and to "furnish us with sixty or Eighty good Dragoon horses."[53] Marion responded in a somewhat angry tone, claiming it was not in his "power to furn[is]h them but it is not nor never have been."[54] He went on to say that if Greene thought it best to dismount the militia, the army would never get their service in the future, and then threatened to resign his militia commission.[55]

Greene's response is interesting. Often, he could be very diplomatic in his correspondence, and at other times, he wasted no time in being blunt. In response to Marion's attempt to resign his post, he said:

> Your state is invaded, your all is at stake. What has been done will signify nothing unless we persevere to the end. I left a family in distress and every thing dear and valuable to come & afford you all the assistance in my power, and if you leave us in the midst of our difficulties while you have it so much in your power to promote the service it must throw a damp upon the spirits of the Army to find the first Men in the State are retiring from the busy scene to indulge themselves in more agreeable amusements. My reasons for writing so pressingly respecting the Dragoon [horses] was from the distress we were in. It is not my wish to take the horses from the Militia if it will injure the public service, the effects and consequences you can better judge of than I can.[56]

In his response, Greene defined the cause and the sacrifices necessary to prevail against the greatest military force on earth. Marion would serve until the end of the war.

On May 10, Greene received startling news. Even though Rawdon had been reinforced from John Watson after evading Marion and Lee, he decided to abandon Camden.

Rawdon was cut off from food and forage by Sumter, Marion, and Pickens. Fort Watson had fallen, and after an unsuccessful attempt to force Greene to fight again, Rawdon wrote to Lieutenant Colonel Cruger to evacuate Ninety Six and join Thomas Browne at Augusta, and to Major Maxwell to abandon Fort Granby and retreat to Orangeburg.[57] Captain Nathaniel Pendleton wrote Sumter that "the General is of the opinion that the same motives which has induced Lord Rawdon, to this step, will induce the evacuation of all the out Posts, which the enemy have at Ninety-Six, Augusta and on the Congaree."[58]

Before he left Camden, Rawdon burned the jail, the mills, several private houses, and all the private stores he could not bring with him.[59] He took with him 500 slaves and the majority of the loyalist population of the town. Initially, he was headed to Nelson's Ferry on the Santee to attack Marion and Lee, who were besieging Fort Motte, the main British supply depot for materials moving between Charleston and Camden, but he was too late. He finally ended up at Monck's Corner, about forty miles north of Charleston. Rawdon's messages to the other commanders were all intercepted and never got through.

After the evacuation of Camden, the British hold on South Carolina began to slip away. The posts of Orangeburg, Fort Motte and Fort Granby all fell to the Americans, the last one falling on May 15. Marion had been dispatched to Georgetown, which he had no problem handling, and it fell on May 29. Of all the British forts in the interior, only Ninety Six remained. That was where Greene was headed, and that was where Lee would meet him after the fall of Augusta.

Colonel Robert Gray, the loyalist, reflected on the loss of the backcountry. He blamed "the want of a sufficient concurrence on the part of the people ... after having missed of crushing Green's [sic] army." He also laid blame at the feet of Cornwallis, for had he "followed Gen. Greene to the Southward or had the reinforcements from Ireland arrived a month sooner, in either of these cases, we should have had an army in the field superior to Greene's & all our posts would have been safe."[60] Gray knew that "the enemies army must be destroyed or driven away, posts must be established & an army kept on the frontiers to prevent any attempts from the Northward, & militia must be embodied."[61]

On May 17, Greene began his movement toward Ninety Six, moving up the north bank of the Saluda River, with instructions to Sumter to keep himself between Rawdon's army, which at this point was on the coast, and his own.[62] Ninety Six was an important place in the backcountry. With an all-important road network, it was a center of commerce and trading between the interior and the coast, and since it had a courthouse, it was a center of power in the area. By 1775, it had a dozen dwellings, with artisans plying their craft, and much of the land was cleared for agriculture and grazing, with corn, wheat, indigo, and flax the primary crops.

But more importantly for Greene, the loyalists who now occupied the town had cut down trees in every direction up to a mile outside of the town, preventing an enemy the ability to use the woods as cover. It was remote, but Greene's objective was to reduce Ninety Six, and then make a move toward Augusta to help remove the British from that post. Greene had just under a thousand men and only three artillery pieces. He had two regiments of Continental troops from Maryland and Delaware totaling 427 men, a Virginia brigade of 431 men, a battalion of sixty-six North Carolinians, and a company of sixty infantrymen under Captain Robert Kirkwood.[63]

The defense of Ninety Six fell to Lieutenant Colonel John Cruger, a New York loyalist with heavy family connections, who had 550 loyalists, 350 from New York and New Jersey, as well as 200 more from South Carolina.[64] At first glance, it would appear that Greene had the advantage. But Cruger's defenses would be a severe test for Greene's troops.

The town itself was surrounded by a stockade, which was surrounded by a deep ditch and abatis, with the earth from the excavations forming a high bank on the outside.[65] On the eastern edge of the village lay the most formidable obstacle, the Star Redoubt. It had eight points and sixteen salient and reentering angles protected by a dry ditch and abatis.[66] A wooden platform was built to hold cannons which were aimed in the direction from which Cruger expected an attack. West of the stockade was a smaller palisaded fort containing two blockhouses, and connecting all of the structures together was a communications trench that was covered and also protected the only supply of water, which came from Spring Branch, a rivulet that was fed by a spring.[67] The star was unique because it allowed its defenders to fire on the enemy from its many angles, and the attackers were immediately in a disadvantageous position because they were caught in a deadly crossfire.

Greene crossed the Saluda River at Island Ford on May 21 and then struck out down the Island Ford road toward Ninety Six, which was ten miles southwest. He arrived in the rainy darkness of the 22nd and immediately went to work. Greene ordered the place encircled, and the Americans made four camps surrounding the fort, all within artillery distance.[68] He also ordered his engineer, Thaddeus Kosciuszko, to reconnoiter the enemy's position. According to Henry Lee, "Lieutenant-Colonel Cruger was informed of the events that had lately taken place; but hearing of Greene's advance upon Camden, he had been industriously engaged in strengthening his fortifications, and was determined not to abandon his post."[69] Cruger ordered artillery platforms to be built in the star redoubt, and moved his men into key positions in the stockade fort and the jail, and occupied blockhouses contained within the stockade.

Greene and Kosciuszko, after a lengthy examination of the fort, realized that the British were "much better fortified and garrison[ed] much stronger in regular troops than was expected."[70] Greene confided to Lafayette that "our success is very doubtful."[71] Greene accepted Kosciuszko's recommendation to begin the approaches against the strongest feature of the fort, the Star Redoubt, igniting a firestorm of controversy later on. Many believed that cutting off Cruger's water supply should have been done instead of attacking at the enemy's strongest point. But Kosciuszko thought cutting off the water supply via the Spring Branch would not have adversely affected the British significantly. Lee disagreed. "Never regarding the importance which was attached to depriving the enemy of water, for which he entirely depended on the rivulet to his left, Kosciuszko applied his undivided attention to the demolition of the star, the strongest point of the enemy's defence."[72]

Gaining control of the Star Redoubt would have made for easy access to the rest of the fort, so Greene commenced his approaches. Kosciuszko attempted to construct a three-gun artillery battery approximately seventy yards north of the star (while others thought it closer to 150 yards). Roderick MacKenzie, a lieutenant in the 71st Foot, who wrote about the siege, noted that "it can hardly be conceived that his engineer, Kosciuszko … would break ground and begin a sap within so small a distance of a regular fortification, if he intended its reduction by the common mode of approaches."[73] Kosciuszko had dug too close. Cruger attacked the entrenchments with a detachment of thirty soldiers, who "in an instant leveled those works, and loaded a number of negroes with the entrenching tools of the Americans."[74] Kosciuszko himself noted that the sallies forward by the British were supported "by the musketry and Artillery from the Fort."[75]

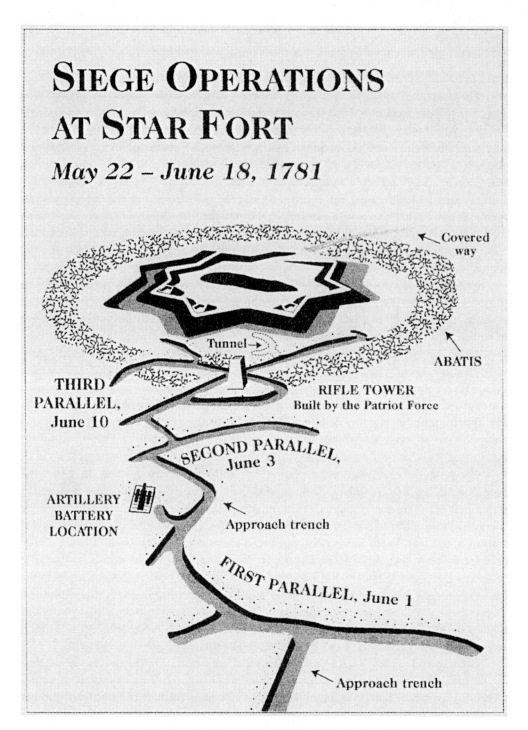

SIEGE OPERATIONS AT STAR FORT

May 22 – June 18, 1781

Covered way

ABATIS

Tunnel →

THIRD PARALLEL, June 10

RIFLE TOWER
Built by the Patriot Force

SECOND PARALLEL, June 3

ARTILLERY BATTERY LOCATION

Approach trench

FIRST PARALLEL, June 1

Approach trench

Fortifications at Ninety Six (National Park Service).

Convinced of the strength of the fortification, Greene began new entrenchments. According to MacKenzie, "the Americans again broke ground, but at the distance of four hundred paces from the Star, and behind a ravine."[76] In siege warfare, a series of trenches that face an enemy's defenses are called parallels. The construction of these trenches was very labor intensive and was mostly done at night. Once a parallel was in place, the men could move artillery forward on wooden platforms so as to batter the enemy's defenses. Once a parallel was constructed, approach trenches known as saps connected the parallels, and were angled so as not to come under direct enemy fire. On the morning of May 24, Greene's 6-pounders opened up on the star redoubt from parapets constructed in the trenches, and as Kosciuszko recounted, "with great effect, Alarmed the Enemy prodigious[ly]."[77]

Work on the saps continued once night fell, and Greene sent out foraging parties to obtain food and other necessities. Others were sent out scouring the countryside for sticks and branches to make fascines, which were large bundles of sticks and branches to help fortify the walls of the trenches. Other teams were creating gabions, large baskets filled with earth. The American works were not the typical earthworks one would find in a textbook siege, as the soldiers had to deal with hard ground, little time, a paucity of men, and a lack of knowledge about siege warfare.[78]

By June 3, the second parallel was finished, and Greene was in a far better position to attack Cruger. It was then, according to etiquette, when an unconditional surrender was requested, "making the commandant *personally* responsible for a fruitless resistance, demanding an immediate and unconditional surrender to the army of the United States of America."[79] The loyalists had suffered few casualties and provisions were plentiful, and the commandant responded that "Ninety Six was committed to his charge, and that both duty and inclination pointed to the propriety of defending to the last extremity."[80]

Though Cruger was surrounded, he was still able to make contact with Rawdon, informing him of the situation at hand. On May 31, he told Rawdon that "he [Greene] is now within one hundred and fifty yards of our Star Redoubt, the principal work, and approaching with great rapidity."[81] Three days later, Cruger's note to Rawdon became a little more serious. "Our neighbors continue industriously at work. They are within less than sixty yards of our Star Redoubt, at which distance they put up a log battery last night and fired from it this morning."[82]

Upon Cruger's refusal to surrender, Greene opened up on the Star Redoubt with a heavy crossfire from three of his batteries.[83] By Monday, June 4, the Americans initiated a new tactic, firing arrows with combustible tips "on the roofs of the British barracks to set them on fire, but this design was immediately counteracted by Lieut. Col. Cruger, who directed all the buildings to be unroofed."[84] Greene was beginning to have doubts about American progress in front of the star.

Henry Lee arrived on June 8, fresh from his victory at Augusta. Accompanying Lee was General Pickens with 400 South Carolina militiamen. He wasted little time, and after conferring with Greene, began operations from the west of the British stockade redoubt.[85] Alexander Garden, of Lee's Legion and aide-de-camp to Greene, thought that Lee was right by attacking from the west "since it commanded the only fountain from which the garrison could procure water; and subsequent events incontestibly proved, that if his plans had been adopted in the first instance, the fort must have fallen."[86]

By the next day, Lee's men had pushed a sap forward close enough to mount a 6-pounder to fire on the British.[87] Meanwhile, Kosciuszko had now reached within forty yards of the star, when he decided to begin work on a mine that he had envisioned since the beginning of the siege. Progress was slow, the heat and humidity of the season helping to hamper operations. The goal was to pack the tunnel with gunpowder with the resulting explosion breaching the star and allowing the Americans to storm the fort. Unfortunately, a lack of gunpowder prevented the execution of this maneuver, and Greene sent off a note to Pickens to obtain some from the capture of a recent fort.

Greene was frustrated by the lack of progress in front of the star. The British continued their sorties against the American works, and Greene had failed to receive reinforcements from the Virginia militia. Greene wrote Samuel Huntington, expressing his frustrations as "the approaches have gone exceeding slow, and our poor Fellows are worne out with fatigue.... The position [is] difficult to approach and the Ground extremely hard."[88] To make matters worse, on June 11, a dispatch brought news that a British fleet had landed in Charleston, providing reinforcements for Rawdon who were already en route to Ninety Six.[89] Greene immediately sent his cavalry and Pickens to join Sumter in delaying Rawdon's advance on Ninety Six, along with a message to Marion to lend a hand.[90] The good news was that the approaches were moving forward at a rapid pace, and the Maham tower was completed.

During the night of June 13, a thirty-foot tower made of interlocking logs was erected under the direction of Kosciuszko, and the Americans were able to gain an advantage. Because the fort was only thirty yards or so from the ditch of the star, riflemen were able to fire down into the fort, and thus created chaos among the British gunners. The British responded quickly. Major Greene, who was commanding in the star, ordered the parapet in front of the star raised three feet higher using sandbags, and small apertures were left in between the sandbags from which riflemen would be able to shoot.[91] The British attempted to destroy the tower but failed.

Water was rapidly becoming an issue for the British as well. Spring Branch, the town's water source, lay outside the star, which was in range of American fire. Cruger attempted to dig a well within the confines of the fort, but at twenty-five feet, no water was found, and Cruger abandoned the project. MacKenzie noted that by the 17th of June, "the sufferings of the garrison were now extreme ... and the only means of procuring this necessary element in a torrid climate ... was to send out naked Negroes, who brought a scanty supply from within pistol shot of the American pickets, their bodies not being distinguishable in the night from the fallen trees, with which the place abounded."[92]

More bad news began to force Greene's hand in front of Ninety Six. Desertions were affecting the operations to stop Rawdon, and William Washington's cavalry had arrived too late to slow his advance. Rawdon had taken an alternate route, further embarrassing Sumter. Greene did not have the manpower to fight Rawdon and Cruger, and the siege had not progressed to the point where he could engage the British.[93] With Rawdon advancing toward Ninety-Six, "it now became necessary to hazard an assault, to meet Rawdon, or to retire," Lee wrote.[94] Greene knew it, too. He decided to attack. "The American army having witnessed the unconquerable spirit which actuated their general, as well as the unexpected results of former battles, could not brook the idea of abandoning the siege without one bold attempt to force a surrender."[95] Stirred by his officers and men to make an assault before Rawdon arrived, Greene reluctantly agreed to an assault.

On June 18, Greene made preparations for his attack. His plan was for two simultaneous assaults. On the left of the star would be Lieutenant Colonel William Campbell of the First Virginia Regiment, with detachments of Maryland and Virginia troops. Fifty men volunteered to lead the charge, also called the Forlorn Hope, led by Lieutenant Isaac Duval of Maryland and Samuel Selden of Virginia. These men would be armed with axes in order to cut through the fort's perimeter so that soldiers following with hooks would pull down the sandbags and breach the defenses of the star with the troops behind them. On the right of the star, Colonel Lee, along with his infantrymen and a detachment of Delaware Continentals under Captain Kirkwood, would move against the stockade.

Shortly before noon, Greene's troops made their way into the third parallel. Time seemed to drag as both sides knew what was imminent. At noon, as Lee so dramatically put it, "The first signal was announced from the centre battery, upon which the assailing columns entered the trenches, manifesting delight in the expectation of carrying by their courage the great prize in view."[96]

American artillery pinned down the British, and sharpshooters in the Maham tower forced the riflemen at the parapet to stay low. But events quickly changed after the initial success. As American soldiers tried to pull down sandbags placed on the parapet, "the riflemen, fixed at the sand-bag apertures, maintained a steady and destructive fire."[97] The Forlorn Hope were pinned down in the ditch, caught in a crossfire by marksmen in the star, and they were suddenly surprised by sixty loyalists who "entered the ditch, divided their men, and advanced, pushing their bayonets till they met each other. This was an effort of gallantry that the Americans could not have expected."[98] What followed was a mass of men engaged in hand-to-hand combat, with bayonets and clubbed muskets.[99]

On the other side, Lee was having more success on his front. His troops advanced on the fort, found it empty, and began to drive across Spring Branch and assault the jail, hoping that Cruger would divert forces from the star to Lee. But it was not to be. Greene could see an hour after the attack that trying to carry the star would be a fruitless endeavor and called off the attack. "The adverse fortune experienced by our left column made the mind of Greene return to his cardinal policy, the preservation of adequate force to keep the field," Lee wrote afterwards.[100] The British had lost approximately twenty-seven killed and fifty-eight wounded, and the American toll was 147 killed, wounded and missing.[101] During the night, "gloom and silence pervaded the American camp; every one disappointed—every one mortified. Three days more, and Ninety-six must have fallen; but this short space was unattainable."[102]

Greene waited in front of Ninety Six as long as he could, trying to conceal his intentions from Colonel Cruger. But he was making his preparations for his departure. "Greene communicated to Sumter the event of the preceding day, advised him of the route of retreat, and ordered the corps in his front, with the cavalry under Washington to join him with celerity."[103] Greene also wrote Pickens trying to assuage the fears of the local inhabitants, giving them "the strongest assurances that it is my intention to maintain our footing in this State."[104] He wanted Pickens to communicate that British reinforcements were not adequate to hold the backcountry, and that "our horse will be continually hovering round the enemy during their stay in this Neighborhood and prevent their plundering the Country."[105]

On the morning of the 20th, Greene moved out and "gained the Saluda, where he was joined by his cavalry."[106] They had gone fourteen miles and camped along the Little River, where Greene busied himself by issuing statements of gratitude to his men, as well as drafting a formal letter to Congress. He thanked Col. Kosciuszko for "planning and prosecuting the approaches [which] would have gained infallible Success, if time had admitted of their being completed."[107] Greene also "announced his grateful sense of the conduct of the troops, as well during the siege as in the attack."[108]

Meanwhile, Greene's cavalry was searching for the latest intelligence on Rawdon's column and discovered that Rawdon had reached Ninety Six on the morning of June 21. Rawdon quickly decided to pursue Greene, and the next day set out to find him. But once Rawdon reached the Enoree, he "acquired information which convinced him of the impracticality of accomplishing his enterprise, and induced him to spare his harassed troops unnecessary increase of fatigue."[109] The heat and humidity of the southern summer were unbearable. Rawdon turned back on the 24th with the American cavalry of Lee and Washington close behind.

Greene, however, moved northeast toward Charlotte "and passed successively the Enoree, the Tiger and Broad rivers, his sick and wounded continuing to precede him."[110] Rawdon had never intended to hold Ninety Six. It was too far from Charleston and far too deep in hostile territory to provide any discernable use. So in July, Cruger was left to destroy the village, and then set out to link up with Rawdon, who had headed to Orangeburg to meet up with Lieutenant Colonel Alexander Stewart, who commanded the 3rd Regiment.[111]

When Greene learned that Ninety Six was evacuated, he promptly made a move to the southeast, hoping to get in between Rawdon and Cruger. But the staggering marches and the extreme heat of the season were taking a toll on both armies. Greene received a letter from Marion on July 7 with intelligence that Rawdon's troops are "so fatigued they cannot possibly move."[112] Rawdon's march from Ninety Six to Orangeburg was in devastating heat and many of the soldiers suffered grievously.

Greene's army had suffered too. As Lee recorded in his memoirs, "The heat of the season had become oppressive, and the troops began to experience its effect in sickness. General Greene determined to repair to some salubrious and convenient spot to pass the sultry season."[113] Greene had decided to end the campaign for the time being and headed to the High Hills of Santee, a line of hills that ran along the north bank of the Santee, and rose about two hundred feet above the surrounding countryside, a place of rest and refitment away from the swamps of the lowcountry.[114] But not everyone was at rest. Greene ordered Sumter, Marion, and Lee to move rapidly to break up British posts at Monck's Corner and Dorchester, and the British subsequently withdrew their forces to the vicinity of Charleston.

The failure at Ninety Six encompassed several factors. Greene had laid some of the blame at the feet of his partisan leaders. Historian Edward McCrady felt that Sumter's inactions were responsible for the failure to harass Rawdon's troops on their march to Ninety Six.[115] In a letter to Henry Lee long after the war, Pickens said Greene was very critical of Sumter and "expressed himself in a manner I had not heard him before or after."[116] Greene had written Marion with an obvious critical tone: "It is my wish to have fought Lord Rawdon before he got to Ninety-six, and could I have collected your force and that of General Sumter and Pickens, I would have done it, and am persuaded we should have defeated him.... I am surprised the people should be so averse to joining in some general plan of operations."[117]

Siege operations against the Star Redoubt remain controversial. Critics of Greene's decision stated he should have focused his operations against the water supply.[118] Greene's desire to construct a battery seventy yards from the star demonstrated a lack of knowledge in siege warfare and a possible overconfidence in the American side.[119]

Lastly, Greene laid part of the blame at the feet of Thomas Jefferson. Two thousand Virginia militia had been raised for the express purpose of reinforcing Greene, but Jefferson had countermanded the order due to the threat of the British invasion. Greene's anger was palpable. In a letter to Jefferson on June 27, Greene was critical of Jefferson's decision. "The tardiness, and finally the countermanding of the Militia ordered to join this army has been attended with the most mortifying and disagreeable consequences."[120] Almost always looking at the bigger picture, Greene noted that it was not consistent "with the common interest that local motives should influence measures for the benefit of a part to the prejudice of the whole."[121] Greene also mentioned to Samuel Huntington that "had the Virginia Militia joined us agreeable to our success would have been compleat."[122]

But as Lee aptly noted, the process had been far more difficult than what had been gained by the actions of Greene's army. Lee waxed poetic in his memoirs, reflecting on the "skill, courage and fidelity" it took to get to this point, but also that "fortune often gives victory; but when the weak oppose the strong, destitute of the essential means of war, it is not chance but sublime genius which guides the intermediate operations, and controls the ultimate event."[123]

Others sang Greene's praises as well. A correspondent in Salisbury noted that "for more than eight months past, [he] so often baffled the British, always superior in numbers and everything else except valor and military talents."[124] Charles Stedman remembered that Greene, "through his own firmness and perseverance the successes of his detachments against the British outposts, and the advantages derived from the general disaffection of the inhabitants to the British, he succeeded in the main object of the campaign."[125]

As the army recovered at the High Hills of Santee, Greene probably took the opportunity to reflect on what had happened since taking command in December of the previous year. The army he assumed command of had been in tatters. He had marched hundreds of miles, short on men and provisions, yet never lost sight of his ultimate goal, which was to drive the British out of the Carolinas.[126] But he knew he was not finished. Greene had been forced to raise the siege of Ninety Six, but more importantly, he had occupied Rawdon's army, so they could not be used in Cornwallis's Yorktown campaign. In addition, his constant pressure against the British had forced them to the coast.[127]

During the course of his tenure as commander, Greene had written many letters to many people regarding the state of affairs with the militia, and his antipathy towards them became a source of contention. The correspondence between Greene and Joseph Reed, president of the Pennsylvania Council, between May and August, put Greene on the defensive. Back in early May, Greene had opined to Reed about the state of affairs near Camden, where thousands of expected militia had failed to show up: "The prospects here are so unpromising, and the difficulties so great, that I am sick of the service, and wish myself out of the Department."[128] Reed responded to three letters he received from Greene, and in a very long letter, he revealed to Greene, supposedly representing the sentiments of various people, that he holds "the Militia in Contempt & are too much inclined to attribute Failures to them."[129] Reed carefully suggested that "the Sucesses which they have obtained to the Northward, at Kings Mountain & elsewhere seem also to give them some meritorus Claims."[130] Quoting an English poet, Reed advised Greene, "Be to their Faults a little blind/ And to their Virtues very kind."[131] Reed plainly told Greene that his comments were not doing him justice nor serving the public good.

Reed also took the opportunity to admonish Greene about blaming Congress for the lack of men and supplies furnished during the war. "Congress cannot support Armies, establish the civil Business of a great Empire & conduct a War with one of the greatest

Powers on Earth without Means. Poor & destitute, how unjust is it in us to blame them for not doing what they have not Power to do."[132] It was not until August 6 that Greene replied, and he gave little ground to Reed. He dismissed the thought that he despised the militia, as he felt they were sacred to the integrity of a free society. He felt that he was "responsible for the war in this quarter, and it was necessary that Congress should know what force was here, in order to determine what additional force would be necessary to send."[133]

Greene also became a little defensive while explaining to Reed that the war in the south was quite a bit different from that of the north. He referred to the war in the north as "a plain business, and the manoeuvres plain and simple, but here they are complicated and various."[134] He was understating the war in the north, but he let Reed know that friends were hard to come by in this theatre of war, the greater part of which was populated by "inveterate enemies."[135]

But Greene was honest in his assessment of the travails that he and his army had been through. "Our difficulties, distresses and perseverance, have been greater than you can imagine, and perhaps no army merited more than this; for had not the officers strove, generally, to promote the service all in their power, we should have been inevitably ruined."[136] At the end of his response, Greene came full circle, noting to Reed that "when I am obliged to speak of men and things, I must speak as I find them."[137] Greene had lived it and Reed had not, and the war went on.

PART III

The Failure of Empire

8

The Tide Ebbs

The camp of repose in the High Hills of Santee was anything but that for Nathanael Greene. He had plenty on his mind and there was good reason for that. His thinking turned toward matters of political and social policy as well as his own military actions and those of his subordinates.[1]

Greene was thinking deeply about the conclusion of the war, and he was keenly aware that in peace negotiations the British might invoke the diplomatic principle of *uti possedetis* (as you possess) that would allow the British to retain territory that they held at the end of the war.[2] During the remainder of this year, Greene would begin using his growing influence to establish political control over the southern states so as to avoid any British claims to territory at the cessation of hostilities. He was active in establishing state governments in South Carolina and Georgia and even asked Governor John Rutledge to return to South Carolina.

Greene also desired to bring back a degree of normalcy to the region, trying to put an end to the plundering and senseless murders that characterized the civil war in the South. He also advocated leniency for loyalists. Nevertheless, the vicious internecine fighting continued. The British hanged militia Colonel Isaac Hayne; partisan William Cunningham and his loyalist followers were raiding the backcountry; and North Carolina Governor Thomas Burke was captured by loyalist David Fanning. While others wanted more severe reprisals, Greene consistently favored leniency in dealing with this issue.[3]

In mid–July, Greene wrote Pickens about the conditions of the inhabitants and the need for action to ameliorate their problems. With no civilian government in place, Greene was initiating a relief policy normally the responsibility of the state. Greene noted that "many of the inhabitants are reduced to beggary and want from the late ravages of the enemy and must suffer exceedingly without some mode is adopted to afford them some relief. I recommend your appointing some person or persons to take from the hand of plenty and apply to the necessities of those people."[4] It is not known if Pickens took any action, but Francis Marion assisted the residents of Georgetown when it was burned in early August.[5] Governor Rutledge acknowledged Marion's efforts by telling him that his actions "respecting the inhabitants who have suffered by the destruction of George Town are very proper; it is our duty to alleviate their distresses as much as possible."[6]

Greene also wrote John Mathews, delegate to the Continental Congress from South Carolina. He was adamant about beginning to recreate state government. Greene wrote: "I wish an attempt could be made to establish Civil Government in South Carolina. The Inhabitants of Georgia are making the attempt. If Governor Rutledge is still in Philadelphia, I wish he would not delay a moment in coming here. All gentlemen of influence should return to this Country to assist in correcting the irregularities prevailing, and try to keep the hopes of the people alive. A printing press is exceedingly wanted. We have struggled hard for the salvation of your Country and spilt our richest blood."[7]

Greene could not have used any more candor in describing the situation in South Carolina. When Rutledge arrived in Greene's camp on August 1, he issued a proclamation outlawing plundering and called on justices of the peace to bring these persons to justice, ordering military officers to assist as necessary.[8] By the end of July, Greene had written Pickens again, "exceedingly distressed that the practice of plundering still continues to rage ... to such a degree that the poor inhabitants tremble the moment a party of men appear in sight. If no check can be given this fatal practice I am perswaded the Inhabitants will think their Miseries are rather increased than lessened."[9] But Greene turned to his thoughts of reconciliation and moderation in the same letter. "It is most certainly our interest to encourage the return of the Tories; and I wish you to give them all the encouragement in your power; and afford them all the protection you can. But oblige the most notorious to give up their arms; which may be put into the hands of good men."[10]

Militarily, Greene gave permission to Sumter to execute a plan to threaten British posts in the low country, known as the Dog Days Expedition. The name of the expedition came from the nineteenth-century historian and novelist William Gilmore Simms, who coined the term to honor the endurance of the South Carolina partisans who were able to march in brutal heat with few losses.[11] The dog days are the period between July 3 and August 11, preceding the rise of the dog star Sirius, the hottest and unhealthiest parts of the whole year. Along with Marion and Lee and roughly 1,000 mounted militiamen and Continental cavalry, Sumter was to capture the British post at Monck's Corner, which was located in Biggin's Church, the parish church of St. John, Berkeley.[12]

Sumter had written to Greene on July 15 and informed him of his preparations and the situation at hand, noting that "the post at the Church ... has been lately reinforced w about a Hundred foot & field piece, And all the Horse they cou'd possibly collect."[13] Sumter informed Greene that had sent out "Large Detachments ... to Approach & Attack the Enemy, in the neighbor[hood] of their post," and had sent Col. Henry Hampton "to destroy the Four Hole Bridge, & maintain that pass to the last Extremity," as that was where British reinforcements would have to pass.[14]

After some initial successes, the expedition ran out of steam. At a place called Shubrick's Plantation, Marion felt the British position too strong to attack, but Sumter insisted on an assault. Marion wrote Greene on the 19th: "I marched my men to a fence about fifty yards of the Enimy under a very heavy fire, we soon made them take shelter in and behind house, but was fired on from the stoop of the Houses & through the doors[,] windows & corners, our Amunition being Intirely Expended I was Oblige to retire."[15] Marion claimed his men were needlessly sacrificed, and Sumter claimed he could not renew the attack the next day because of his proximity to Charleston and the threat of British reinforcements arriving at a moment's notice.[16] Regardless, the expedition failed and allowed the British to retreat further into the low country.

Greene publicly commended Sumter, exclaiming that "the gallantry of the Troops deserves the highest commendation. I only lament that the exertions had not been crowned with more deserved success."[17] Privately, he thought the expedition was mismanaged by Sumter. However, it was a psychological victory, severely affecting British morale. But Greene was thinking ahead to the next campaign, and let Sumter know that "once reinforcements arrive and the Troops have had a little opportunity for relaxation, we will draw our force to a point and attack the enemy where ever they may be found."[18]

Another distraction that marked the camp of repose was the execution of Isaac Hayne, a militia colonel. Taken prisoner in the siege of Charleston, he had taken an oath of loyalty to the Crown. But later, deciding the enemy had violated his parole, Hayne returned to the patriot side and was captured in battle on July 7. Condemned for violating his parole, he was hanged on August 4. The repercussions were enormous, and Greene's correspondence during the summer reflects his anger over the execution. On August 10, he informed Marion not to "take any measures in the matter towards retaliation, for I don't intend to retaliate upon the Tory officers but the british."[19] Greene wrote a blistering letter to Lieutenant Colonel Nisbet Balfour, the commandant in Charleston, injecting his republican principles into his protest: "For the honor of humanity, from an abhorrence for every thing that bears the mark of cruelty, and with a desire to give every man an opportunity to act agreeable to his principles and inclination, it was my wish to have all considered as prisoners of war who should be found in Arms and made captives on either side."[20]

That same day, Greene penned a proclamation announcing that he would "make British Regular Officers, and not the deluded Inhabitants who have joined their Army, Subjects of Retaliation."[21] He concluded by taking the moral high ground, stating that he "cannot but regret the Necessity of appealing to Measures so hurtful to the feeling of Humanity, and so contrary to those liberal Principles" on which he would carry on the war.[22] His threat hinted at a keenly developed political sense as well. Greene's threat would help quell the fears of South Carolina militiamen who left the field after the execution of Hayne, and it is thought that this incident and Greene's reaction to it helped end executions on both sides.[23] Greene never retaliated against an enemy officer.

Greene had rested his weary troops for six weeks and had supplemented his army with new recruits. This time Lord Rawdon would not be in command of British troops. He would leave for England because of ill health, leaving Greene to face Lieutenant Colonel Alexander Stewart. According to Lee, "on the 21st [August] the American general decamped from the benign hills of Santee, for the avowed purpose of seeking his enemy."[24] Stewart was at the confluence of the Congaree and Wateree Rivers with his British troops, where it would be easier for him to receive supplies; many of his supplies were intercepted or annoyed by partisans, and here, large rivers were his best chance of resupply.[25]

When Greene broke camp, he marched north to the nearest ford at Camden, crossed the Wateree and marched down the west bank to Howell's Ferry on the Congaree, intending to cross there and pursue Stewart.[26] But when Greene crossed the Congaree on August 28, "Lieutenant-Colonel Lee, still preceding the army, soon found that Stewart had sat down at the Eutaw Springs, forty miles below his late position."[27] Greene had learned that the British "were making preparations to establish a permanent post there. To prevent this I was determined rather to hazard an Action, notwithstanding our numbers were greatly inferior to theirs."[28] In fact, many historians have calculated the relative strength of the armies as somewhat equal, with Greene's force slightly larger. But historian Jim Piecuch has calculated that Greene actually had a two-to-one advantage over Stewart, with 2,773 men compared to Stewart's 1,396.[29] If accurate, this is an important factor, as it demonstrates that Greene was finally able to develop a numerical superiority over his enemy. Marion's partisans joined the army on the evening of the 7th at Burdell's plantation, and Greene moved slowly toward Eutaw Springs, marching at four o'clock in the morning on September 8.

As Greene crept forward, Stewart had no idea he was close by, as partisans had interrupted lines of communication for the British and blocked all Stewart's efforts to gather intelligence. With no effort to conceal the advance of the army, "Lee became convinced, strange as it appeared, that the British commander was uninformed of our proximity."[30] With the British short of provisions, Stewart had sent out a "rooting party" that was made up of approximately 310 men and officers to dig sweet potatoes from the plantations near the Santee River, unaware that Greene was close by. These men were armed with only a few rounds of ammunition each.

Meanwhile, at six o'clock, two deserters from Greene's army made their way to Stewart's camp and informed him that the Americans were closing in. Stewart responded quickly, sending his cavalry commander, Major John Coffin, with fifty cavalrymen and 140 light infantrymen to investigate.[31] Coffin had advanced four miles down the road when he ran into the advance of Greene's army, Lee's Legion infantry commanded by Captain James Armstrong, and South Carolina state troops led by Colonel John Henderson. The British attacked immediately, "but were soon convinced of their mistake by the reception they met with."[32] Lee had instructed Armstrong to post his Legion across the road with the cavalry in the open woods to the right, with Henderson's men in the woods on the left.[33] Four of Coffin's infantry were killed in the attack and forty others were captured.[34] Captain Robert Kirkwood wrote of the rooting party that came to help, that "60 men ... were either Killed, wounded or taken. We met no further opposition, until we arrived with one mile of their Encampment."[35] In actuality, most of the rooting party were made prisoners, with several killed or wounded.

The British position bordered Eutaw Creek on their right, a tributary of the Santee River. It was thickly bordered with brush and undergrowth. The only open ground was a large field cleared of timber on both sides of the River Road, with a brick house in the rear of the field holding a commanding position. On the north side of the house was a garden, surrounded by a strong palisade that extended most of the way toward the creek, and a road had been recently opened forming a fork, one leg of which led to Charleston and the other to a plantation on the Santee, which branched off opposite the brick house. The British camp was located in the open field under cover of the house and occupied both sides of the road.[36] Stewart placed a detachment of infantry about a mile in front of his camp to delay the American advance before they came to the main line of resistance. The British right was anchored on the steep riverbank with 300 light infantry and grenadiers under Major John Marjoribanks, protected by a dense thicket of blackjack oaks. It was an area in which it was difficult for cavalry and infantry to operate.[37] It formed an angle, almost perpendicular to the rest of the British main lines. On the left flank, in reserve, were the remnants of Coffin's cavalry and infantry.[38] On the British left were the 64th and 63rd Regiments, with Lieutenant Colonel Cruger's Loyalists in the middle flanking each side of the road, with the 3rd Regiment on the British right nearest Marjoribanks.[39]

Greene's front line consisted of "four small Battalions of Militia, two of North, and two of South Carolinians."[40] Marion was in command on the right, Colonel Malmedy in the center, and Pickens on the left. The second line consisted of three small brigades of

Opposite: **Battle of Eutaw Springs, September 8, 1781 (U.S. Military Academy).**

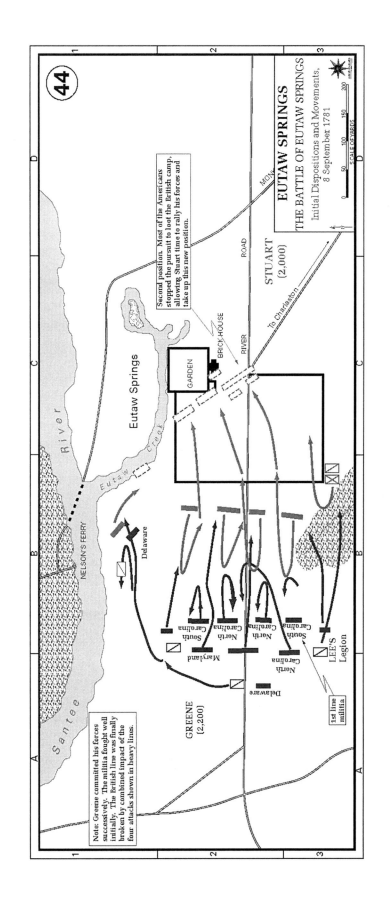

44

Santee

River

NELSON'S FERRY

Eutaw Springs

Eutaw Creek

Note: Greene committed his forces successively. The militia fought well initially. The British line was finally broken by combined impact of the four attacks shown in heavy lines.

GREENE (2,200)

Delaware

Delaware

Maryland

South Carolina

North Carolina

North Carolina

South Carolina

North Carolina

1st line militia

LEE'S Legion

GARDEN

BRICK HOUSE

RIVER

MONC...

ROAD

To Charleston

STUART (2,000)

Second position. Most of the Americans stopped the pursuit to loot the British camp, allowing Stuart time to rally his forces and take up this new position.

EUTAW SPRINGS
THE BATTLE OF EUTAW SPRINGS
Initial Dispositions and Movements,
8 September 1781

SCALE OF YARDS
0   50   100   150   200

Continental troops, three regiments of North Carolinians on the right, the Virginians' two regiments in the center, and the two regiments of Marylanders on the left. Lee covered the right flank, and Henderson's South Carolina state troops on the left. Wade Hampton and several other colonels were under Henderson's command on the left. William Washington and Robert Kirkwood's Delaware troops formed the reserve.

The Americans moved forward through open woods, Otho Williams noting that the "whole country on both sides of the road, being in woods, the lines could not move with much expedition consistently with preserving their order ... producing occasional derangements in the connection of lines."[41] The battle began with firing from both sides, and "a steady and desperate conflict ensued. That between the artillery of the first line and that of the enemy was bloody and obstinate in the extreme."[42] Greene noted as well that "a most tremendous fire began on both sides from right to left, and the Legion and State Troops were closely engaged."[43] The militia advanced under heavy fire, and were performing far beyond expectations. "Governor Rutledge, who was anxiously attending the event of the battle ... wrote to the South Carolina delegates that the militia fired seventeen rounds before they retired."[44]

But the severity of the enemy's firepower began to force the North Carolina militia to give way. Greene acted quickly, and the "North Carolina Brigade under General Sumner was ordered up to their support," the Continentals replacing the retreating militia in the center of the first line.[45] According to Greene, while the battle was raging intensely, this unit fought with gallantry and even drove the enemy back to their original position. But these reinforcements and Pickens and Marion's South Carolinians eventually began to waver under British pressure.

Stewart had committed his reserves before the battle began, keeping only Coffin's cavalry in reserve, and they were not engaged in this part of the battle until they were attacked by the Legion cavalry. As Pickens and Marion began to give way, the British rushed forward without orders. But, "Greene determining to strike a decisive blow, brought up the Marylanders and Virginians: when our line became dense, and pressing forward with a shout, the battle raged with redoubled fury."[46] They advanced with bayonets, and at the same time, Lee's infantry turned upon the British left and poured on a heavy fire. Henry Lee remembered that "the enemy's left could not sustain the approaching shock, assailed as it was in front as it was in flank, and it instantly began to give way, which quickly afterward took place along the whole line, in some parts of which the hostile ranks contended with the bayonet."[47] But on the British right, events were not proving as successful. Marjoribanks stood firm and formed a new line with his left on the palisaded garden and his rear to the creek.[48] It seemed for the moment that Marjoribanks was unassailable.

However, the situation was changing by the minute. The British were now in full retreat through their own camp. Stewart claimed that finding the Virginia and Maryland lines already formed and his troops receiving a heavy fire from them, "it was ... necessary to retire a little distance to an open field, in order to form, which was instantly done."[49] The Americans followed in hot pursuit, but the camp itself created a formidable obstacle with all the standing tents and equipment. It stunted the American advance, and while the Americans were making their way through the camp, Major Sheridan of Cruger's force "had thrown himself into the house ... from ... which they could direct their fire with security and effect."[50] He was also aided by two swivel guns that raked the American forces.

Now, the British began to get the upper hand. An American attempt to batter down the house with artillery failed; the gunners were killed or retreated.

Meanwhile, Stewart was reorganizing his troops for a counterattack. "Marjoribanks and Coffin ... now made simultaneous movements; the former from his thicket on the left, and the latter from the wood on the right of the American line."[51] Greene reacted quickly to the movement and ordered Lee's Legion cavalry to move through the clear terrain south of the camp and push into the British rear, engaging Coffin's troops. Marjoribanks had still had maintained his position, so Greene ordered William Washington forward, because he saw if Marjoribanks was not dislodged, "the Maryland flank would soon be exposed to his fire."[52]

Washington's forces, which included Wade Hampton and horsemen from South Carolina, could not penetrate the blackjack thicket, but he saw an open space in the rear. Riding across Marjoribanks's front, his unit was cut to pieces, and Washington himself was captured. Kirkwood's troops came quickly, but failed to dislodge the enemy. Greene's aide, Captain Nathaniel Pendleton, was dispatched to deliver the message, but Lee was not with his cavalry. It was said that "Col. Lee was very little, if at all, with his own corps after the enemy fled. He took some dragoons with him ... and rode about the field, giving orders and directions, in a manner the General did not approve of. Gen Greene was, apparently, disappointed when I informed him Col. Lee was not with his cavalry."[53] Lee's second-in-command, Major Joseph Eggleston, was ordered to attack and was repulsed. Greene was running out of options and Stewart began to rally his men. Coffin moved forward from the woods on the American right and attacked the scattered American infantry, and Marjoribanks moved out from his solid position in the blackjack thicket, seized the American guns, and then fell under the protection of the brick house.

Greene knew it was time to pull back and he ordered a retreat. "I thought proper to retire out of the fire of the House and draw up the Troops at a little distance in the Woods, not thinking it adviseable to push our advantages farther," he wrote.[54] Water was in short supply, and with the battle lasting almost four hours on an unusually hot day, Greene was forced to return to Burdell's plantation, seven miles from the field of battle. According to Otho Williams, Greene decided to end the battle because his artillery was dismounted, and it was futile to attempt anything further against the house with nothing other than small arms fire.[55] Stewart maintained the enemy "retired with great precipitation ... seven miles from the field of action," and the victory would have been more complete "had not the want of Cavalry prevented me from taking the advantage which the gallantry of my Infantry threw in my way."[56] Although he had to move seven miles from the field, Greene had every intention of renewing the battle.

Losses were heavy on both sides. Greene lost 139 killed, 375 wounded and eight missing. Stewart's losses were even greater, eighty-five killed, 351 wounded and 430 missing, including those of the rooting party.[57] He had lost 42 percent of his force. Stewart's letter to Cornwallis also sheds some light on the British condition after the battle. The lack of cavalry had hindered British attempts at a more complete defeat of Greene. Feeding the army was also an issue; the troops had "for some time been much in want of bread, there being no old corn or mills near me," he wrote to Cornwallis.[58] When listing casualties from the battle, Stewart did not hesitate to inform Cornwallis his army was not as large as it appeared, for "the army was much reduced by sickness and otherwise."[59]

Lee also mentioned that sickness was an issue for the Americans, as "never had we experienced so much sickness at any one time as we did now."[60] He did not fail to mention that "the British army did not escape the insalubrity of the season and the climate ... their chief attention too being called to the restoration of the sick and wounded."[61]

This was the last great battle of the Revolution in the Carolinas. The consequences of it were enormous. Stewart, like his predecessors, was operating in enemy country, and after the tremendous losses at Eutaw Springs, he could no longer remain there, and fell back to Monck's Corner.[62] Greene acted quickly, and "Marion and Lee were to move on the 9th, and turn the enemy's left, with a view of seizing the first strong pass on the road to Charleston, below the Eutaw Spring, as to interrupt Colonel Stewart when retreating, as to repel any re-enforcement which might be detached from the garrison of Charleston."[63] At Ferguson's Swamp, Stewart linked up with Major Archibald McArthur with a detachment of 300 men, and Lee was unable to take advantage of the situation. Greene determined to "halt a Day or two to refresh; and then take our old position on the High Hills of Santee."[64]

Even though each side claimed victory, most historians view the battle as a draw. For Greene, it may be considered a strategic victory, as the British were forced to move their army back to the safe environs of Charleston, leaving Greene in control of most of South Carolina.[65] Even though Stewart held the field at the end of the battle, Otho Williams claimed that "the best criterion of victory is to be found in consequences; and here the evidence is altogether on the American side. For the enemy abandoned his position, relinquished the country it commanded, and although largely re-enforced, still retired."[66] Charles Stedman noted that "this was the last action of any consequence that happened in South Carolina between the king's troops and the Americans: The former from this time, chiefly confined themselves to Charlestown Neck and some posts in its neighborhood; the security of that town appearing to be their principal object."[67] The British now held only Charleston, Savannah and Wilmington, and had been driven out of the Carolina backcountry. On September 9, a French fleet sailed into Chesapeake Bay; it would have further implications in the Southern campaign.

Meanwhile, on the coast, Cornwallis was making an important and consequential move. Despite all the conflict and apprehensions, Cornwallis left Wilmington on April 25 and headed north for Virginia. He told Clinton two days before he left that even though his infantry and cavalry were not ready to march, he must begin: "[I]t is very disagreeable to me to decide upon measures so important and of such consequence to the general conduct of the war without an opportunity of procuring your Excellency's directions or approbation, but the delay and difficulty of conveying letters and the impossibility of waiting for answers render it indispensably necessary."[68] To Phillips, he wrote the day before his departure, "I shall therefore immediately march up the country by Duplin Court House, pointing towards Hillsborough, in hopes to withdraw Greene."[69] Cornwallis would be marching to the lowest ford of the Roanoke, which was about twenty miles above Taylor's Ferry, because as he noted in his letter, "in a hostile country ferries cannot be depended upon," but he would "try to surprise the boats at some of the ferries from Halifax upwards."[70]

The possibility of returning to South Carolina did not seem to occur to Cornwallis. Even though he could not provide any immediate assistance to Rawdon at Camden, if Cornwallis had marched there in relief, Rawdon would have probably been able to hold the town. Cornwallis's commissary, Captain Gregory Townsend, had written Cornwallis on April 14, noting that "it appears by the returns from thence [Wilmington], 26th March, there are for 6,000 men bread and flour sixty nine days, pork and beef thirty three days, rum 69 days, and a good supply of salt, which I hope with the cattle of the country will make up the deficiency of salt provisions."[71]

It would have certainly been possible for Cornwallis to have returned from Wilmington into South Carolina, but Balfour questioned the practicality of the march in a letter to Cornwallis on May 21. Balfour had dispatched a schooner with provisions for Cornwallis's army, and when it was seized, "and not being able to procure any mode of safe conveyance to you at that critical period," he wrote to Cornwallis, "was most distressing, as your return would then, I presume, have been determined upon when you knew it might have been so easily effected from these asistances."[72] Cornwallis never received Balfour's letter, but it was clear that the march to Virginia created angst among some subordinates.

Another possible reason for Cornwallis's departure from the Carolinas was his distaste for what the war had become. Defensive warfare never suited Cornwallis; he was a man fully at ease with offensive operations. The descent into civil war and the barbarity that accompanied it had taken its toll, and the year's campaigning leading up to this point had become stressful and anxiety-producing. With nothing to show for his efforts, Cornwallis was looking for another avenue to exploit his strengths, and to conduct offensive operations in Virginia rather than suffer through another difficult campaign in the Carolinas was more to his liking. His correspondence from this time period is riddled with reasons why he should abandon the Carolinas. Looming large at this point was Tarleton's loss of the light troops at Cowpens. Perhaps with the light troops in hand, Cornwallis could have experienced a different outcome to the campaign, and the march to Virginia may not have been contemplated in the first place.[73]

Cornwallis had learned of the difficulties of crossing rivers from his pursuit of Greene to the Dan River. Ahead of his main body, "Lieutenant-colonel Tarleton, with the advanced guard, was directed to seize as many boats as possible on the north-east branch of Cape-fear river, and collect them at a place about fifteen miles above Wilmington."[74] Throughout the march, Cornwallis would be keeping a wary eye on the availability of supplies and adequate forage for his troops, doubtless unwilling to repeat the hardships of marching his undersupplied army through North Carolina the previous winter. Tarleton would be employed doing what he did best—leading light troops ahead of the main army to seize supplies at strategic locations.

Thus far, the march north had had limited success with the usual array of problems. Cornwallis notified Balfour on May 3 that "the troops [are] becoming sickly and many of the mills being useless by the dryness of the season, which prevents my keeping up my stock of provisions so as to enable me to return if necessary from any point of the march to Wilmington."[75] The second part of his letter is truly heartless and self-serving and indicative of the fact that Cornwallis was never going to win the hearts and minds of the people. "Perhaps it will be proper for you to lay an embargo on provisions, to turn out of town all parole men and disaffected people with their families and many Negroes, and to shut your gates against many of the poor country people and all Negroes [so] that your stock of provisions may hold out."[76] Cornwallis ordered Balfour to dispatch transports and provisions at once to his army. Tarleton had informed Cornwallis on May 4 that "the country is alarm'd but the militia will not turn out. They were very near securing their leaders. Many people this day apply'd for paroles."[77] No longer would he utilize loyalists as he did in South Carolina.

On May 5, Cornwallis ordered Tarleton to advance towards Halifax. "On his route he ordered the inhabitants to collect great quantities of provisions for the King's troops, whose number he magnified in order to awe the militia."[78] Tarleton seized several mills along his march, which would be crucial in grinding flour for the advancing British army. Writing to Cornwallis from the mill, Tarleton reported that "here you will find 4000 weight of flour. Cobb's, Lamb's, Viverett's, Muffin's and another mill are all busily employ'd and will furnish supplies."[79] Traveling from Cobb's Mill, Tarleton took Halifax on May 7 with very few casualties and reported that "some stores of continental cloathing and other supplies were found in the place."[80] Cornwallis arrived in Halifax on May 10.

While the difficulty of finding supplies in the southern department could prove fatal to an advancing army, the difficulty of finding reliable information could prove just as challenging. While making a rendezvous with Major General Phillips had always been the objective since leaving Wilmington, actually finding Phillips was easier said than done. Both Cornwallis and Tarleton wrote frequent letters to Phillips as they advanced across North Carolina and into Virginia, but neither heard back, instead having to rely on rumors which spread wildly across the countryside. Shortly before reaching Halifax, enough of these rumors had reached Cornwallis concerning Lord Rawdon's victory over Greene at Hobkirk's Hill that he believed South Carolina to be safe. Nevertheless, he sought to unite the two British armies.

Two days after Cornwallis arrived in Halifax, General Benedict Arnold penned a letter to him. Arnold, the famous American turncoat and newly minted British general, had joined his army with General Phillips in Virginia and finally provided Cornwallis with some concrete information. "General Phillips is here in force to cooperate agreeable with your Lordship's wishes. The Marquis La Fayette is on the opposite shore with, as is said, fifteen hundred Continental troops and some militia."[81] At last satisfied with his plan, on the 14th, Cornwallis wrote an encrypted message on a piece of American currency for General Phillips—"I march tomorrow to join you."[82] Cornwallis's army left Halifax on May 15 bound for Petersburg, seventy miles away. The following day, a letter from Arnold arrived explaining Phillips's long silence. "I am very sorry to inform your Lordship that Major General Phillips died the 14th instant after an illness of about a fortnight. His loss is greatly lamented as he was universally beloved and esteemed by the army."[83] Arnold had assumed command over the British troops at Petersburg, and also sought to unite the British armies in the area.

Cornwallis reached Petersburg by May 20 and assumed command over the united British armies. With 5,000 troops behind him, he at last had the sort of army at his disposal which he needed to conduct an offensive war. Across the river was a new opponent in the form of the young Marquis de Lafayette and a relatively small army. Cornwallis quickly left Petersburg and marched in force to Westover to cross the two-mile-wide James River. Despite the vast numbers of troops and the width of the river, Tarleton remembered "such were the exertions of the detachments of sailors, under the orders of Captains Aplin and Dundass, the passage was completed in less than three days."[84] Setting his sights on Richmond, Cornwallis embarked on a destructive campaign intent on disrupting the rebel supply lines in Virginia.

On May 26, Cornwallis wrote to Clinton to explain his new strategy. "I shall now proceed to dislodge La Fayette from Richmond and with my light troops to destroy any magazines or stores which may have been collected either for his use or for General Greene's army. From thence I purpose to move to the neck at Williamsburgh ... and keep myself unengaged from operations which might interfere with our plan for the campaign, until I have the satisfaction from hearing from you."[85] The destruction of rebel supplies was a task well-suited for Tarleton and the British Legion. With the union of the British armies, Cornwallis also gained command of a similar asset—Lieutenant Colonel John Graves Simcoe and the Queen's Rangers.

Simcoe was the son of a naval officer and like Cornwallis, had been educated at Eton. Although he enjoyed his studies, he wanted to follow in his father's footsteps and devoted himself to the study of the military arts, which he considered "as the most extensive and profound of sciences."[86] He was first commissioned in 1770, and his regiment set sail for the colonies in 1775; he arrived in Boston two days after the Battle of Bunker Hill. He saw action in several engagements over the next few years, including at Brandywine. Convinced of the necessity of light troops for success in the American war, he was placed in charge of the Queen's Rangers.[87] The Rangers were a frontier unit comprised of loyalists, which traced its roots to the brutal battlefields of the French and Indian War. The irregular style of warfare for which the Rangers were trained was well-suited for the sort of destructive campaign which Cornwallis was planning.

Without sufficient numbers to engage Cornwallis in a pitched battle, Lafayette avoided Cornwallis's advance past Richmond. Tarleton wrote in his memoirs that "at this period, the superiority of the army, and the great superiority of the light troops, were such as to have enabled the British to traverse the country without apprehension or difficulty, either to destroy stores and tobacco in the neighborhood of the rivers, or to undertake more important expeditions."[88] In early June, Cornwallis was presented with the opportunity to do both. The Earl received word that the Virginia assembly was to meet in Charlottesville, and that Baron von Steuben was guarding a significant rebel store at the Point of Fork, forty miles west of Richmond. Having two light units suited for these operations, Cornwallis dispatched Tarleton with the British Legion to deal with the assembly, and he dispatched Simcoe with the Queen's Rangers to deal with Steuben.

South Carolina was never that far away from Cornwallis. Balfour had written him in late May still hopeful, but feeling a sense of desperation. "The country may still be regained if we are in force sufficient to repossess it," he wrote Cornwallis, "but if the enemy are allowed to remain any time in it, they will annihilate every remaining vestige of loyalty and by the vigor of their measures prevent our being joined by a single man."[89] Balfour urged Cornwallis to send reinforcements immediately. In the same letter, Balfour reflected on the efforts made by so many to hold on to South Carolina, lamenting, "I only cannot help regretting the leaving a country where so many exertions have been made to keep it and establish our friends in it."[90] So many officers and men had invested their lives in maintaining British control, and now it all seemed for naught.

Several weeks later, a more serious tone from Balfour emerged about a different problem. "Our want of money increases to a great degree. The expences of purchasing horses for the infantry, the sums paid to the distress'd refugees and militia, added to other contingencies, swells the expenditure of public money to a very great amount."[91] Cornwallis also took time to write to Lord Rawdon, who was essentially making excuses for staying within the environs of Charleston. He also framed a very pessimistic outlook for the

future in South Carolina, blaming loyalists for the lack of military assistance and reiterat-
ing that "a strong garrison in Charlestown with a small corps in the country will prevent
the enemy from reaping any advantage from it unless they keep a considerable body of
Continentals in the country for that purpose."[92]

Since leaving Wilmington, Cornwallis had brutalized the countryside and its citizens. A portion of a letter from Richard Henry Lee to Arthur Lee sums up the situation
in Virginia:

> The enemy affect to leave harmless the poor and they take everything from those they call the
> rich. Tis said that 2 or 3000 Negroes march in their train, that every kind of stock which they
> cannot remove they destroy—eating up the green wheat and by destroying of the fences expose
> to destruction the other growing grains. They have burnt a great number of warehouses full of
> tobacco and they are now pressing on to the large ones on the Rappahanock and Potomac rivers
> and the valuable iron works in our northern parts. The fine horses on James River have furnished
> them with a numerous and powerful cavalry.[93]

After a rapid march, Simcoe reached the Point of Fork on June 5. Hoping to be able to
capture the Baron, several rangers advanced in the uniforms of Steuben's dragoons whom
they had taken prisoner upon their arrival. When the rangers reached Steuben's main
body, they found them on the far side of the river, trying to escape with the stores. Simcoe
decided to try to trick Steuben into hastening his retreat and leaving his supplies. "Every
method was now taken to persuade the enemy, that the party was Earl Cornwallis's army,
that they might leave the opposite shore, which was covered with arms and stores," wrote
Simcoe in his journal, "the baggage and women halted among the woods, on the summit
of the hill, and, in that position, made the appearance of a numerous corps."[94] That night,
the British heard the enemy destroying their boats so that they could not be used to ferry
the British across in their pursuit.

The morning brought a welcome sight. "A deserter and a little drummer boy came
from the enemy in a canoe, and gave information that Steuben marched off on the road
by Cumberland Court-house, towards North Carolina. It is remarkable this boy belonged
to the 71st regiment: he had been taken prisoner at Cow-pens, enlisted with the enemy,
and now, making his escape, was received by the piquet which his father commanded."[95]
In addition to this unlikely reunion, Simcoe seized and destroyed "two thousand five hundred stands of arms [and] a large quantity of gunpowder," and shared in the spoils of
much-needed supplies, including "upwards of sixty hogsheads of rum and brandy, several
chests of carpenters' tools, with casks of flints, sail cloth and wagons, and a great variety of
small stores, necessary for the equipment of cavalry and infantry."[96] The successful corps
reunited with Cornwallis on June 7.

Tarleton, in the meantime, headed towards Charlottesville with his sights set on
Thomas Jefferson and the Virginia Assembly. Although it was not his primary objective,
he still took advantage of any opportunities to disrupt the movement of rebel supplies in
the area. Along the way, "he fell in with twelve wagons that were on their journey, under
a weak guard, from the upper parts of Virginia and Maryland, with arms and clothing for
the continental troops in South Carolina. The wagons and stores were burnt, that no time
might be lost, or diminuation of force made by giving them an escort."[97] Hoping to effect
a surprise attack, Tarleton had marched at a furious pace and reached Charlottesville on
June 4.

After clearing the rebel advance guards, Tarleton ordered his cavalry to charge into the town. Surprised by the sudden appearance of the British, the Americans offered little resistance. "Seven members of the assembly were secured: A Brigadier-general Scott, and several officers and men, were killed, wounded or taken. The attempt to secure Mr. Jefferson was ineffectual; he discovered the British dragoons from his house, which stands on the point of a mountain, before they could approach him, and he provided for his personal liberty by a precipitate retreat."[98] Although Jefferson escaped, the capture of seven members of the assembly was a clear victory for the British and a blow to the rebel government in the area.

Tarleton also continued his destruction of rebel stockpiles. "One thousand new firelocks that had been manufactured at Fredericksburg were broken: Upwards of four hundred barrels of powder were destroyed: Several hogsheads of tobacco, and some continental clothing and accouterments, shared the same fate."[99] Tarleton could not help but notice that following the victory, he began to see locals wanting to join the British, but he was unable to stay in the area long enough to raise a significant number. Following the raid, Tarleton rejoined Cornwallis.

Having successfully carried out the simultaneous raids in the area west of Richmond, and successfully destroying many rebel supplies and stores, Cornwallis moved towards Williamsburg to await orders from Clinton. Largely due to the difficult nature of reliably sending letters, Cornwallis had not heard from his commander-in-chief since he moved into Virginia. This unreliable system was to cause a great deal of confusion between the two British officers over the coming weeks. Clinton had heard about the army's move into Virginia in late May, writing an angry letter showing his displeasure with Cornwallis on the 29th, but that letter would not reach the earl for some time, on June 26 in Williamsburg, to be exact. Clinton was direct and to the point: "I shall dread what may be the consequences of your Lordship's move, unless a reinforcement arrives soon in South Carolina.... I should certainly have endeavored to have stopped you, as I did then, as well as now, consider such a move to be dangerous to our interests in the Southern Colonies."[100]

Outside of New York, Clinton was feeling the pinch from George Washington and Comte de Rochambeau, the commander-in-chief of the French Expeditionary Force that had arrived in America. Convinced of the necessity of holding New York against an army, which may have been as large as 20,000, and the potential effects of a siege, Clinton desired additional troops to bolster the 10,931 he had guarding the city. From Cornwallis's army he wanted as many as 3,000 troops. Cornwallis was ordered "to take a defensive station in any healthy situation you chuse (be it at Williamsburg or York Town)."[101] Cornwallis was ordered to set up a naval base for this express purpose.

Clinton went on to emphasize that he had not changed his mind about British strategy in the South, and that there was no possibility of reestablishing order in any rebellious province on the continent without the hearty assistance of numerous friends. "These, my Lord, are not I think to be found in Virginia, nor dare I positively assert that under our present circumstances they are to be found in great numbers any where else ... except the southern provinces. In these your Lordship has already made the experiment. It has there failed. They are gone from us and I fear not to be recovered."[102] Faced with clear orders from an unhappy commander, Cornwallis had little choice. Cornwallis readied the troops for transportation from Portsmouth to New York.

Four days later, Cornwallis wrote to Clinton to inform him of the army's moving towards Portsmouth to comply with Clinton's need for reinforcements. In his letter,

Cornwallis could not help but rather prophetically question the value "of a defensive post in this country which cannot have the smallest influence on the war in Carolina and which only gives us some acres of an unhealthy swamp and is for ever liable to become a prey to a foreign enemy with a temporary superiority at sea."[103] Despite his apprehensions, on July 4, Cornwallis departed for Portsmouth, where General Leslie was stationed

Shortly before the convoy was ready to sail, a cyphered dispatch from Clinton was handed to Cornwallis at one in the morning on July 20. The dispatch was brief but ordered Cornwallis to halt any troops bound for New York and wait for new orders. Those orders were delivered the next day. Clinton and the British navy were concerned about the lack of deep-water ports in the area to support ships-of-the-line, and such a port had to be secured before any troops were sent to New York. Clinton himself seemed uneasy about the situation. "I am as much mortified as your Lordship can possibly be at the necessity there is at present for leaving you upon the defensive in Chesapeak.... When, therefore your Lordship has finally determined upon the force you think sufficient for such works as you shall erect at Old Point Comfort and the number you judge requisite to cover them at York Town and for their other services of the Chesapeak during the unhealthy season, you will be pleased to send me the remainder."[104]

After a long period of stalemate, with the last major battle in the north having been fought at Monmouth, New Jersey, in 1778, Washington finally had his opportunity. It is beyond the scope of this book to discuss the intricacies of the siege that took place at Yorktown. Suffice it to say, on August 14, Washington received word that a French fleet of the Comte de Grasse was sailing for the Chesapeake with twenty-nine ships and 3,000 men.[105] Washington jumped into action, and he and Rochambeau marched French and American troops south to Virginia, all the while appearing as if he were making preparations to attack New York in order to hold Clinton in place.

In an amazing coordination of land and sea operations, the French appeared off the Chesapeake capes on August 26, defeating the British in an encounter, preventing Cornwallis from receiving reinforcements from or access to the sea. By the end of September, Cornwallis's 8,000 men were completely surrounded by nearly 17,000 American and French troops. Cornwallis had no options left. On October 19, 1781, he surrendered. Major combat had ended, and the war in the South, which has become the unknown American Revolution in the history books, had proved itself to be the deciding theater of battle. The Carolinas were the proving ground of American resolve.

Washington, with all that he brought to the American Revolution, the absolute center of the political and military struggle for independence, was not the decisive figure in the war in the South. Nathanael Greene, whose fortunes after the fall of New York reached rock bottom, climbed to the highest heights of success that he could have imagined. Cornwallis, the professional soldier and leading one of the greatest armies of the eighteenth century, the clear favorite in the contest in the South, had fallen like Goliath. Charles O'Hara summed it all up after Yorktown: "America is irretrievably lost."[106]

9

"The Play, Sir, Is Over"

Greene was occupied with several key matters during this lull in the campaign. The situation with Cornwallis was one of them. The arrival of the French fleet in the Chesapeake had forced Greene to consider the possibility of assembling "considerable" land forces, "all of which are to be employed against Lord Cornwallis who it is supposed will endeavor to make good his retreat through North Carolina to Charlestown."[1] To prepare for that eventuality, Greene implored Colonels Shelby and Sevier to recruit "as large a body of riflemen" as they could and come to Charlotte and to inform Greene when they left and when they arrived. His goal was plain enough: "If we can intercept his Lordship it will put a finishing stroke to the war in the Southern States."[2]

To Marion, he made a similar plea. He informed Marion of the arrival of French forces and Washington in Virginia, and asked him to assemble as large a militia body as he could if Cornwallis attempted to make a retreat toward Charleston. Greene said Marion must act "immediately" and "join the army at the shortest notice."[3] But several days later, on September 19, Greene informed Marion that a retreat of Cornwallis was not now likely, but "don't relax your preparations for fear of Accident, & we may want the Militia here for our own defence."[4]

By September 23, with events moving rapidly in Virginia, Greene received a letter from Colonel Lewis Morris, Jr., stating that "the troops from the Northward are all arrived and two or three days will produce a very interesting scene. His Lordship [i.e., Cornwallis] has fortified himself very strongly at York and no doubt will make a spirited and obstinate resistance. It is possible he may be relieved, but the probability is against him."[5] For the time being, Greene's chances of engaging again with Cornwallis were fading each day.

Greene was anxious for Colonels Shelby and Sevier to join him. He wrote them on October 11, explaining that "the Enemy are ravaging the country in the Stephens Parish [South Carolina] to prevent which and to straiten them in the articles of supplies, I wish to collect a force to drive them into Town [i.e., Charleston]."[6] He also knew about Count de Grasse's victory over the British fleet in the Chesapeake, and was in "hopes the [French] fleet and army will move this way, and lay siege to Charles Town." He noted that "all the Militia are coming out for this purpose and we only await your arrival to begin our operations."[7] Sevier and Shelby both joined Greene's army in late October. Contrary to Greene's hopes, neither Washington's army nor the French fleet moved towards Charleston after the capitulation at Yorktown.[8]

Lack of supplies continued to plague the army, which was running low on salt. Greene wrote Colonel William Davie and spared no words for the importance of this commodity. "I shall only observe that an army which has receivd no pay for more than two years[,] distressed for want of clothing, subsisted without spirits and often short in the usual allowances of meat and bread will mutiny if we fail in the article of salt; [and] would soon produce such a variety of diseases and complaints that the greater part would soon be transferred from the field to the hospital."[9] Greene was correct about mutiny. The very conditions Greene described in his letter to Davie led to unrest among the Maryland Continentals. They were unpaid, hungry and poorly clothed, and there were only 200 survivors left from the original seven regiments.[10] A South Carolina soldier, who was drunk, encouraged others to confront their officers while on the parade ground. He was seized, convicted and shot the next day in front of the whole army.[11] Any other thoughts of mutiny were quelled.

Other routine military and civilian matters occupied Greene's time after Eutaw Springs as well. He told the president of the Continental Congress the condition of the sick and wounded was worsening, as he had visited all the hospitals from the High Hills to Charlotte. "The extent of our Hospitals, the malignity of disorders, & increasing sick since the battle of Eutaw, together with the numerous wounded on hand, the little means we had to provide for them, & the great number of surgeons which fell sick in our service, have left our sick & wounded in a most deplorable situation."[12] He indicated his force was too small and sickly to initiate any major movements unless it was in the "partizan way."[13]

Greene informed the commander-in-chief that he had been planning the reduction of Wilmington in concert with Governor Thomas Burke, but the "Enemy have left the place, and now occupy Brunswick, about thirty miles below." Judging by the preparations of small transports in Charleston, Greene thought it "highly probable the Enemy intend to take off the Garrison."[14]

The ever-present issue of violence in the countryside also had Greene's attention. North Carolina Governor Thomas Burke, along with other government officials, was captured by a Tory raiding party in Hillsborough in September, and turned over to the British.[15] Retaliation by Whigs was swift, and reports of reprisals began to filter into Greene's headquarters. According to reports, the men under General Griffith Rutherford were mistreating civilians and destroying property.[16] Greene, ever conscious about postwar reconciliation between Whigs and Tories, did not mince words in a letter to Rutherford. Greene felt "those measures highly unwarrantable which carries the marks of cruelty and increases our enemies. If we persue the tories indiscriminately and drive them to a state [of] desperation we shall make them from a weak and feeble foe a sure and determined enemy."[17] As it turned out, Rutherford's men were not as guilty as Greene had supposed, but nonetheless, in a follow-up letter to Rutherford, Greene reiterated his point that "cruelty always marks the authors with disgrace and is generally attended with disadvantage; however, it is very right to hold out great vengeance to the disaffected that they may receive grace with a greater sense of obligation."[18]

Greene also knew that the issues with the disaffected population were not just a problem in the Carolinas. His approach was to support a national solution, and he believed that if the "Governors of every state would correspond with each other and adopt nearly a similar policy with respect to the proper mode of treating the disaffected," justice and unification would be the result.[19] Greene approved of measures in moderation, and when South Carolina Governor John Rutledge offered a pardon to Tories in his state, Greene applauded. But when acting Governor Alexander Martin refused to issue pardons,

Greene did not force the issue, respecting the primacy of the civilian authorities over the military.

The news of the surrender of Yorktown spread through the camp like wildfire. Celebrations rang out as Cornwallis finally flew the white flag on October 19. But Greene was not celebrating. Wilmington, Charleston, and Savannah were still in British hands, and he needed men if he were to finish the business at hand. Greene had driven the British almost into the confines of Charleston, and it was time to shut the door to British occupation in the south. Washington wrote Greene on the 31st to let him know that reinforcements were on their way in a few days "under the Command of Major Gen. St. Clair, and will consist of the Pennsylvania, Maryland & Virginia Continental Troops, including their Cavalry."[20] Greene would be receiving 700 men and it would be two months before they arrived. Much to Greene's chagrin, de Grasse was returning to the West Indies, and with him the chance to blockade Charleston and end the British occupation.[21] As he had always done, Greene would have to make do with what he had.

At last, the men under Colonels Shelby and Sevier made it to camp, and Greene decided it was time to descend into the low country. Greene sent the mountain men down to Marion to help hold back the new British field commander, Major John Doyle, who had replaced the wounded Alexander Stewart. By mid–November, Greene was on the move. He tasked Marion with giving him intelligence of his position and "guarding our left after we get down as low as Four Holes."[22] Greene crossed the Wateree, then moved south down the west side of the river and crossed the Congaree.[23] Here he learned that the riflemen he had wanted so badly had all gone home. Greene was crushed, but he had to move on.

British Major General Alexander Leslie had arrived in Charleston to take over command in the South and had twice as many men as Greene. This presented a potential problem, but Greene continued advancing. Marion informed him that the British had withdrawn from Monck's Corner to "below the Goos Creek Bridge," fifteen miles from Charleston.[24] The British had been out foraging, and "they leave nothing for the inhabitants," said Marion, as provisions were very scarce.[25] The village of Dorchester was exposed now, and Greene made that his immediate objective.

Major Doyle had 850 men under his command, and Greene decided that he would attack. He left Otho Williams with the rest of the army to move toward Four Holes, and with 400 infantry and cavalry, he entered the town accompanying his troops. After an initial skirmish, Greene was recognized. Believing that he was under siege from the entire American army, Doyle withdrew, and in doing so, he destroyed his stores, sank his guns in the Ashley River, and fled in the direction of Charleston.[26] Greene thought they had "disgraced themselves not a little by their precipitate retreat."[27]

The British retreated behind the Quarter House, a famous tavern at the northern end of the six-mile-long isthmus, which had Charleston at its southern end. Gen. Leslie ordered the house fortified, canals were dug between the Ashley and Cooper Rivers, and trees were felled to form abatis and clear fields of fire for the defenders.[28] The British would be able to conduct raids from either flank into the countryside with the house inaccessible from the front except for a narrow path.[29] The British were now confined to the outskirts of Charleston, and it appeared they were heading for the ultimate siege. John's Island was being stocked with cattle in preparation for the worst.[30]

But Greene was cautious as well as observant about British strength. He told Governor John Rutledge that "their force is formidable and they can make sudden incursions into the Country without being encumbered with a heavy baggage we must be careful not to give them an opportunity of doing us an injury."[31] In the meantime, Greene was headed to Round O, where he would meet Williams with the rest of the army. Round O was forty miles from Charleston and directly between Savannah and Charleston, between the Edisto and Ashepoo Rivers. Greene strategically placed "Sumter at Orangburgh and the Four Holes[,] General Marion in St. Stephens & St Thomas Parish and ... a flying Army of the Cavalry and a detachment of Infantry for the security of the Country between Ashley & Edisto."[32] Lee was specifically instructed by Greene to prevent the inhabitants from being plundered in the greater interests of the American cause. He also concerned himself with the Africans, "from whom the enemy get all their best intelligence and who will be either more or less useful to them as they are treated well or ill by us."[33] Greene emphasized that he was to pay particular attention to this matter, because as Greene's thinking progressed, it would become a bigger issue as the war came to a climax.

As Greene pondered the military situation in South Carolina, he wrote John Rutledge and began to contemplate the use of Africans in the defense of the state. Greene had no doubt that they would make great soldiers and the states were unable to provide sufficient reinforcements without them. Greene drove home his point with Rutledge when he mentioned that "the number of whites in this State are too small, and the State of the finances too low, to attempt to raise a force in any other way. Should this measure be adopted, It may prove a great means of preventing the Enemy from further attempts upon this country, when they find they have not only the whites, but the blacks to contend with."[34] Greene was induced to think about unique solutions to problems of manpower when rumors swept through camp that the British were on their way to Charleston with thousands of troops from New York and Ireland.[35] Greene had implored Washington and Rochambeau to send more reinforcements, but both refused, arguing that Virginia needed to remain secure.[36]

Greene had an ally in the quest to arm slaves, and that was in the person of Colonel John Laurens, a Continental officer, a member of the South Carolina House of Representatives, and the son of Henry Laurens, a South Carolina planter who had also been president of the Continental Congress. Laurens, who had first formulated such a plan and had been unsuccessfully pushing its adoption for years, helped Greene by introducing a bill to the newly convened legislature to recruit 2,500 slaves, but the measure was defeated. The idea was too radical. After much debate, the legislature approved a measure to have them serve the army not as soldiers but as "waggoners, Pioneers, Artificers and servants for the officers," never again returning to the proposal of arming them for combat.[37]

The beginning of 1782 brought some other important developments to the region, even though major combat was no longer a possibility. General "Mad" Anthony Wayne arrived in camp with the Pennsylvania Line on January 4, and General Arthur St. Clair with 1,200 Maryland and Delaware troops arrived shortly thereafter, with far fewer troops than were expected. In the wake of the approach of St. Clair's men, the British commander in Wilmington, Major James Craig, had evacuated the town and headed to Charleston.[38] Now, Greene "began to enter more particularly into his long-mediated design of relieving the state of Georgia, by forcing the enemy to evacuate Savannah."[39] By the 9th, Greene sent Wayne with infantry and cavalry to Savannah to do just that. After Wayne suppressed an Indian uprising and quelled Whig and Tory violence, the British finally evacuated the city on July 11. Now only Charleston remained in British hands.

On the political front, the South Carolina General Assembly finally convened on January 18, 1782, at Jacksonborough, a town located ten miles south of Round O and about thirty miles from Charleston. Greene had convinced Gov. Rutledge to make the seat of power on Charleston's doorstep in order to create the picture that British power had been ended in South Carolina. In a speech opening the Assembly, according to Lee, Rutledge praised the militia for its "enterprising spirit and unremitted perseverance," noting the efforts of Sumter and Marion, and of course, he warmly mentioned "the pleasing change of affairs, which under the blessing of God, the wisdom, prudence, address, and bravery of the great and gallant General Greene, and the intrepidity of the officers and men under his command, has been happily effected."[40] Greene took the opportunity to move his camp to Skirving's plantation, a few miles east of Jacksonborough, on the 16th to ensure the legislature's meeting would take place uninterrupted.[41]

On the military front, Lee had proposed an expedition in December against John's Island, where the British held herds of cattle to feed the garrison at Charleston. The guard posted on the island numbered between 400 and 500 men. Lee told Greene that "if the enemy do not exceed 400, [John] Laurens & my self will be adequate to the attempt provided."[42] Greene would provide 700 men, but he was hesitant about the operation, and with good reason. In order to reach John's Island, it was necessary to cross from the mainland at low tide, with British galleys patrolling the perimeter. It would also mean that Lee would have to cross back at low tide when he finished with the operation. Greene noted in his letter to Lee that he hated "all Island[s] for Military operations where we do not command the water."[43] Greene added with caution: "But if you get cut off, and we driven back, the consequences would be dreadful from the effect it would have upon the Country."[44]

On January 11, the attempt was made, and Greene's concerns about the mission came to fruition. "One column led by Lt Col Lee got over, but unfortunately the other Column … got lost … yet it was so long before they found that the tide had rizen so high as to be impossible and the other troops were obliged to recross."[45] Interestingly, the British retreated to James Island, leaving some provisions behind and destroying others, but the British evacuation did confirm for many of Greene's troops that the unwillingness of the British to fight the Americans was indicative of the poor morale of the British garrison in Charleston.[46]

This stage of the war also began the changing of the nature of the relationships between Greene and his subordinates. Francis Marion left the army to serve in the new Assembly, and Pickens and Sumter became members of the Assembly as well. Otho Williams as well as John Eager Howard, recovering from a serious wound suffered at Eutaw Springs, also left and headed back to Maryland.[47]

But the biggest news was that Henry Lee, Greene's reliable cavalry commander, was resigning from the army. In a letter to Greene on January 26, Lee claimed that "disquietude of mind and body unite in giving birth to my request. The first arises from the indifference with which my efforts to advance the cause of my country is considered by my friends, the persecution of my foes, and my consciousness that it is not in my power to efface the disagreeable impression."[48] The correspondence between the two went back and forth, and Greene was quick to point out to Lee that "few officers either in America or Europe are held in so high a point of estimation as you are."[49] Greene implored Lee not to leave the army, but Lee would have none of it.

According to historian Gregory Massey, Lee had been dissatisfied because of his contention of not receiving enough credit in Greene's official reports of the Southern Campaign, and Lee was sensitive to any perceived slights.[50] Charles Royster, one of Lee's biographers, asserted that Lee also resented the fact that John Laurens, a younger man who joined the Southern Army, enjoyed the seniority he did because he was a former member of Washington's staff.[51] In one of Lee's letters to Greene, Lee noted: "I read some of your reports with distress, because some officers & corps were held out to the world with a lustre superior to others, who to say the least deserved equally."[52] Greene magnanimously responded, "I shall leave you at liberty to think of me as you please and whatever sentiments you may entertain of me I will always do justice to your merit, and shall always be happy to share your friendship and confidence when it can be had on terms reciprocal and honorable."[53]

In his official report on the Eutaw Springs action, Greene had commented in a positive fashion on Lee's conduct during the battle. However, Royster claims that Lee's fellow officers in the militia as well as the Continental Army resented Lee's status in the army. In addition, rumors of Lee's supposed lack of courage in several engagements, the failure of the John's Island expedition, and Lee's perception that Greene showed favoritism toward Lieutenant Colonel William Washington, a relative of the commander-in-chief, all combined to create feelings of discord and resentment in Lee.[54]

It can also be said, with some degree of certainty, that years of combat had taken their toll, and Lee may also have been suffering from battle fatigue.[55] Lee's resignation also spurred on another controversy. Greene had appointed Laurens to command Lee's Legion, and that decision was met with indignity from the officers, who tendered their resignations, but withdrew them when Greene accepted them.[56] Greene would have none of it. He would not allow his hand to be forced.

The legislature, in addition to conducting state business, had awarded Greene a confiscated estate. The South Carolina General Assembly adopted confiscation and amercement acts, seizing the estates of 375 loyalists and establishing a tax of twelve percent on almost fifty other loyalist estates.[57] Greene had been wary of mass confiscations and believed them to be anathema to building postwar bonds. But Greene's feelings on political matters were overlooked, and after evaluating his own financial situation, he accepted the confiscated estate. Greene was awarded a confiscated rice plantation on the Edisto River known as Boone Barony. "They [the Assembly] have voted me their thanks unanimously," he wrote to Joseph Reed, "accompanied with a vote vesting me with an estate of ten thousand guineas."[58]

With the war winding down, Greene was beginning to take stock of his financial future. "This [estate] with the shattered remains of my little fortune will lay a foundation for a decent support in the decline of life."[59] Greene began to cultivate a new interest in this region, and with business prospects in the North lacking, perhaps this was an opportunity he could not refuse.[60] Acknowledgments for Greene's efforts in securing the South continued to pour in. North Carolina had presented him with a 25,000-acre estate, and Georgia presented him with a 2,000-acre estate called Mulberry Grove, which would become Greene's new home after the war.

The spring brought a visit from Catharine Greene, which somewhat cheered the general, but he was still concerned with the British threat in Charleston.

Even with the war winding down, Greene was facing myriad problems. Morale was suffering, and increased squabbling had led to a mutiny, which Greene put down by hanging the instigator. Captain Walter Finney, who had been sent down from York-town after Cornwallis's surrender, noted in his diary that the troops were "badly fed, and wretchedly Clothed, at least one third of the men as naked as they came into the world, their Blanket & Hat excepted, which they belted round them to defend from the clemency of the weather, as well as to preserve that Decency which custom has introduced in that part of the Globe."[61]

The situation in the countryside was still grave, and it was unsafe to travel without an escort. "The disaffected are numerous and their Situation so desparate that they confine themselves to their private haunts and conceal themselves in the Swamps from whence they issue forth and murder and rob every person on the road."[62] Desertions were mounting, and Greene issued an order on April 20 describing the situation as "disgraceful" and tried to appeal to his men. "What can those Deserters propose to themselves who abandon the Army ... to Join one shut up in a garrison under daily apprehension of a siege & where the refugees are groaning under every specie's of distress, suffering and want."[63] Despite Greene's appeals, desertions continued, and men disappeared into the Carolina backcountry.

Greene was still in desperate need of supplies, and he wrote to Robert Morris about the critical nature of the problem. Morris, however, was not sympathetic. He told Greene that he should "continue [his] Exertions with, or without Men, Provisions, Cloathing or pay, in hopes that all Things will come right at last."[64] He told Greene that the states had done everything they could, and taxation was out of the question.

Word leaked out that the British were actually going to withdraw from Charleston. The British government had made a decision to evacuate Charleston and other British posts on April 4, but General Leslie did not receive those instructions until June.[65] Both sides continued to wait.

In May, Greene received a copy of a newspaper, supposedly the *Charleston Royal Gazette* of May 18, which contained a request from Parliament to King George III to terminate offensive operations in America.[66] King George's response was to follow the "advice" of the House of Commons and "take such measures" to restore "harmony between Great Britain and the revolted Colonies."[67] Events were moving quickly, but for Greene, not quickly enough. He was barely able to hold his ragged troops together.

More big news had reached his ears as Clinton submitted his resignation and left New York for England on May 13. Sir Guy Carleton was the new British commander and had been named to succeed Clinton before Lord North's ministry collapsed on March 27 and a new government led by the Marquis of Rockingham took over. By the spring of 1782, Lord North's ministry was being challenged as to whether the American war should continue. British successes were not resulting in control of territory, and the belief that loyalists would rise up had failed to materialize.[68] By March, the North ministry had collapsed, and the entry of France and Spain into the war had doomed Great Britain to failure.[69] The new ministry ordered Carleton to withdraw British forces from America.[70] Carleton's primary mission was to evacuate Savannah, Charleston, and New York.[71]

On July 7, the army moved further south toward Charleston, to the Ashley Hill plantation. Encamped at Bacon's Bridge since March, Greene was searching for a healthier camp for his men, and although Ashley Hill was considered a better site, many men continued to be plagued by malaria. Greene wrote Washington while in camp there, and continued to doubt the veracity of the actual departure of the British. "The people of this country have their expectations raised and are sanguine in their hopes," he wrote, "that Charlestown will be speedily abandoned. There are some preparations on which these opinions are founded but I must confess they seem to be rather contracting their works than abandoning the place."[72] It was not until early August that Greene finally believed it was true.[73] Savannah was evacuated the same day Greene wrote his letter to the commander-in-chief.

Minor skirmishes marked the period of time after Eutaw Springs until the evacuation of Charleston. With the British confined to Charleston in the latter part of 1782, it was hard for them to get supplies without piercing American lines. In August, General Leslie asked Greene for a cessation of hostilities in order to buy provisions for the garrison and the residents of Charleston. With "American soldiers ... covered by tattered garments, destitute of shoes, and scarcely furnished with blankets," Greene nonetheless rejected the request.[74] Leslie, "foiled in accomplishing his object in the way desired, ... prepared to effect by force the procurement of those supplies."[75] Greene, unwilling to give the British any leeway, organized a combat operation to prevent British incursions into the countryside.

Greene dispatched General Mordecai Gist of Maryland and Lieutenant Colonel John Laurens to oppose Leslie's advances to the plantations along the Combahee River. Many men came down with fever, the British were able to net 300 barrels of rice, and most importantly of all, John Laurens was killed in an ambush.[76] Greene had warned Laurens about being too brazen in military engagements and too desirous of military glory for his own good. In his short career, he had demonstrated his worth as an officer, and now, months before the war was over, Laurens was gone, the victim in an insignificant skirmish with the enemy over food.

The embarkation of the British was finally accomplished on December 14, 1782. Thousands of slaves from both Tory and Whig plantations, as well as loyalists numbering in the thousands, had boarded British ships and left. On the morning of the 14th, the British troops began marching down to the dock onto awaiting transports. At eleven o'clock, Leslie's rear guard made their way to the dock to board awaiting transports, and were followed 200 yards behind by a corps of American infantry, dragoons and artillery commanded by Anthony Wayne.[77] At approximately three o'clock, Nathanael Greene entered the city with Governor Mathews and a column of Continental troops. "On the next day the civil authority resumed its former functions, and the din of arms yielded to the innocent and pleasing occupations of peace."[78] Greene had beaten all the odds and had defeated the greatest military power on earth.

As the war drew to a close, Greene was looking ahead to his postwar life, and his finances occupied much of his attention. The laurels he won in the South were no substitute for the ability to provide for his family. The family business back in Warwick was in the hands of his brothers and was not doing as well as he had hoped. In 1779, Greene had entered a partnership with former commissary general Jeremiah Wadsworth and Barnabas Deane, the brother of the Continental Congress delegate from Connecticut, Silas Deane. Greene and Wadsworth had invested 10,000 pounds sterling each, mostly in shipping and privateering ventures, but by September 1782, Deane informed Greene he had lost most of the money invested.[79] When the company disbanded in 1784, Greene was left with nine hundred sixty pounds sterling.[80]

Greene had also turned to two of his friends, Colonel Cox and Colonel Pettit, who had been businessmen in civilian life, and his investments with them went sour. Essentially,

Greene was broke. In August 1783, he confided to Catharine about how bleak their financial future looked. "Col. Wadsworth informs me that all my stocks put into his hands four years ago, have been lost; and that out of upwards of a thousand pounds put into his hands four years ago, I have not fifty left. This loss and those heavy losses with my brothers distresses my private affairs exceedingly."[81]

The awarding of confiscated plantations to him advanced his thought process on how he could make money and be financially independent. Mulberry Grove was over 2,000 acres, and the only way to operate a plantation of that size and to create a profit was to do it with slave labor. Desperate to avoid a life of financial enslavement, Greene turned to slavery itself.

If Greene had anxiety over the question, his friends saw his new way of life as a slippery slope for Greene. Reverend William Gordon, a Congregationalist minister from Roxbury, Massachusetts, gave Greene his point of view on the issue of living on a southern plantation: "I hope You & your Lady will not sit down to enjoy the sweets of your toils & dangers in such a hot climate, & where slaves are more numerous than Freemen. You are a Citizen of America, but the Rhode Island & Providence Plantations have the first right to your services as a citizen."[82]

Joseph Reed waxed philosophical with two questions that required Greene to think about the direction in which he was heading. "Will you be a Planter with a Retinue of Slaves? Or will you come Northward to enjoy more Ease, but less Splendor?"[83] Warner Mifflin, a devout Quaker from Delaware, reminded Greene that the Declaration of Independence set forth the natural rights of all men and to "countenance slavery it would be a stigma to thy character in the Annals of History."[84]

Greene's response clearly indicated the direction he was heading and there was no looking back. "The generosity of the southern states has placed an interest of this sort in my hands, and I trust their [slaves'] condition will not be worse but better. They are, generally, as much attached to a plantation as a man to his family; and to remove them from one to another is their greatest punishment."[85] It was pure fantasy and Greene had completely deluded himself. It was a far cry from 1775, when, writing Catharine after being called forth to defend the common rights of Americans, Greene wrote the following about slavery: "Slavery shuts up every avenue that leads to knowledge, and leaves the soul ignorant of its own importance; it is rendered incapable of promoting human happiness, piety or virtue; and he that betrays that trust, being once acquainted with the pleasure and advantages of Knowledge and freedom, is guilty of spiritual suicide."[86]

For the estate he was to live on, Mulberry Grove, outside Savannah, Greene borrowed money from superintendent of finance Robert Morris and former commissary general Jeremiah Wadsworth to buy slaves and other accouterments for his estate.[87] Greene had to have on his mind the letter he received from Dr. Benjamin Rush in September 1782, about prohibiting the future importation of slaves. One line was particularly poignant: "For God's Sake do not exhibit a new Spectacle to the World, of men just emerging from a war of liberty with their cloathes not yet washed from the blood which was Shed in copious & willing streams in its defence, fitting out vessels to import their fellow creatures from Africa to reduce them afterwards to Slavery."[88] Greene had tried to obtain a loan in Holland for the needs of his plantations but was denied. Robert Morris broke the news that there was a more "general want of Money both in Europe & America than I ever knew, and every attempt at relief that I have heard of has proved abortive."[89]

With the imminent departure of the British in late 1782, Greene was concerned about the British taking slaves with them. Unfortunately, his motives were selfish. Publicly, Greene was pessimistic of British intentions, telling Otho Williams that he "would believe nothing until it was signed[,] sealed and deliverd. The Nation that is wicked enough to begin an unjust war will be base enough to practice every deception."[90] However, in a letter to Francis Marion, Greene expressed his suspicion about British intentions to evacuate Charleston, but his real concern was not only that they leave quickly, but with as few slaves as possible. "I am persuaded it will take place soon and the more scanty we can render their supplies of provisions the sooner it will take place and the fewer Negroes they will have it in their power to take with them."[91]

By November 1783, Greene had learned a hard lesson about the planter lifestyle. Heavy rains led to disappointing crop production, and it continued a downward spiral for Greene's finances from which he never recovered.[92] The plantation at Mulberry Grove became synonymous with personal setbacks and tragedies. Gravely concerned about his finances, he wrote Catharine, "I tremble at my own situation when I think of the enormous sums I owe and the great difficulty of obtaining Money. I seem to be doomed to a life of slavery and anxiety."[93] It was an interesting choice of words.

Greene headed back to Rhode Island in the summer of 1785 to gather his wife and children. Caty Greene had given birth to their sixth child, only to see the baby die before Greene arrived. While still mourning, the family left Rhode Island and headed to Mulberry Grove to settle down. Continuing to fret over finances, Greene lost ninety-five barrels of rice in several accidents and Caty once again lost another baby in infancy in 1786.[94] Greene had been under tremendous pressure, not only in this sphere of his life, but also dating back to the early winter of 1782–1783, when trying to clothe his army, his path collided with that of one John Banks.

The early winter of 1782 found Greene in a terrible position trying to supply his army, and he was forced to send out foraging parties to obtain provisions. Even after the evacuation of Charleston, "we have been obliged to subsist the Troops at the point of the bayonet," Greene wrote to Benjamin Lincoln.[95] Robert Morris sent Greene directions to arrange the supply of his army with a private contractor in 1783. The only contractor willing to participate in this process was John Banks, a merchant from the firm Hunter, Banks & Company out of Fredericksburg, Virginia.

Greene wrote Lincoln in February confirming that "Lt Col Carrington has closed a contract with Mr Banks for the subsistence of the Army at something less than eleven pence sterling. It is high but it could not be had lower. There was not an offer made but by Mr Banks altho I wrote to all the principal Men in the Country. People have not that spirit for engaging in business here as with us."[96] Banks was not a reputable merchant and Greene must have sensed it, for in a letter to Robert Morris informing him of the deal, Greene noted that "the Army in a starving condition Mr Banks knew his advantages too well not to avail himself of it."[97]

It was not long after this agreement that Banks's credit with his suppliers ran out. In order to supply his men, Greene took the ominous step of cosigning the notes, as there was no other way. After Greene signed on with Banks, the army was clothed and provisioned for the winter and all seemed well. But the bottom fell through quickly, which added to Greene's despair. Two of Greene's aides secretly became partners with Banks, and when a private letter to his partner in Virginia became public, Greene's reputation became severely damaged, especially when Banks had mentioned that Greene was giving him special consideration and he was going to include Greene in his firm after the war.[98]

When Greene learned of the contents of the letter, he moved swiftly to control the damage. Greene forced Banks to publicly retract the statements, in which Banks declared that "he [Greene] neither has, or ever had, any commercial connexion with me of a private nature, or intimated a wish or desire of the kind."[99] Greene then asked two of his subordinates to examine the evidence and corroborate Banks's retraction. Anthony Wayne and Col. Edward Carrington issued a joint statement and publicly defended Greene, hoping it would "remove every impression those letters may have occasioned to the injury of General Greene, to whom it must be mortifying to have his conduct made a subject of public discussion, from a transaction which had the public good, and the relief of the suffering soldiers for its objects." They added that sometimes "private jealousy saps public confidence" so that this letter "may be of public utility."[100]

Allegations of wrongdoing began to mount as Greene became involved in yet another controversy. In this case, cavalry officers began appropriating army property for their own benefit from the public sphere.[101] When Greene learned that Captain James Gunn had appropriated a new horse from the Continental Army, Greene pursued the matter with vigor. Eager to make an example of him, Greene denounced the court that had sided with Gunn and reprimanded Gunn publicly in general orders.[102] Greene sent the records of the proceeding to Congress, which upheld Greene's view that officers had no right to sell army property without orders. This backfired on Greene and many officers identified with Gunn's cause, and with rumors swirling that Greene had speculated with army funds, they became bitter and resentful.[103]

It was also thought that Greene had been awarded land and slaves by the Southern governments and had been rewarded for his work, though Greene was viewed as denying his men the same privilege.[104] When it became known that Greene had signed notes for Banks guaranteeing payment to his creditors, it further isolated Greene from his men.[105] Even after this controversy, Greene continued his relationship with Banks because he was the only supplier for his army. When Banks died in 1783, creditors began pursuing Greene to recover their losses. Greene's financial future was crippled, and it was not until years after his death that his widow Catharine was able to obtain a reimbursement from Congress.[106] After all the hardships of war—the triumphs and laurels that came with victory—it hardly seemed fair that Greene's life would take this turn and financial difficulties would plague him until his dying day.

Greene himself had become a slave, in paradoxical terms. As a slaveholder, he was now dependent on others for his independence, but the labor of others, weather, and fluctuating crop prices created more uncertainty in his life.[107] Consumed by his own debt, Greene would never attain the status of independent farmer, forever vigilant for his and his family's economic survival as well as his children's legacy. In hindsight, returning to Rhode Island and turning around the family business may have held more potential, but this is pure speculation. Greene was out of his element in Southern society. He was an outsider and everyone knew it. Desperation drove him, and what might have been his postwar legacy had he never settled those confiscated plantations we will never know. The independence movement that he fought for with such vigor, military skill, and political finesse became for him an elusive dream which he never realized. On a certain level, it was a tragedy unbefitting a man who had such great talents and the zeal and ardor of his mentor, George Washington.

The end came for Greene on June 19, 1786. After touring the rice fields of his neighbor, Mr. William Gibbons, on a scorching day, Greene took ill and lingered, apparently suffering sunstroke, but it is possible that other maladies may have been at play.[108] He passed away at only forty-four years of age.

Tributes came in from all corners of the country. The *Charleston Evening Gazette* noted that "the General was courteous, affable and accomplished; in sentiment, exceedingly liberal, ever judging with candor of those who differed in opinion with himself."[109] Alexander Hamilton eulogized Greene "as a patriot ... in the foremost rank," and noted that "we have a succession of deeds as glorious as they are unequivocal to attest his greatness and perpetuate the honors of his name."[110] Lafayette wrote to Jefferson, and was heartfelt in his feelings about the passing of Greene: "Poor Greene! His last letter was particularly affectionate to me, particularly Expressive of His Concern in the affairs of His Country."[111] Henry Knox, in a letter to Washington, wrote simply, "The death of our common & invaluable friend genl Greene, has been too melancholy and affecting a theme to write upon."[112] Washington himself noted that "the Public, as well as his family & friends, has met with severe loss. He was a great & good man indeed."[113]

William Johnson, an early biographer of Greene, described his command of the Southern Department as demonstrating "uncommon vigilance and foresight."[114] Historian William Gordon characterized Greene as a man "of a humane disposition; but resolutely severe when the same was necessary. He was of a firm and intrepid, and independent mind. He abhorred the cruelties that were practiced by the partizans of each side, and strongly inculcated a spirit of moderation."[115]

Francis Vinton Greene, a veteran, historian, and distant relative of the general, praised the campaign of 1781 led by Greene: "The eleven months' campaign—January to December, 1781, from the Catawba to the Dan and from the Dan back to Charleston and Augusta ... has always been considered one of the most brilliant in American annals."[116] J.W. Fortescue, the British historian, was equally effusive with his thoughts on Greene and his campaign: "His keen insight into the heart of Cornwallis' blunders and his skillful use of his guerilla troops are the most notable features of his work, and stamp him as a general of patience, resolution and profound common sense, qualities which go far towards making a great general."[117]

Greene had done the impossible. He began his tenure in the South with an inferior army, destitute of food and supplies, and through the worst of times, had outmaneuvered the British and forced them from the region. He was relentless in acquiring resources from the states or Congress, and never let up on his quest to rid America of the British. At first glance, his early demise seems like a cruel twist of fate, given what he poured into his command and into his country. But perhaps that was his destiny. He had come a long way since the early days of 1775. From the disaster at Fort Washington, it was thought he might never recover, but he did, and in grand style. His actions in the southern theatre of war are what determined the outcome of one of the most critical time periods in American history.

10

The Men and the Legacy
of the Southern Campaign

The factors that contributed to the British defeat in America, and particularly the south, are myriad. The southern strategy became a dismal failure because of the many aspects of the strategic plan that failed to materialize for the British. The British calculated that invading Georgia to secure British Florida's northern border, and then occupying each state north from there, would require the assistance of two specific groups that occupied the south: loyalists and Native Americans. Lord George Germain believed that burgeoning loyalist support would help with the subjugation of the south and the Cherokees and the Creeks would ally themselves with the British cause as well. The calamitous Cherokee-American War of 1776 effectively ended any hope of a Native American alliance with the British because Indian nations were no longer interested in risking their demise as a people.[1] Germain also believed that the American economy would be devastated by the British invasion and thus incapable of providing sufficient war material to counter the British.[2] But critical miscalculations of British planners of the Southern Campaign concerned their expectations about support from loyalists.

The loss of Burgoyne's army at Saratoga and the entry of France into the war forced Britain to utilize loyalists to compensate for losses on the battlefield and to alleviate mounting concerns at Whitehall about the cost of the war and the dwindling funds in the treasury.[3] Difficulty in levying new taxes and fears about home defense against the French also stoked the growing opposition to sending more regular army troops to America.[4] Assurances from the former governors of Georgia and the Carolinas that a majority of loyalists would be able to restore the royal governments of the southern colonies to their rightful authority supported the argument for increased reliance on loyalist cohorts.[5]

Although the British overestimated loyalist support, it was based on what at the time was solid evidence. Oaths of allegiance sworn by Americans at New York, Philadelphia, Savannah and Charleston convinced the British that there were cracks in the pro-independence veneer.[6] Cornwallis believed that with loyalist assistance, he would be able to not only defend South Carolina, but subdue North Carolina and support Clinton's plan to raid the Chesapeake.[7] Unfortunately, the implementation of the British strategy was delayed for eight months because the 1778 signing of the Franco-American Treaty of Alliance forced the British to postpone their Southern Campaign in order to reinforce their bases in the Floridas and counter the French in the Caribbean. So, the British began operations against St. Lucia and to reinforce the Floridas.[8]

In any case, British plans to utilize the loyalists began to unravel. One cause for this was because some loyalists' allegiances were constantly changing. Some loyalists defected, gratefully supplying rebel militias with much-needed weapons and ammunition as well as other supplies.[9] Other loyalists discredited their cause because they were bent on avenging rebel insults by engaging in a civil war that resulted in mass cruelty and violence perpetrated by both sides.[10] As time went by, loyalists and patriots moved further away from one another, no longer connected by a similar ethnicity, as increasingly distant as citizens from two different countries.[11]

As it turned out, Cornwallis found that he could place little hope in loyalists to pacify local regions and to reestablish royal government. Consequently, he did nothing of significance to create a combat-ready force from loyalists, and as a result, militia companies were more likely to be relegated to guarding the baggage train while regulars manned the network of outposts running through South Carolina and northern Georgia.[12] The British never felt that loyalist regiments were equal to the task of the traditional British soldier, and thus they were not incorporated into the regular army.

Lord Rawdon and Patrick Ferguson were perfect examples of men who did not receive the rank of their British contemporaries. Indeed, lack of promotion, poor equipment, inadequate supplies, and few opportunities to distinguish oneself in the field caused many able-bodied loyalists to desert British service or simply not to enlist as Cornwallis's auxiliaries. The fact was that in dealing with loyalists, Britain made two huge errors: they turned to them too late and ultimately could rely on them too little. Basic ignorance of colonial conditions and sheer incompetence led to these errors. Foreign intervention, political pressure, and poor intelligence led to the adoption of a strategy which had major limitations.[13]

The British strategy was to seize and maintain, but Cornwallis never achieved this goal. Groups of partisans could never be eliminated from the field. They hid in inaccessible swamps and mountains and based themselves in areas that had not been pacified by loyalist militia. More importantly, partisan groups could achieve numerical superiority against any local militia groups and cause havoc.[14] In addition, the British failed to organize civil government in their areas of occupation, and the local population became weary of confiscation and plunder of food and other military necessities. Even Cornwallis failed to heed the complaints of plundered citizenry, writing, "I cannot defend every man's house from being plundered; and I must say that when I see a whole settlement running away from twenty or thirty robbers, I think they deserve to be robbed."[15] With this statement, Cornwallis clearly revealed himself to be unable to provide order and security for the backcountry, and thus sympathy for the British cause ebbed.

In addition, the British lacked the numbers and mobility to be able to police the Carolinas with their contingent of troops, including their German mercenaries. Vast distances and often troublesome terrain and climate further complicated the British ability to take and retain territory. That inability to control territory forced the British government to struggle with the logistics necessary to provide for the most basic needs of the troops in the field, such as food, forage, animals, lumber, and coal.[16] Partisans, poor roads, great distances, and a land stripped of its bounty deprived Cornwallis's force of the necessities on which operational success depended.[17]

The failure to pacify the countryside caused Cornwallis to adopt more conventional military tactics in his pursuit of Greene and attempting to draw him into battle.[18] Greene was always reluctant to engage Cornwallis in the traditional set-piece battle. Greene knew that in such a confrontation, he would never keep his army intact. In their pursuit of Greene, Cornwallis's forces experienced attrition due to constant skirmishes and partisan hit-and-run attacks, referred to in the eighteenth century as *la petite guerre*.[19] With his exhausted army, Cornwallis could not counter the conventional threat of the main army and the unconventional threat of the partisans at the same time. With loyalists unwilling to join the army, Cornwallis and his troops remained remote and exposed.[20] The intense summer heat and humidity wreaked havoc on an army that never acclimated to the conditions. Disease played an important part in the decimation of the British fighting forces. J.R. McNeil, an environmental historian from Georgetown University, described the critical role played by mosquitoes. "Cornwallis' army was simply melting away," he wrote, with a critical role being played by "revolutionary mosquitoes."[21]

Clinton had also failed to allocate his forces properly. He was hyper-focused on New York City, where he kept 20,000 troops, and only sent one-quarter of the available British forces to Cornwallis. Given the attrition suffered by Cornwallis, he was unable to garrison British centers of control once he left for Virginia. Cornwallis completely lost the initiative to Greene once he departed for Virginia, and Greene seized upon Cornwallis's departure by picking off the British backcountry outposts. He then drove the retreating regulars back into Charleston, from which they were evacuated in December 1782.

Another reason for the failure of Cornwallis's campaign in the South was the sometimes brutal treatment of civilians. The bloody forays of Banastre Tarleton's Legion drove neutral civilians into the rebel camp for protection.[22] Often, the presence of the British army actually created a lack of harmony among civilians. Some were intimidated by it and pretended to be loyal, for which they suffered later. Others committed covert acts of violence against British troops, which assured them of patriot sympathy. Refusal to give quarter to surrendering patriot soldiers, especially at the Waxhaws, undermined British moral and political authority.[23] Many who might have remained neutral became committed patriots, and Ferguson's defeat at King's Mountain can be linked to this devastating event.

The lack of a unified command structure hindered the British ability to wage war as well. Henry Clinton believed that controlling Georgia and South Carolina were the keys to southern strategy, while Cornwallis held that Virginia was rightly the primary objective. Unfortunately for the commander-in-chief, Lord Germain sided with Cornwallis.[24] After Cornwallis defeated Greene at Guilford Court House, instead of pursuing Greene's retreating force, he headed to the coast to refit, and then decided to move into Virginia without consulting Clinton. Clinton condemned this break with his grand strategy, a departure that presaged the campaign's defeat at Yorktown.[25]

Another cause of the British defeat was Clinton's proclamation of June 3, 1780, which sowed the seeds of discontent among those prisoners of war on parole who thought they could sit out the war as neutrals. Clinton declared that all who did not declare allegiance to the king would be treated as enemies. In this way, Clinton had broken his original pledge, and thus returned to New York leaving Cornwallis with a South Carolina seething with resentment.[26] The British had also failed to understand the geographical as well as political factions that existed within South Carolina itself. The merchants along the coast tended to have revolutionary tendencies, for their profits on the trade of goods was subject to British taxes and trade restrictions. Plantation owners who had profited from selling cash crops to Britain tended to be loyalists in the low country. The backcountry mostly supported the revolution, as it was mostly populated by settlers interested in expanding westward against British policy.

Clinton's original scheme for subduing Georgia and South Carolina greatly miscarried. Instead of conquering those states and then organizing royal governments in them, British armies that defeated the rebels moved on, leaving behind minimally manned outposts. As a consequence of this strategy, local loyalists were not adequately protected from partisan harassment.[27] In this way, loyalty to the Crown became virtually life-threatening. Clinton had failed to develop a military policy to rally the loyalists, and remained too far away in New York to give efficient and effective commands to the army in the field.

As for Nathanael Greene, the Southern Campaign was a defining moment. It showed that Greene was not only a successful military commander in the field, but also an effective manager in many other aspects of the war that would prove to be as important as the military victory itself. There is little question that Greene's experience in the northern theatre in the early part of the war was a precondition to his success in the South. His direct experience as quartermaster in this area was essential. Greene demonstrated organization, an understanding of logistics and supply honed from managing the approximately one hundred workers at the forge at the Greene homestead back in Coventry, Rhode Island. He had a keen knowledge of effectively supplying the army, which he derived from his experience in the war that dated back to 1775.

Greene's actions upon taking command of the Southern Department were in stark contrast to his predecessor, Horatio Gates. Greene moved quickly and confidently to ascertain his own situation and to determine how to move against Cornwallis. Within weeks of taking command, Greene inspired confidence among his subordinates, grasping the complexities of the political and military situation in the Carolinas.[28] Greene's focus on keeping his army fed and preventing his opponents from doing the same was one of the keys to victory. Greene was able to acquire every boat in central North Carolina in order to secure his withdrawal to the Dan River and prevent Cornwallis from catching him.[29] Like his mentor, George Washington, Greene was skilled at managing a diverse and sometimes quarrelsome cast with a steady political hand. His handling of inflated egos and those of grandiose ambitions was masterful. His constant contact with Washington and the Congress kept them fully informed, and on the battlefield, Greene was able to keep the American army fed, clothed, supplied, and paid, albeit not always to Greene's standards of decency.[30]

Greene's handling of the militia in the south was deft and required a great deal of political skill and finesse. His overall view of the militia was negative, and numerous letters written by Greene support that premise. However, Greene knew that the Continental Army was not large enough to fight the British solely on its own merit, but required militia units not only to join in battles, but to engage in irregular warfare, protecting lines of supply and communication, denying the enemy the ability to forage in the countryside, and gaining intelligence about enemy movements.[31]

Unfortunately for Greene, controlling the militia was a far different task from controlling Continental troops. Greene knew he could not dictate to militia leaders, so instead he phrased his orders in the form of collegial requests, and not direct orders.[32] Sumter's inability to cooperate with Greene's objectives created tension between the two that led to a more difficult relationship, but Marion was an excellent example of someone who worked well with Greene. Marion recognized the symbiosis that existed between the Continental army and the militia and was willing to subordinate himself to Greene, although he sometimes could become irritated when he had conceived of other ideas on how to handle a particular situation.[33]

Greene's initial letter to Marion upon taking command demonstrates the tenuous hold he had over the militia and how political acumen would go a long way in encouraging support. "I like your plan of frequently shifting your Ground," Greene wrote in a complimentary fashion. "It frequently prevents a Surprise and perhaps a total Loss of your Party. Untill a more permanent Army can be collected than is in the Field at present we must endeavor to keep up a Partizan War and preserve the Tide of Sentiment among the People as much as possible in our Favour."[34] Unlike Gates, Greene made the partisan bands an integral part of his vision and knew that irregular warfare would be a more effective weapon against the formal tactics of the British.[35]

One of Greene's most salient strengths was his ability to steer a course of moderation and restraint in dealing with a number of issues, such as how the impact of the barbarities committed by both sides would threaten future peace and the ability to establish order in the southern states. After the execution of Isaac Hayne, fellow militia leaders seethed with a desire for seeking vengeance, but Greene was able to demonstrate restraint and thereby avoid retaliation, which helped him cement popular support for the Whig cause in the South.[36] The establishment of law and order was essential to Greene. He was able to gain the support of the local populace for troops as well as access to supplies only if they stood to benefit from Whig rule. His troops, particularly the Continentals, therefore had to conduct themselves on a higher moral footing than the enemy by refraining from plundering the locals and mistreating the prisoners.[37]

Greene's policy toward loyalists was not as punitive as that of political leaders in the South. For example, Greene favored a policy that provided pardons for Tories who bore arms against their Whig neighbors with the stipulation that they had served in a military capacity and not as roving bandits with no recognized affiliation.[38] While Greene was promoting reconciliation, he certainly did not advocate for total pardons. With recruiting efforts falling short in 1782 especially, Greene needed men to fill the ranks, so loyalist militiamen who had left British ranks were welcome to serve with the patriots and take oaths of allegiance.[39] Greene knew that a smoother transition to peace would be possible if some degree of clemency was part of the equation.

Unfortunately, Greene's council on clemency was not universally accepted by all political leaders in the South. Greene had heard that the North Carolina legislature did not intend to deal kindly with loyalists, and the terrible state of loyalists in Charleston, he feared, would be exacerbated by the departure of the redcoats at the end of the war. "Many in Charlestown beg for mercy but cannot obtain it," Greene wrote to George Weedon.[40] South Carolina and Georgia were showing some degree of leniency to loyalists, but overall, events elsewhere indicated that Greene's advice was not widely followed. Other states passed punitive legislation against Tories, confiscated property, and equally disturbing, did not allow many Tories to return to their homes after the war.[41] Although Greene never relented in his quest for the humanity of all and a peaceful return to effective state government, he never quite achieved this goal.

One of Greene's most important commitments was for the military to transfer power to a legitimate civilian government and then subordinate itself to that government. Loyalists often complained that the British had never constructed a civilian government, and furthermore, they never integrated other important groups, such as Native Americans and African-Americans, into their strategy for conquering the South.[42] But Greene, for the latter part of 1781, had been seeking the reestablishment of civil government in South Carolina and Georgia while keeping the British restricted to the smallest area possible because of *uti possidetis*. Indeed, Greene prompted Governor John Rutledge of South Carolina to hold elections for a new legislature while Georgia did the same.[43]

Although relations during the war with civilian officials were very tense at times, Greene had finally begun rebuilding relations and returning these states to their former conditions. Congress recognized Greene for "the measures he has pursued for the general security of the southern states, and for dispossessing the enemy of the several posts occupied by them," noting that these efforts "afford such proofs of his judgement, vigilance, and firmness."[44] But Greene's influence began to ebb late in the war over the constant problem of supplying his troops in the field as well as his stance on raising African-American regiments. This proposition had always remained unpopular among many whites.

Greene was a leader who responded well to the needs of his subordinates during the war. This was because of his leadership style, giving leeway to his subordinates so they could exercise initiative. For instance, when Daniel Morgan was granted an independent command prior to Cowpens, Greene gave him the latitude to take on Tarleton and defeat him, but of course, not without explicit instructions multiple times.[45] He entrusted great confidence in Otho Williams, especially in those final stages of the Race to the Dan, and in his most trusted subordinate, Henry Lee, whose ego he had to assuage on occasion. Lee would not be shielded from criticism from Greene when the situation demanded it, but Greene saw Lee as an essential cog in the Southern Campaign and ranked him near the top as one of his "heroes of the South."[46]

Conversely, after the Battle of Hobkirk's Hill, Greene's scapegoating of Col. John Gunby reveals one of the worst episodes of his relationship with subordinates. Greene was unyielding in his ill treatment of Gunby with his correspondence. It revealed a serious flaw in his personality, considering that Greene himself had experienced scathing criticism of his defense of Fort Washington in the New York campaign. Fortunately, Washington had been a more loyal and understanding superior. Even though Washington had taken responsibility for the disaster at Fort Washington, Greene failed to model his behavior accordingly with Gunby, instead trying to protect himself and ruining the career and reputation of a subordinate who subsequently failed to recover that reputation during his lifetime.[47] Mostly, Greene had solid relationships with his subordinates throughout the Southern Campaign. His letters are filled with praise for those directly under him and those who were not. With the exception of his treatment of Gunby, positive relations were instrumental in the American victory in the south.[48]

Paradoxically, as a military commander, Greene lost all of his battles, but during his tenure as southern commander, the British had been forced out of the interior of the Carolinas into the logistical protections afforded them on the coast, particularly Charleston and Savannah. One of Greene's greatest skills was the ability to adapt to changing situations, improvising against his far superior British opponents.[49] One of the most important aspects to Greene's generalship was his ability to withdraw his army so as to keep it intact while inflicting casualties on the enemy. Greene summed up his campaigns by his famous line: "We fight get beat rise and fight again."[50]

He also mastered the skill of deploying his cavalry on the open terrain of the Carolinas so as to avoid unnecessary combat. Unlike Gates, Greene understood the open terrain of the southern battlefields and the superior value that cavalry brought. He wrote to Washington: "To the northward, cavalry is nothing ... but to the Southward a disorder by a superior cavalry may be improved into a deficit, and a defeat into a rout. The cavalry [are] the security of the army and the safety of a country."[51]

Greene also made several wise command decisions in the course of his command. To begin with, as a former quartermaster, Greene recognized the importance of supply and made consequential decisions about the location of magazines by studying the topography and supply possibilities in the Carolinas.[52] Next, he managed the Continental troops as well as militias in battle and as forces operating independently.[53] In addition, he was able to split his army in the face of a numerically superior enemy, a violation of military doctrine, with Daniel Morgan at Cowpens, and then seize the initiative to put the British on the defensive. Likewise, his masterful retreat to the Dan River dragged Cornwallis and his depleted army further away from its base of support. Lastly, his foresight enabled all the available boats to be brought to the opposite side of the river, depriving Cornwallis of his capacity to destroy Greene's army for good. Because of his skilled leadership, Greene lost no men to desertion and was able to regroup and face Cornwallis at Guilford Courthouse, the final contest that drove Cornwallis to the coast to refit.

As a tactician, Greene made some mistakes along the way, and he also experienced some bad luck. At Guilford Courthouse, Greene made a tactical error by placing the raw Second Maryland Regiment on the flank instead of the experienced and battle-tested First Maryland Regiment, and while trying to rally his men he lost touch with his cavalry units.[54] Though not of Greene's doing, Lee had withdrawn from his initial position at an angle that left Greene's flank exposed. At Hobkirk's Hill the following month, Greene performed very well, but the incident with Colonel Gunby, and William Washington's disregard for Greene's order to protect the American flank during a counterattack, helped contribute to another American loss. At Ninety Six, Greene began siege operations, but when British reinforcements were closing in, he determined on a risky frontal attack that failed, forcing him to withdraw. Eventually, Cruger's isolated position in the backcountry would be abandoned, giving Greene what he wanted.

The final major battle of the Revolution at Eutaw Springs featured Greene with a solid performance, skillfully managing the battle, but again Lee and Washington were found to be acting in disregard of his orders and failed to deliver on the battlefield. Greene had not reined in his cavalry commanders, which angered other subordinates, but here the fault lies with Greene for not admonishing them for their lackluster performance.

But no matter what, Greene forced his opponents to play mostly by his rules. Greene's army kept the British off-balance by moving quickly, applying pressure at just the right times, and using a variety of methods to wear his opponent down. Greene masterfully used partisans and regulars in fixed battles, sieges, and hit-and-run raids while refraining from taking huge risks that could have resulted in the demise of his army.[55] Greene was extremely organized, disciplined, and relentless in his pursuit of revolutionary ideals, and he recognized that the war was not about conquering territory, but rather winning the hearts and minds of the people. Washington may have been the indispensable man of the American Revolution, but Greene was the indispensable man of the Southern Campaign. Washington's victory at Yorktown had everything to do with Nathanael Greene.

October 17, 1781, marked an anniversary which the British would have preferred to forget. Only four years earlier, Gentlemen Johnny Burgoyne had surrendered his army at Saratoga to an American army led by Horatio Gates and Benedict Arnold. The vanquished British army was afforded the full ceremonial honors of war. The soldiers marched past the victors with their colors flying and their bands playing. As a show of respect for his opponent, Gates did not take the sword that Burgoyne offered him. However, the subsequent four years of savage warfare had altered the landscape—and both the antagonists and their conventions of conduct—to an almost unrecognizable degree. Officers trained in traditional European methods of warfare fell victim to the American style of war. Burgoyne left America, never to return. Gates had been disgraced at Camden by Cornwallis, and consequently never held command again. Arnold now wore a British uniform, allied to the Earl Cornwallis, who found himself surrounded at Yorktown, writing to General Washington to discuss articles of capitulation.

How Cornwallis got to this point in time and circumstance is multi-layered. He was an aggressive and decisive leader, and he always wanted to deliver the crowning blow. From his letters, it was apparent that Cornwallis was looking for that climactic battle that would terminate the conflict in the South.[56] But Cornwallis's personality traits affected his judgment and his actions. Cornwallis had a tendency to be arrogant, and at times sulky, and he ignored certain events and strategic aims. The southern strategy called for specific steps to be taken to secure the ground won in the Carolinas, but Cornwallis took no steps to control the backcountry.[57] He ignored the fact that sitting down at the coast put him at risk for an inescapable trap and never believed that the French and the Americans could ever coordinate land and sea operations to bring the war to a close. For such an aggressive commander, it is quite astounding that he was ensnared at Yorktown.

Cornwallis blamed his failures on orders that were inflexible and that denied him the latitude to accomplish his goals as the situation demanded. Thus, he largely ignored the chain of command and communicated directly with Lord George Germain instead of Clinton during the campaign. As he began to reassess the situation in the Carolinas, he saw the lack of support from loyalists and became certain that the only way to end resistance in South Carolina was to destroy the supply of men and material coming from the north.[58] He set out to do that by invading North Carolina and the following year, Virginia. Interestingly, he never indicated any concern over how a larger enemy fleet might affect his situation on the ground.[59]

However, like many great commanders, Cornwallis kept his public persona on a completely professional level. Never one to criticize subordinates in public, he was hesitant to discipline them in private, preferring to spur them to greater heights than to find fault for failures they had experienced in command.[60] But many times, events would leave his control, such as the depredations committed on civilians by British soldiers. He knew as an experienced commander that this would hamper his efforts to gain popular support, but with the size of the southern theatre, the physical geography and the vast distances between British points of control, Cornwallis was unable to exert discipline over his subordinates in order to put a halt to atrocities. Nonetheless, the responsibility for these events falls squarely with the commander.

After Cornwallis burned his wagons at Ramsour's Mills, his men were without some of the extra comforts that helped smooth a rugged journey overland. But his men had faith in him, and Cornwallis demonstrated that he too would share the hardships of the common soldier. British Sergeant Roger Lamb recorded that during the Guilford Courthouse campaign, Cornwallis "would admit of no distinction."[61] When food became in short supply and men were compelled to eat turnips and ground Indian corn, "in all this his lordship participated, nor did he indulge himself even in the distinction of a tent; but in all things partook our sufferings, and seemed much more to feel for us than himself."[62]

The Race for the Dan River was a decisive series of events that severely impacted Cornwallis's ability to wage war. His desperation to catch Greene and force him to battle had a number of ramifications. First, burning his wagons in order to pursue Greene across a barren landscape was reckless and foolhardy. After most of his light troops were lost at Cowpens, Cornwallis lost the ability to acquire intelligence about Greene's movements and to navigate the local geography.[63] By the time he reached the Dan, and Greene had successfully escaped, loyalist support had vanished as fast as the rebel army. Cornwallis's lack of judgment cost him dearly, as well as his lack of communication with Clinton, for both men should have been aware that they would not be receiving the naval support of the British. Nor did they calculate the size and strength of the French fleet until it was far too late.[64] Even as Cornwallis committed some serious blunders, he persisted in his intense drive to erase Greene and his army from the Carolinas, driving him from the field in their last encounter while outmanned. Cornwallis, throughout the campaign, kept his loyal base among the soldiery by his constant physical courage even when the odds were stacked against him. Cornwallis was to be found on the battlefield where the action was, directing his men under fire. Courage was never lacking in the Earl.

At Yorktown, Cornwallis requested the same terms under which Burgoyne had surrendered his army, namely that the British and German officers be allowed passage back to their home countries, but the events which had unfolded since Cornwallis arrived in the South made that impossible. Washington made that known in a swift reply: "The condition annexed of sending the British and German troops to the parts of Europe to which they respectively belong is inadmissible. Instead of this, they will be marched to such parts of the country as can conveniently provide their subsistence…. The same honors will be granted to the surrendering army as were granted to the garrison of Charlestown."[65] Unable to hold out much longer, Cornwallis accepted Washington's terms and surrendered his army on October 19.

Claiming illness, Cornwallis himself did not attend the ceremony. It is possible that this was true, as Cornwallis had been sidelined by a long illness early in the North Carolina campaign, and disease had ravaged the British encampment at Yorktown. Indeed, of the 5,950 rank and file present at the surrender, over 1,900 were listed under "sick and wounded."[66] In Cornwallis's place stood Charles O'Hara, of whom he often spoke so highly. Washington refused to accept Cornwallis's sword from O'Hara, instead allowing Benjamin Lincoln, who commanded the Charleston garrison and had also been present at Saratoga, to accept it.

Whether or not Cornwallis was ill, he still had to perform the unenviable task of informing his superiors of his surrender. On October 20, 1781, Cornwallis penned a letter to Clinton, beginning thus: "I have the mortification to inform your Excellency that I have been forced to give up the posts of York and Gloucester and to surrender the troops under my command by capitulation on the 19th instant as prisoners of war to the combined forces of America and France."[67] Cornwallis was taken into the custody of John Laurens, whose father Henry had been a former president of Congress. Henry had been imprisoned by the British in the Tower of London, after his ship was seized in 1780 while sailing to Amsterdam to negotiate for Dutch support of the American cause, of which Cornwallis was still the constable.[68]

Cornwallis did not remain in Yorktown for long, departing to New York soon after the surrender. Unable to participate in the war under the terms of his parole, Cornwallis sailed for England accompanied by Benedict Arnold. As would be expected following such a humiliating defeat for Great Britain, someone would have to be blamed. The two candidates, it seemed, were to be Cornwallis and Clinton.

Nevertheless, even in defeat, Cornwallis's positive reputation at home and abroad seemed relatively unaffected. An article from the *Public Advertiser* of January 11, 1782, described Cornwallis as someone "whose Judgement and Penetration, whose Valour and Enterprize have been acknowledged with Admiration by our own Officers." The paper noted that Cornwallis was "lamented and beloved by his Countrymen, esteemed by the common Enemy, and admired by the whole world."[69] That Cornwallis enjoyed the support of the British citizenry was evident in another article the following week, after many of the returning officers first met with the King. The *Whitehall Evening Post* reported that "so overjoyed were the people at his arrival there, that he was carried from London in to the Guildhall on men's shoulders, accompanied with an incredible number of spectators, whose acclamation upon the occasion can be better conceived than described. The occasion was also marked by the Archbishop of Canterbury, who happened to be the Earl's uncle, [and who] noted his nephew's return by a ringing of bells at his palace of Lambeth."[70]

In the face of Cornwallis's popular support, Clinton strove to pass off blame for the war to his subordinate. In early 1783, Henry Clinton published his narrative of events of the 1781 campaign, in which he attempted to exonerate himself in the public eye. Clinton was upset by the publication of Cornwallis's letter of October 20 reporting his surrender without any of Clinton's letters accompanying it. In the letter, the Earl had made sure to remind Clinton that he "never saw the post in a very favourable light" and that he would never have attempted a defense of the position had he not believed relief from Clinton was imminent.[71] Clinton, on the other hand, contradicted this assertion, affirming "that none of the misfortunes of the very unfortunate campaign of 1781 can, with the smallest degree of justice, be imputed to me."[72]

Back in May 1781, Clinton wrote Cornwallis expressing the "apprehensions I felt on reading your letter to me ... wherein you inform me of the critical situation you supposed the Carolinas to be in, and that you should probably attempt to effect a junction with Major General Phillips."[73] He scolded Cornwallis for not informing him of his intentions in a previous letter, and noted, "I should certainly have endeavored to have stopped you—as I did then ... consider such a move as likely to be dangerous to our interests in the southern colonies."[74]

Cornwallis engaged in a point-counterpoint letter exchange with Clinton, trying to cover his tracks for not engaging his superior with his intentions. Cornwallis responded to Clinton's letter a month later, arguing that "after the experiment I had made had failed, [and] until Virginia was to a degree subjected, we could not reduce North Carolina or have any hold of the backcountry of South Carolina, the want of navigation rendering it impossible to maintain a sufficient army in either of these provinces at a considerable distance from the coast, and the men and riches of Virginia furnishing ample supplies to the rebel southern army."[75] Cornwallis made a pathetic reach in explaining his actions by telling

Clinton of "General Greene's intention of coming to the northward, and that part of the reinforcements destined for his army was stopped in consequence of my arrival here."[76]

After receiving Clinton's narrative of the campaign of 1781, Cornwallis wrote to Alexander Ross, his former aide-de-camp and close friend: "I received Sir H's narrative last night, and have read it in a cursory manner. It is a bad performance, and I think-not likely to do the cause much good with people of judgement, yet I think it may be necessary to take some notice of it, as he so often arraigns my march into Virginia, as a measure undertaken without waiting for his consent."[77] Cornwallis indeed took notice of Clinton's pamphlet, publishing his own answer to Clinton's narrative. The year 1783 saw both generals engage in a public display of finger pointing. While Clinton insisted that Cornwallis had acted independently of his command, Cornwallis countered that Clinton's strategy of courting southern loyalists was doomed from the start. "Our failure in North Carolina was not occasioned by want of force to protect the rising of our friends, but by their timidity, and unwillingness to take an active and useful part."[78]

Using the pseudonym Themistocles—the name of an Athenian democratic politician—a third unknown author engaged in a savage attack on Clinton for his role in the loss of America and accused him of digging up a past that was better forgotten, namely non-aristocratic rule: "To be serious, Sir Henry ... so rotten a subject, permit me to assure you, never in the course of all my practice ... have I handled. It will smell vilely in the nostrils of the people. It was a thing long defunct, and it were, therefore, better that it had remained for ever buried in the grave of oblivion."[79]

While historian Benjamin Franklin Stevens's pamphlet is invaluable to the modern historian, Steven's commentary is heavily biased in favor of Cornwallis. Stevens was an important bibliographer of materials that were found in European archives and relating to the American Revolution. He dismissed Clinton's argument with nearly the same dramatic and hyperbolic tone Themistocles had used in his pamphlet. More modern examinations suggest that blame should be shared by both generals.

The correspondence of Lord George Germain reveals that same sentiment. Germain felt that "if Earl Cornwallis had possessed the phlegm of Sir Henry Clinton, he would have remained in possession of South Carolina and Georgia, but ambitious for new laurels he has blighted those already won. On the other hand, if Sir Henry had the zeal and activity of Cornwallis, he would have marched with all his forces to join the latter while there was yet time, as Cornwallis advised, and with 20,000 good troops they would have overthrown all who opposed them."[80] Both generals, after all, had fallen victim to the difficult, sometimes impassable geography of the Carolina backcountry. Such terrain had actively impeded communication, not only between Clinton and Cornwallis, but also between the Earl and his troops in the field. In the same way, it was difficult to relay intelligence and supplies to armies in the field. There was often no way of knowing how long it would take for a letter to reach its intended recipient, if it reached him at all.

Cornwallis had indeed abandoned the Carolinas without authority from Clinton, but had done so after a catastrophic winter campaign that had devastated his army. This move directly opposed what Clinton was trying to accomplish in the South. Clinton, however, was overly concerned about the safety of New York, and he failed to reinforce Cornwallis once he was stationed at Yorktown. Cornwallis had been uneasy about the strategic position of Yorktown, and he had argued that he had been "induced to remain in them by the prospect of relief."[81] Indeed, Clinton had been preparing a relief effort, but it did not sail until the very same day Cornwallis surrendered. The arrival of the French fleet at the mouth of the York River had rendered that a moot point. Even Cornwallis realized this, writing on October 15 to Clinton that "the safety of this place is therefore so precarious that I cannot recommend that the fleet and the army should run great risque in endeavoring to save us."[82] In view of Clinton's lack of promptness in dispatching reinforcement to Yorktown, and Cornwallis's precipitous and reckless decision to invade Virginia in the first place, neither general was blameless.

Despite the controversies of the postwar period, Cornwallis was able to maintain many other influential political connections, most importantly King George III. After Cornwallis requested to resign from his position at the Tower of London, believing it to conflict with the terms of his parole, the King asked him to stay, and in doing so displayed his confidence in the Earl: "My lord, The whole tenor of your conduct has so manifestly shown, that Attachment to My Person, to Your Country, and to the Military Profession, are the motives of Your Actions, that I am certain no fresh proof is necessary to the World for justice to be done You on that head."[83] This unwavering monarchical support doubtless helped Cornwallis to emerge the better from the controversy with Clinton.

Cornwallis enjoyed a long and successful career following the Treaty of Paris. In 1786, he was knighted by George III. He also returned to military service, being appointed governor-general and commander in chief of the army in India. He soon wrote to Alexander Ross for assistance. "The proposal of going to India has been pressed upon me so strongly ... and with grief of heart, I have been obliged to say yes, and to exchange a life of ease and content, to encounter all the plagues and miseries of command and public station."[84] Cornwallis had first been suggested for the governor-generalship in 1782, but had passed on this opportunity until the appointment gave him command over the British army in India.[85]

Upon his arrival on the subcontinent, Cornwallis was met with a nearly incomprehensible bureaucracy of political and military offices that needed to be sorted out. The situation in India was vastly different from anything Cornwallis had been accustomed to, with officers and soldiers owing their loyalty to the [East India] Company instead of the Crown. Both the army and the local administrative offices needed attention.

At the core of the army in India were units of European infantry, which Cornwallis viewed with disgust. Not only did they lack discipline, the Earl believed that they actually hindered progress in India by discrediting the colonizers. "Nothing can be more prejudicial to our interests and safety, than to degrade the character of Europeans, in a country where a handful of them are to hold millions in subjection. The contemptible trash of which the Company's European force is composed, makes me shudder."[86]

The next several years saw Cornwallis attempt to enact widespread reforms to improve the Company's and the army's hold over the colony. His reforms were put to the test in the Third Mysore War (1790–1792). Going as far as to include elephants to haul supplies, an exotic innovation, Cornwallis decisively defeated the army of Tipu Sultan and solidified the British hold on the region. He returned to England a hero.[87]

Not destined to rest for long, Cornwallis returned to England to learn of a rebellion brewing in Ireland. Having proved his mettle as a problem solver in India, Cornwallis became Lord Lieutenant of Ireland, where again he was charged with overseeing both the military and civil administration. Although proving to be an effective leader again, Cornwallis was unhappy in his new position. Writing to Ross, now a major general, he lamented his situation. "The life of a Lord-Lieutenant of Ireland comes up to my idea of perfect misery, but if I can accomplish the great object of consolidating the British Empire, I shall be sufficiently repaid."[88]

Cornwallis's disdain may have had to do with the similarity of the Irish rebellion to his time in the Carolinas. "Although there is no enemy here to oppose a large body of our troops in the field, we are still engaged in a war of plunder and massacre, but I am in great hopes that partly by force, and partly by conciliation, we shall bring it to a speedy termination."[89] The speedy termination Cornwallis was hoping for was impeded by the landing of a small force from France in Ireland. Again leading troops in the field, he crushed the invading army from France and helped to bring about the Act of Union in 1800. Cornwallis solidified himself as a diplomat on the international stage when he served as the British signatory to the Treaty of Amiens, which temporarily brought a halt to the French Revolutionary Wars.

Following this success, Cornwallis was once again appointed governor-general in India, but he died shortly after arriving in 1805. He was buried in India. Following his death, several statues were erected in his honor both in England and India. A mausoleum in the Roman style in Ghazipur bears the inscription, "This monument, raised by the British inhabitants of Calcutta, attests their sense of those virtues, which will live in the remembrance of grateful millions, long after it shall have mouldered in the dust."[90] Although never able to move past his surrender at Yorktown in the minds of most Americans, Charles Cornwallis enjoyed a longer and more fruitful career than most of those responsible for the British defeat in America, and went on to become one of the most successful and respected defenders of the Empire.

In the years after the close of the war, the South finally began its recovery from the terrible state of war that had existed there for so long. It experienced the beginnings of economic prosperity and population growth, and by 1788, the majority of southern states moved their capitals to the interior, better able to address the concerns of more of their citizens.[91] Former loyalists eventually became part of the fabric of society, and the back-country was not only growing more populous, but also developing an important crop. The Constitution was ratified quickly by Georgia and South Carolina, followed by Virginia and North Carolina, with slavery now protected and the Bill of Rights in place.[92] The stage was set for a new conflict that would emerge in the nineteenth century.

In the end, Greene and Cornwallis had changed the face of the war in the backcountry of the Carolinas and the fate of their respective countries. The difficulties they faced and the fortitude in which they fought the campaign challenged them in the extreme. However, despite Cornwallis's previous service on the battlefields of Europe during the Seven Years' War and his being the more experienced commander, he did not fare as well as the relatively inexperienced Greene. Greene effectively used the geography of the area to his advantage. The Carolinas were too vast, the settlements greatly dispersed and separated by terrain too difficult to be subdued by the single army led by Cornwallis. As seen by his later career, the Earl was a gifted commander when given a large force and the objective to destroy a singular opposing army. However, such a strategy was doomed in the southern theatre. His ostensible victories in such battles as the fight at Guilford Courthouse actually resulted in casualties that made success of the Southern Campaign less and less likely. In the end, Cornwallis's disastrous loss of light troops, particularly at Cowpens, removed any hope for subjugating the Carolinas.

Much can be said about being the underdog, and Greene played that role to perfection. His life story that began with a simple Quaker from Rhode Island who ended up playing a major role in the defeat of the greatest military power on earth at the time is mind-boggling. It is more remarkable that most of his experience came as Washington's principal lieutenant in the northern theatre and not in an independent command.

A postwar portrait at the Greene homestead in Coventry, Rhode Island, depicts a worn and haggard commander. Although he was in his forties when he sat for the portrait, Greene appears to be much older. Greene had given every ounce of his being for the cause. Thus, his exploits in the South can no longer remain part of the "unknown Revolution" that much of the Southern Campaign has become in the public eye. His meteoric rise in his short lifetime deserves the same recognition as all those other great American heroes in the struggle for independence.

Chapter Notes

Introduction

1. John C. Dann, ed., *The Revolution Remembered: Eyewitness Accounts of the War for Independence* (Chicago: University of Chicago Press, 1980), 50.
2. *Ibid.*, 98.
3. *Ibid.*, 195.
4. John Robert Shaw, quoted in Don Hagist, *British Soldiers, American War: Voices of the American Revolution* (Yardley, PA: Westholme, 2012), 29.
5. Banastre Tarleton, *A History of the Campaigns of 1780 and 1781 in the Southern Provinces of North America* (Dublin: Colles, Exshaw, et al., 1787), 4.
6. William Moultrie to Benjamin Lincoln, 17 November 1779, in William Moultrie, *Memoirs of the American Revolution, So Far as It Related to the States of North Carolina and South Carolina, and Georgia* (New York: David Longworth, 1802), 2:43.
7. Moultrie to Lincoln, 22 February 1780, *ibid.*, 2:47.

Chapter 1

1. Richard J. Hooker, ed. *The Carolina Backcountry on the Eve of the Revolution: The Journal of Charles Woodmason, Anglican Itinerant* (Chapel Hill: University of North Carolina Press, 1953), xxi.
2. Robert L. Meriwether, *The Expansion of South Carolina, 1729–1765* (Kingsport: Southern Publishers, 1940), 114.
3. Hooker, *Woodmason*, xxi.
4. Robert Weir, *Colonial South Carolina* (New York: KTO Press, 1983), 39.
5. Walter Edgar, *South Carolina: A History* (Columbia: University of South Carolina Press, 1998), 4.
6. *Ibid.*, 8.
7. Christopher Ward, *The War of the Revolution*, ed. John Richard Alden, vol. 2 (New York: Macmillan, 1952), 656.
8. Richard Tyler, "The South Carolina Middle Country, 1754–1763," *The Picket Post*, no. 87 (1965): 37.
9. Walter Edgar, *Partisans and Redcoats: The Southern Conflict That Turned the Tide of the American Revolution* (New York: William Morrow, 2001), 2.
10. *Ibid.*, 39.
11. Rachel N. Klein, "Ordering the Backcountry: The South Carolina Regulation," *The William and Mary Quarterly* 38, no. 4 (1981): 666.
12. *Ibid.*, 41.
13. Rachel N. Klein, *Unification of a Slave State: The Rise of the Planter Class in the South Carolina Backcountry, 1760–1808* (Chapel Hill: University of North Carolina Press, 1990), 9.
14. Meriwether, *South Carolina*, 48.
15. *Ibid.*, 49.
16. *Ibid.*, 106.
17. *Ibid.*, 83.
18. Tyler, *Middle Country*, 41.
19. Meriwether, *South Carolina*, 114.
20. *Ibid.*, 115.
21. William S. Powell, *North Carolina Through Four Centuries* (Chapel Hill: University of North Carolina Press, 1989), 1.
22. Marjoleine Kars, *Breaking Loose Together: The Regulator Rebellion in Pre-Revolutionary North Carolina* (Chapel Hill: University of North Carolina Press, 2002), 18.
23. *Ibid.*, 20.
24. *Ibid.*, 21.
25. Roger A. Ekirch. "'A New Government of Liberty': Hermon Husband's Vision of Backcountry North Carolina, 1755," *The William and Mary Quarterly* 34, no. 4 (1977): 638.
26. Powell, *North Carolina*, 4.
27. *Ibid.*, 132.
28. Kars, *Breaking Loose*, 22.
29. Jerome Nadelhaft, *The Disorders of War: The Revolution in South Carolina* (Orono: University of Maine at Orono Press, 1981), 14.
30. *Ibid.*, 14.
31. *Ibid.*, 14.
32. Edward McCrady, *The History of South Carolina Under the Royal Government 1719–1776* (New York: MacMillan, 1897), 121.
33. *Ibid.*, 122.
34. Gregory H. Nobles, "Breaking into the Backcountry: New Approaches to the Early American Frontier, 1750–1800," *The William and Mary Quarterly* 46, no. 4 (1989): 650.
35. Edgar, *Partisans and Redcoats*, 2.
36. *Ibid.*, 3.
37. *Ibid.*, 12.
38. Nadelhaft, *Disorders of War*, 14.
39. *Ibid.*, 13.
40. Nobles, "Breaking into the Backcountry," 652–653.
41. McCrady, *South Carolina*, 313.
42. *Ibid.*, 318.
43. *Ibid.*, 624.
44. T.W. Moody, "The Ulster Scots in Colonial and Revolutionary America," *Studies: An Irish Quarterly Review* 34, no. 133 (1945): 89.
45. William K. Boyd, ed., *Some Eighteenth-Century Tracts Concerning North Carolina*

(Raleigh: Edwards & Broughton, 1927), 420–421.

46. *Ibid.*, 420–421.
47. *Ibid.*, 421.
48. Moody, "Ulster Scots," 90.
49. E.R.R. Green, "The Scotch-Irish and the Coming of the Revolution in North Carolina," *Irish Historical Studies* 7, no. 26 (1950): 79.
50. Moody, "Ulster Scots," 91.
51. Green, "Scotch-Irish," 77.
52. Edgar, *South Carolina*, 56.
53. Edgar, *Partisans and Redcoats*, 3.
54. *Ibid.*, 5
55. *Ibid.*, 9.
56. Jenna Weissman Joselit, *Immigration and American Religion* (New York: Oxford University Press, 2001), 31.
57. *Ibid.*, 32.
58. Adelaide L. Fries, ed., *Records of the Moravians in North Carolina* (Raleigh: Edwards & Broughton, 1926), 3:1206.
59. *Ibid.*, 1206.
60. Joselit, *Immigration*, 34.
61. Ruth Blackwelder, "The Attitude of the North Carolina Moravians Toward the American Revolution," *The North Carolina Historical Review* 9, no. 1 (1932): 12.
62. Fries, *Records of the Moravians*, 3:1044.
63. *Ibid.*, 14.
64. *Ibid.*, 16.
65. Blackwelder, "North Carolina Moravians," 20.
66. *Ibid.*, 20–21.
67. Rufus M. Jones, *The Quakers in the American Colonies* (London: Macmillan, 1911), 295.
68. *Ibid.*, 338.
69. *Ibid.*, 352–353.
70. Roger E. Sappington, "North Carolina and the Non-Resistant Sects During the American Revolution," *Quaker History* 60, no. 1 (1971): 33.
71. *Ibid.*, 33.
72. *Ibid.*, 38.
73. Francis Charles Anscombe, *I Have Called You Friends: The Story of Quakerism in North Carolina* (Boston: The Christopher Publishing House, 1959), 154.
74. *Ibid.*, 154.
75. *Ibid.*, 107.
76. Dorothy Gilbert Thorne, "North Carolina Friends and the Revolution," *The North Car-*

olina *Historical Review* 38, no. 3 (1961): 337–338.
77. W.H. Snowden, "General Greene and the Friends at Guilford," *The American Friend* 2 (March 28, 1895): 307.
78. *Ibid.*, 307.
79. Hooker, *Woodmason*, xi–xii.
80. *Ibid.*, xxi.
81. *Ibid.*, xxvii–xxviii.
82. Edgar, *Partisans and Redcoats*, 10.
83. *Ibid.*, 6.
84. *Ibid.*,39.
85. *Ibid.*, 11.
86. *Ibid.*, 13.
87. *Ibid.*, 87.
88. Tyler, "Middle Country," 36.
89. Hooker, *Woodmason*, 32–33.
90. Frederick Jackson Turner, *The Frontier in American History* (Tucson: University of Arizona Press, 1997), 107.
91. Jack P. Greene, "Independence, Improvement and Authority: Toward a Framework for Understanding the Histories of the Southern Backcountry during the Era of the American Revolution," in Ronald Hoffman, Thad Tate, and Peter Albert, eds., *An Uncivil War: The Southern Backcountry during the American Revolution* (Charlottesville: University of Virginia Press, 1985), 17.
92. *Ibid.*, 18.
93. *Ibid.*, 31.
94. T.W. Moody, "The Ulster Scots in Colonial and Revolutionary America: Part II," *Studies: An Irish Quarterly Review* 34, No. 134 (1945): 211.
95. Klein, *Unification of a Slave State*, 36.
96. Moody, "Ulster Scots, Part II," 212–213.
97. Ronald Hoffman, "The 'Disaffected' in the Revolutionary South," in Alfred F. Young, ed., *The American Revolution: Explorations in the History of American Radicalism* (Dekalb: Northern Illinois University Press, 1976), 290–291.
98. *Ibid.*, 291.
99. Kaylene Hughes, "Populating the Backcountry: The Demographic and Social Characteristics of the Colonial South Carolina Frontier, 1730–1760" (Ph.D. diss., Florida State University, 1985), 153.

100. *Boston Chronicle,* December 5–12, 1768, in H. Roy Merrens, ed., *The Colonial South Carolina Scene: Contemporary Views, 1697–1774* (Columbia: University of South Carolina Press, 1977), 247.
101. Klein, *Unification of a Slave State*, 37–38.
102. George Lloyd Johnson, *The Frontier in the Colonial South: South Carolina Backcountry, 1736–1800* (Westport: Greenwood Press, 1997), 114–115.
103. *Ibid.*, 115.
104. *Ibid.*, 115.
105. Edgar, *South Carolina*, 211–212.
106. Klein, *Unification of a Slave State*, 47.
107. Alexander Gregg, *History of the Old Cheraws* (New York: Richardson, 1867), 134.
108. *Ibid.*, 134–135.
109. *South Carolina and American Gazette*, August 7, 1767, no. 456.
110. Hooker, *Woodmason*, 214.
111. Edgar, *South Carolina*, 214.
112. *Ibid.*, 224.
113. Richard Maxwell Brown, *The South Carolina Regulators* (Cambridge: The Belknap Press of Harvard University, 1963), 190.
114. Hooker, *Woodmason*, 226.
115. *Ibid.*, 220.
116. *Ibid.*
117. Gregg, *Old Cheraws*, 133.
118. Johnson, *Colonial South*, 117.
119. Klein, *Unification of a Slave State*, 52.
120. Johnson, *Colonial South*, 120.
121. Klein, *Unification of a Slave State*, 51.
122. *Ibid.*, 50–51.
123. Johnson, *Colonial South*, 127.
124. Edgar, *South Carolina*, 216.
125. Klein, *Unification of a Slave State*, 65.
126. James P. Whittenberg, "Planters, Merchants, and Lawyers: Social Change and the Origins of the North Carolina Regulation," *The William and Mary Quarterly* 34, No. 2 (1977): 220.
127. Roger A. Ekirch, *"Poor Carolina": Politics and Society in Colonial North Carolina,*

1729–1776 (Chapel Hill: University of North Carolina Press, 1981), 164.

128. *Ibid.*, 168.
129. Boyd, *Eighteenth-Century Tracts*, 255.
130. *Ibid.*, 256.
131. Ekirch, *Poor Carolina*, 187.
132. Marvin L. Michael Kay and Lorin Lee Cary, "Class, Mobility, and Conflict in North Carolina on the Eve of the Revolution," in Jeffrey J. Crow and Larry E. Tise, eds., *The Southern Experience in the American Revolution* (Chapel Hill: University of North Carolina Press, 1978), 134.
133. William S. Powell, ed., *The Regulators in North Carolina: A Documentary History, 1759–1776* (Raleigh: State Department of Archives and History, 1971), 5.
134. William Saunders, ed., *The Colonial Records of North Carolina* (Raleigh: Josephus Daniels, reprint, 1968), 8:245.
135. *Ibid.*
136. Ekirch, *Poor Carolina*, 169.
137. *Ibid.*, 172.
138. *Ibid.*, 173–174.
139. Powell, *Regulators in North Carolina*, 226.
140. *Ibid.*, 162.
141. Boyd, *Eighteenth-Century Tracts*, 271.
142. Ekirch, *Poor Carolina*, 194.
143. *Ibid.*, 245.
144. *Ibid.*, 245–246.
145. *Ibid.*, 195.
146. *Ibid.*, 197.
147. Powell, *Regulators in North Carolina*, 378.
148. *Ibid.*, 458.
149. *Ibid.*, 459.
150. *Ibid.*, 462.
151. Ekirch, *Poor Carolina*, 203.
152. Charles Francis Adams, *The Works of John Adams, Second President of the United States: With a Life of the Author, Notes, and Illustrations* (Boston: Little, Brown, and Company, 1852), 7:284.
153. *Colonial Records of North Carolina*, 8:639.
154. Powell, *North Carolina*, 159.
155. Ekirch, *Poor Carolina*, 203.
156. *Ibid.*, 205–206.

157. *Ibid.*, 207.
158. Roger Ekirch, "Whig Authority and Public Order in Backcountry North Carolina, 1776–1783," in Hoffman, et al., *Uncivil War*, 103.
159. *Ibid.*, 209.
160. Weir, *Colonial South Carolina*, 282.
161. Klein, *Unification of a Slave State*, 81.
162. Ekirch, *Poor Carolina*, 210.
163. Klein, *Unification of a Slave State*, 82.
164. Rebecca Brannon, *From Revolution to Reunion: The Reintegration of South Carolina* (Columbia: University of South Carolina Press, 2016), 16.
165. *Ibid.*
166. *Ibid.*
167. Harry M. Ward, *The War for Independence and the Transformation of American Society* (London: UCL Press, 1999), 37.
168. *Ibid.*
169. Peter N. Moore, "The Local Origins of Allegiance in Revolutionary South Carolina: The Waxhaws as a Case Study," *The South Carolina Historical Magazine* 107, No. 1 (2006): 27–28.
170. *Ibid.*, 28.
171. *Ibid.*, 29.
172. *Ibid.*, 36.
173. *Ibid.*, 37.
174. *Ibid.*
175. *Ibid.*, 40–41.
176. John S. Pancake, *This Destructive War: The British Campaign in the Carolinas, 1780–1782* (Tuscaloosa: University of Alabama Press, 1985), 89.
177. Robert Gray, "Colonel Robert Gray's Observations on the War in Carolina," *South Carolina Historical and Genealogical Magazine* 11, no. 3 (1910): 141.
178. Brannon, *Revolution to Reunion*, 16.
179. Jeffrey J. Crow, "Liberty Men and Loyalists: Disorder and Disaffection in the North Carolina Backcountry," in Hoffman, et al., *Uncivil War*, 128.
180. Rebecca Brannon, "Reconciling the Revolution: Resolving Conflict and Rebuilding Community in the Wake of Civil War in South Carolina" (Ph.D. diss., University of Michigan, 2007), 18.

181. *Ibid.*
182. Crow, "Liberty Men and Loyalists," 139.
183. Alan S. Brown, "James Simpson's Reports on the Carolina Loyalists, 1779–1780," *Journal of Southern History* 21, No. 4 (1955): 513.
184. *Ibid.*, 518.
185. *Ibid.*
186. *Ibid.*
187. Weir, *Colonial South Carolina*, 322.
188. Edgar, *South Carolina*, 229
189. Nadelhaft, *Disorders of War*, 51.
190. Brannon, *Revolution to Reunion*, 24.
191. *Ibid.*, 25.
192. Crow, "Liberty Men and Loyalists," 159.

Chapter 2

1. William T. Bulger, "The British Expedition to Charleston, 1779–1780" (Ph.D. diss., University of Michigan, 1957), 35.
2. *Ibid.*, 36.
3. K.G. Davies, ed. *Documents of the American Revolution 1770–1783* (Dublin: Irish University Press, 1976), 15:61.
4. John Shy, *A People Numerous and Armed: Reflections on The Military Struggle for American Independence* (New York: Oxford University Press, 1976), 209.
5. Davies, *Documents*, 15: 60.
6. David K. Wilson, *The Southern Strategy: Britain's Conquest of South Carolina and Georgia 1775–1780* (Columbia: University of South Carolina Press, 2005), 62.
7. Paul H. Smith, *Loyalists and Redcoats: A Study in British Revolutionary Policy* (Chapel Hill: University of North Carolina Press, 1964), 98.
8. *Ibid.*, 98–99.
9. *Ibid.*, 115.
10. Stephen Conway, "From Fellow-Nationals to Foreigners: British Perceptions of the Americans, circa 1739–1783," *The William and Mary Quarterly* 59, no. 1 (2002): 94.
11. *Ibid.*, 97.
12. Smith, *Loyalists and Redcoats*, 123.

13. William B. Willcox, *Portrait of a General: Sir Henry Clinton in the War of Independence* (New York: Alfred A. Knopf, 1962), 294.

14. *Ibid.*, 297.
15. *Ibid.*, 294.
16. *Ibid.*, 298.
17. Davies, *Documents*, 18:46.
18. *Ibid.*
19. *Ibid.*
20. *Ibid.*
21. *Ibid.*
22. Bulger, "British Expedition to Charleston," 81.
23. *Ibid.*, 82.
24. *Ibid.*, 83.
25. Willcox, *Portrait of a General*, 352.
26. Bruce E. Burgoyne, ed. and trans., *Diaries of Two Ansbach Jaegers* (Westminster: Heritage Books, 2007), 87.
27. *Ibid.*, 88.
28. *Ibid.*
29. Wilson, *Southern Strategy*, 63.
30. Conway, "Fellow-Nationals," 98.
31. Richard S. Dunn, *Sugar and Slaves: The Rise of the Planter Class in the English West Indies, 1624–1713* (Chapel Hill: University of North Carolina Press, 1972), 97.
32. *Ibid.*, 112–113.
33. *Year Book–1880, City of Charleston* (Charleston: The News and Courier Book Presses, 1880), 244.
34. *Ibid.*, 254.
35. Carl P. Borick, *A Gallant Defense: The Siege of Charleston, 1780* (Columbia: University of South Carolina Press, 2003), 18.
36. *Ibid.*, 19.
37. Bernhard A. Uhlendorf, ed. and trans., *The Siege of Charleston, With an Account of the Province of South Carolina: Diaries and Letters of Hessian Officers from the von Jungkenn Papers in the William L. Clements Library* (Ann Arbor: University of Michigan Press, 1938), 327.
38. *Ibid.*, 325.
39. *Ibid.*, 329.
40. *Year Book–1880*, 256.
41. Uhlendorf, *Siege of Charleston*, 335.
42. *Ibid.*
43. *Ibid.*, 321.
44. Borick, *A Gallant Defense*, 26.

45. Ward, *War of the Revolution*, 2:695.
46. Borick, *A Gallant Defense*, 27.
47. Ward, *War of the Revolution*, 2:696.
48. Lilla Mills Hawes, ed. *Lachlan McIntosh Papers in the University of Georgia Libraries* (Athens: University of Georgia Press, 1968), Miscellanea Publications, No. 7, 96.
49. Ward, *War of the Revolution*, 2:697.
50. Pancake, *Destructive War*, 63.
51. Bulger, "British Expedition to Charleston," 70.
52. Borick, *A Gallant Defense*, 36; Ward, *War of the Revolution*, 2:697.
53. Bulger, "British Expedition to Charleston," 89.
54. Borick, *A Gallant Defense*, 41.
55. Ward, *War of the Revolution*, 2:697.
56. *Ibid.*
57. Borick, *A Gallant Defense*, 71.
58. General Benjamin Lincoln. Letter to Commodore Abraham Whipple, January 30, 1780, Abraham Whipple Collection. MSS 802, Box 1, Folder 1, Rhode Island Historical Society.
59. *Ibid.*, February 7, 1780.
60. *Ibid.*, February 13, 1780.
61. Borick, *A Gallant Defense*, 76.
62. Ira D. Gruber, ed., *John Peebles' American War: The Diary of a Scottish Grenadier, 1776–1782* (Mechanicsburg: Stackpole Books, 1998), 343.
63. Clinton to Germain, 9 March 1780 in Davies, *Documents*, 18:53–54.
64. *Ibid.*, 54.
65. *Ibid.*
66. Ward, *War of the Revolution*, 2:698.
67. Jared Sparks, ed. *Correspondence of the American Revolution: Being Letters of Eminent Men to George Washington. From the time of his Taking Command of the Army to the End of his Presidency* (Boston: Little, Brown, & Co., 1853), 2:413–415.
68. *Ibid.*
69. Hawes, *Lachlan McIntosh Papers*, 98.
70. Samuel Baldwin, "Diary of Events, In Charleston, SC,

from March 20th to April 20th, 1780," in *Proceedings of the New Jersey Historical Society* 1, 1845–1846 (Newark: Daily Advertiser, 1847), 78.
71. *Ibid.*, 79.
72. Ward, *War of the Revolution*, 2:698.
73. Johann Ewald, Joseph P. Tustin, ed. and trans., *Diary of the American War: A Hessian Journal* (New Haven: Yale University Press, 1979), 210.
74. Borick, *A Gallant Defense*, 82.
75. Ward, *War of the Revolution*, 2:698.
76. Francis Marion to Benjamin Lincoln, 5 March 1780, reel 5, *Benjamin Lincoln Papers*, microfilm edition, 16 reels (Boston: Massachusetts Historical Society, 1967).
77. Mark Mayo Boatner III, *Encyclopedia of the American Revolution* (New York: David McKay, 1966), 676.
78. Henry Lee, *Memoirs of the War in the Southern Department of the United States* (New York: University Publishing Company, 1869), 1:174.
79. *Ibid.*
80. Lyman C. Draper, *King's Mountain and Its Heroes: History of the Battle of King's Mountain, October 7th, 1780, and the Events Which Led to It* (Cincinnati: Peter G. Thomson, Publisher, 1881), 489.
81. Baldwin, "Diary of Events," 80.
82. Ewald, *Diary of the American War*, 221.
83. Draper, *King's Mountain*, 490.
84. Bulger, "British Expedition to Charleston," 112.
85. Borick, *A Gallant Defense*, 104.
86. Clinton to Germain, 13 May 1780, in Davies, *Documents*, 18:87.
87. Borick, *A Gallant Defense*, 115.
88. *Ibid.*, 116.
89. Ewald, *Diary of the American War*, 227.
90. Tarleton, *A History of the Campaigns*, 15.
91. *Ibid.*, 14–15.
92. *Ibid.*, 16.
93. Clinton to Germain, 13 May 1780, in Davies, *Documents*, 18:87.

94. Gruber, *John Peebles' American War*, 358.

95. Hawes, *Lachlan McIntosh Papers*, 99.

96. *Ibid.*, 101.

97. Borick, *A Gallant Defense*, 138–139.

98. Baldwin, "Diary of Events," 84.

99. Borick, *A Gallant Defense*, 172.

100. Draper, *King's Mountain*, 493.

101. Ewald, *Diary of the American War*, 234.

102. William Moultrie, as quoted in George Scheer and Hugh Rankin, *Rebels and Redcoats: The American Revolution Through the Eyes of Those Who Fought and Lived It* (New York: DaCapo Press, 1957), 398.

103. Hawes, *Lachlan McIntosh Papers*, 118.

104. Draper, *King's Mountain*, 495.

105. Gruber, *John Peebles' American War*, 372.

106. Borick, *A Gallant Defense*, 201.

107. *Ibid.*, 216.

108. United States, Continental Army, Southern Department, Continental Army Southern Department Records, 1778–1790, (34/201 OvrSz) South Carolina Historical Society, April 15, 1780.

109. Bulger, "British Expedition to Charleston," 176.

110. Burgoyne, *Ansbach Jaegers*, 145.

111. Ewald, *Diary of the American War*, 238.

112. Gruber, *John Peebles' American War*, 373.

113. *Ibid.*, 377.

114. Moultrie, as quoted in Scheer, 400.

115. Ewald, *Diary of the American War*, 238.

116. *Ibid.*, 241–242.

117. Henry B. Carrington, *Battle of the American Revolution 1775–1781* (New York: A.S. Barnes, 1876), 497.

118. Bulger, "British Expedition to Charleston," 177–178.

119. Borick, *A Gallant Defense*, 226.

120. *Ibid.*, 227.

121. Willcox, *Portrait of a General*, 495.

122. Frank Moore, *Diary of the American Revolution: From Newspapers and Original Documents* (New York: Charles Scribner, 1860), 2:430.

123. Diary of Captain von der Malsberg, Lidgerwood Collection, Morristown National Historical Park, *Hessian Documents of the American Revolution, 1776–1783*, Fiche Number 333, in the collections of the David Library of the American Revolution.

Chapter 3

1. Henry Laurens to Richard Henry Lee, March 10, 1780 in *The Papers of Henry Laurens*, eds., David R. Chestnutt and C. James Taylor (Columbia: University of South Carolina Press, 2000), 15:247.

2. *Ibid.*, 15:297.

3. *Ibid.*, 15:300.

4. Lieut. Colonel Banastre Tarleton to Lieut. General Earl Cornwallis, May 30, 1780, as quoted in Davies, *Documents*, 18:100.

5. *Ibid.*

6. Dr. Robert Brownsfield to William D. James in William Dobein James, *A Sketch of the Life of Brig. Gen. Francis Marion* (Charleston: Gould and Milet, 1821), appendix, 3.

7. *Ibid.*

8. Tarleton, *History of the Campaigns*, 31.

9. *Ibid.*

10. Borick, *A Gallant Defense*, 231.

11. Charles Royster, *The Revolutionary People at War: The Continental Army and American Character, 1775–1783* (New York: W.W. Norton, 1979), 321.

12. *Ibid.*

13. Willcox, *The American Rebellion*, 175.

14. *Ibid.*, 181.

15. *Ibid.*

16. *Ibid.*, 175.

17. *Ibid.*

18. *Ibid.*, 186.

19. *Ibid.*, 186–187.

20. C.A. Bayly and Katherine Prior, "Cornwallis, Charles, first Marquess Cornwallis (1738–1805), governor-general of India and lord lieutenant of Ireland." *Oxford Dictionary of National Biography*, https://doi.org/10.1093/ref:odnb/6338. Web. August 30, 2018.

21. Charles Ross, ed., *Correspondence of Charles, First Marquis Cornwallis* (London: John Murray, 1859), 1:3.

22. *Ibid.*, 1:11.

23. Henry Morse Stevens, "Charles Cornwallis (1738–1805)," *Oxford Dictionary of National Biography*, 7 (London, 1887), 234–241.

24. "Charles Cornwallis, 1st Marquess and 2nd Earl Cornwallis," *Encyclopedia Britannica*. Encyclopedia Britannica Online. Encyclopedia Britannica, Inc., 2018. Web. August 30, 2018.

25. Edgar, *Partisans and Redcoats*, 65.

26. Nadelhaft, *Disorders of War*, 57.

27. Francis Marion, as quoted in Edward McCrady, *The History of South Carolina in the Revolution, 1780–1783* (New York: MacMillan, 1902), 641.

28. Eliza Wilkinson, *Letters of Eliza Wilkinson, during the Invasion and Possession of Charleston, SC by the British in the Revolutionary War* (New York: Arno Press Reprint, 1969 [orig. publ. 1839]), 29.

29. *Ibid.*

30. Gray, "Observations on the War in Carolina," 153–154.

31. Don Higginbotham, *The War of American Independence: Military Attitudes, Policies, and Practice, 1763–1789* (New York: Macmillan, 1971), 362.

32. Donald Barr Chidsey, *The War in the South: An On-the-Scene Account of the Carolinas and Georgia in the American Revolution* (New York: Crown, 1969), 87.

33. Wayne Lee, "Restraint and Retaliation: The North Carolina Militias and the Backcountry War of 1780–1782," in John Resch and Walter Sargent, eds., *War and Society in the American Revolution* (DeKalb: Northern Illinois University Press, 2007), 172.

34. *Ibid.*, 173.

35. *Ibid.*, 175.

36. Andrew Dauphinee, "Lord Charles Cornwallis and the Loyalists: A Study in British Pacification During the American Revolution, 1775–1781" (master's thesis, Temple University, 2011), 22–23.

37. *Ibid.*, 25.

38. *Ibid.*, 26.

39. Jim Piecuch, "Incompatible Allies: Loyalists, Slaves, and Indians in Revolutionary South Carolina," in Resch and Sargent, *War and Society in the American Revolution*, 210.

40. *Ibid.*

41. Ward, *War of the Revolution*, 2:715–716.

42. Paul David Nelson, "Horatio Gates in the Southern Department, 1780: Serious Errors and a Costly Defeat," *The North Carolina Review* 50, no. 3 (1973): 260.

43. Paul David Nelson, *General Horatio Gates: A Biography* (Baton Rouge: Louisiana State University Press, 1976), 222.

44. Paul David Nelson, "Major Horatio Gates as a Military Leader: The Southern Experience," in W. Robert Higgins, ed., *The Revolutionary War in the South: Power, Conflict and Leadership* (Durham: Duke University Press, 1979), 136.

45. Nelson, "Horatio Gates in the Southern Department," 262.

46. George Washington Greene, *The Life of Nathanael Greene, Major-General in the Army of the Revolution* (Freeport: Books for Libraries Press, 1972), 3:108, reprint.

47. Nelson, "Horatio Gates in the Southern Department," 262.

48. Nelson, "Gates as a Military Leader," 137.

49. *Ibid.*, 138.

50. Boatner, *Encyclopedia*, 1078.

51. Lee, *Memoirs*, 1:175.

52. Boatner, *Encyclopedia*, 1077.

53. Robert Scott Davis, Jr., "Thomas Pinckney and the Last Campaign of Horatio Gates," *The South Carolina Historical Magazine* 86, no. 2 (1985): 76.

54. *Ibid.*, 78.

55. Colonel Otho Williams, "A Narrative of the Campaign of 1780," in William Johnson, *Sketches of the Life and Correspondence of Nathanael Greene* (Charleston: A.E. Miller, 1822), 1:487.

56. John Buchanan, *The Road to Guilford Courthouse: The American Revolution in the Carolinas* (New York: John Wiley & Sons, 1997), 155.

57. Davis, "Last Campaign," 75.

58. *Ibid.*, 79.

59. Nelson, "Horatio Gates in the Southern Department," 266.

60. William Seymour, "A Journal of the Southern Expedition, 1780–1783," *The Pennsylvania Magazine of History and Biography* 7, no. 3 (1883): 287.

61. Williams, "Narrative," 1: 493.

62. Cornwallis to Germain, August 21, 1780, in Ian Saberton, ed. *The Cornwallis Papers: The Campaigns of 1780 and 1781 in The Southern Theatre of the American Revolutionary War* (Uckfield, East Sussex: The Naval and Military Press Ltd., 2010) 2:12.

63. John Robert Shaw, *A Narrative of the Life & Travels of John Robert Shaw* (Lexington: Daniel Bradford, 1807), 29.

64. *Ibid.*

65. Buchanan, *Road to Guilford Courthouse*, 162.

66. Account of Garret Watts in Dann, *The Revolution Remembered*, 194.

67. John A. Stevens, "The Southern Campaign," *Magazine of American History* 5, no. 4 (1880): 303.

68. Cornwallis to Germain, August 21, 1780, in Saberton, *Cornwallis Papers*, 2:13.

69. Watts, in *Revolution Remembered*, 195.

70. Stevens, "The Southern Campaign," 303–304.

71. Cornwallis to Germain, August 21, 1780, in Saberton, *Cornwallis Papers*, 2:13.

72. John Senf, "Plan of the Battle near Camden," *Magazine of American History* 5 (1880): 278.

73. Blackwell P. Robinson, *The Revolutionary War Sketches of William R. Davie* (Raleigh: Department of Cultural Resources, 1976), 17.

74. *Ibid.*, 18.

75. "Thomas Pinckney to William Johnson," *Historical Magazine* 10, no. 8 (1886), 245.

76. *Ibid.*

77. *Ibid.*, 247.

78. Davis, "Last Campaign of Horatio Gates," 80.

79. Nelson, "Gates as a Military Leader," 147.

80. Nelson, "Horatio Gates in the Southern Department," 269.

81. *Ibid.*, 270.

82. *Ibid.*, 272.

83. David Ramsay, *The History of the American Revolution* (Philadelphia: R. Aitkin & Son, 1789), vol. 2:170.

84. *Ibid.*

85. *Ibid.*, 171.

86. Tarleton, *History of the Campaigns*, 155.

87. Cornwallis to Germain, August 20, 1780, in Saberton, *Cornwallis Papers*, 144.

88. Tarleton, *History of the Campaigns*, 155.

89. Saberton, *Cornwallis Papers*, 2:28.

90. Cornwallis to Germain, August 20, 1780, in Davies, *Documents*, 18:145.

91. *Ibid.*

92. *Ibid.*

93. Williams, "Narrative," 1:500.

94. *Ibid.*

95. *Ibid.*, 501.

96. *Ibid.*

97. *Ibid.*, 502.

98. Tarleton, *History of the Campaigns*, 158.

99. Robinson, *William R. Davie*, 24.

100. Tarleton, *History of the Campaigns*, 159.

101. *Ibid.*

102. Walter Clark, ed. *The State Records of North Carolina* (Goldsboro: Nash Bros., Book and Job Printers, 1898), 15:171–172.

103. Tarleton, *History of the Campaigns*, 160.

104. Gray, "Observations on the War," 142.

105. Walter Clark, *The State Records of North Carolina* (Winston: M.L. & J.C. Stewart, 1806), 14:434.

106. *Ibid.*

107. George C. Rogers and Charles O'Hara, "Letters of Charles O'Hara to Duke of Grafton," *South Carolina Historical Magazine* 65, no. 3 (1964): 168.

108. Cornwallis to Germain, September 19 and 21, 1780, in Saberton, *Cornwallis Papers*, 2:37–39.

109. Pancake, *Destructive War*, 116.

110. Draper, *Kings Mountain*, 169.

111. George C. MacKenzie, *Kings Mountain National Military Park, National Park Historical Handbook Series* (Washington,

D.C.: U.S. Government Printing Office, 1955), No. 22, 11.

112. Draper, *King's Mountain*, 170.

113. Randall Jones, *The Overmountain Men and the Battle of Kings Mountain*, http://www.learnnc.org/lp/editions/nchist-revolution/4272 (accessed April 8, 2018).

114. Buchanan, *Guilford Courthouse*, 206–207.

115. *Ibid.*

116. *Ibid.*

117. Wade Kolb and Robert Weir, eds., *Captured at Kings Mountain: The Journal of Uzal Johnson, A Loyalist Surgeon* (Columbia: University of South Carolina Press, 2011), 28.

118. *Ibid.*

119. Ferguson to Cornwallis, September 14, 1780, in Saberton, *Cornwallis Papers*, 2:150–152.

120. Ferguson to Cornwallis, September 30, 1780, in Saberton, *Cornwallis Papers*, 2:160–161.

121. Ferguson to Cornwallis, October 5, 1780, in Saberton, *Cornwallis Papers*, 2:164.

122. Jones, *Overmountain Men*, www.learnnc.org.

123. Cornwallis to Balfour, October 7, 1780, in Saberton, *Cornwallis Papers*, 2:116.

124. Cornwallis to Ferguson, October 8, 1780 in Saberton, Cornwallis Papers, 2:166.

125. Benson J. Lossing, *The Pictorial Field-Book of the Revolution*, 2 vols. (Rutland: Charles E. Tuttle, 1972, reprint), 2:423.

126. *Ibid.*, 423.

127. *Ibid.*

128. John Roberts, *A Revolutionary Soldier* (Clinton, LA: Feliciana Democrat, Print, 1859), 51.

129. *Ibid.*, 50.

130. *Ibid.*

131. Ensign Robert Campbell, Draper Manuscript, 17 DD 25, in Robert M. Dunkerly, *The Battle of Kings Mountain: Eyewitness Accounts* (Charleston: The History Press, 2007), 20.

132. Colonel Issac Shelby's account in Draper, *King's Mountain*, 543.

133. A.S. Salley, Jr., *Col. William Hill's Memoirs of the Revolution* (Columbia: The State Company, 1921), 23.

134. Campbell, Draper Manuscript, 17 DD 25 in Dunkerly, *Kings Mountain*, 20.

135. Col. William Campbell to Col. Arthur Campbell in Dunkerly, *Kings Mountain*, 27.

136. Roberts, *Revolutionary Soldier*, 50–54.

137. Charles Bowen Pension, Draper Manuscript Collection, 2 DD 228, in Dunkerly, *Kings Mountain*, 18.

138. Leonard Hice pension application, S8713, in Dunkerly, *Kings Mountain*, 49.

139. Thomas Young's account, Memoirs of Thomas Young, in Dunkerly, *Kings Mountain*, 91–93.

140. *Ibid.*

141. Colonel Issac Shelby to Evan Shelby in Draper, *Kings Mountain*, 524.

142. William Campbell, in Draper, *Kings Mountain*, 526.

143. Samuel Williams, "The Battle of Kings Mountain: As Seen by the British Officers," *Tennessee Historical Magazine* 7, no. 1 (1921): 58.

144. James Collins, in Dunkerly, *Kings Mountain*, 34.

145. Colonel Issac Shelby's Pamphlet to the Public, 1823, in Draper, *Kings Mountain*, 566.

146. Bobby Gilmer Moss, ed., *The Journal of Alexander Chesney* (Roanoke Rapids, NC: Scotia-Hibernia Press, 2002), 29–34.

147. *Ibid.*, 31.

148. Col. Arthur Campbell in Draper, *Kings Mountain*, 531.

149. Charles O'Hara to Duke of Grafton, "Letters of Charles O'Hara," 162.

150. Col. Arthur Campbell in Draper, *Kings Mountain*, 527–528.

151. Sir Henry Clinton in Buchanan, *Road to Guilford Courthouse*, 241.

152. Robert Gray, "Observations on the War," 142–143.

153. *Ibid.*, 144.

154. Salley, *Memoirs of the Revolution*, 23.

155. *Ibid.*

156. Alfred E. Jones, ed., "The Journal of Alexander Chesney, a South Carolina Loyalist in the Revolution and After," *The Ohio State University Bulletin* 26, no. 4, 17.

Chapter 4

1. Tarleton, *History of the Campaigns*, 169.

2. Cornwallis to Clinton, December 3, 1780, in Clark, *State Records*, 15:303.

3. Tarleton, *History of the Campaigns*, 171.

4. Dauphinee, "Cornwallis and the Loyalists," 45.

5. *Ibid.*

6. Gray, "Observations on the War," 143.

7. *Ibid.*, 145.

8. Lord Rawdon to Alexander Leslie, October 24, 1780, in Davies, *Documents*, 18:190–191.

9. Willcox, *Clinton's Narrative*, 227–228.

10. *Ibid.*, 228.

11. Washington to Hancock, March 18, 1777, in Frank E. Grizzard, Jr., *The Papers of George Washington*, Revolutionary War Series, January–March 1777 (Charlottesville: University of Virginia Press, 1998), 8:597.

12. *Ibid.*

13. Lee, *Memoirs*, 1:212.

14. *General Nathanael Greene and His Homestead* (Coventry: Nathanael Greene Homestead Association, 2016).

15. *Ibid.*

16. Theodore Thayer, *Nathanael Greene: Strategist of the American Revolution* (New York: Twayne, 1960), 23.

17. Greene to Samuel Ward, October 9, 1772, in Richard K Showman, ed., *The Papers of Nathanael Greene* (Chapel Hill: University of North Carolina Press, 1976), 1:47.

18. *Ibid.*, 1:50*n*.

19. Thayer, *Greene*, 45.

20. *Ibid.*, 50.

21. Greene to Adams, May 26, 1776, in Showman, *Papers*, 1:219.

22. Adams to Greene, June 22, 1776, in Showman, *Papers*, 1:238.

23. Greene to Knox, 17 November 1776, in Showman, *Papers*, 1:354*n*.

24. *Ibid.*, 1:352.

25. Greene to Catherine Greene, December 30, 1776, in Showman, *Papers*, 1:379*n*.

26. *Ibid.*

27. Thayer, *Greene*, 24.

28. Lee, *Memoirs*, 1:221.

29. *Ibid.*, 220.

30. *Ibid.*, 220–221.

31. Terry Golway, *Washington's General: Nathanael Greene and the Triumph of the American Revolution* (New York: Henry Holt, 2006), 121.

32. *Ibid.*, 128.

33. *Ibid.*, 155.

34. James Thomas Flexner, *George Washington in the American Revolution* (Boston: Little, Brown, 1967), 226.

35. John C. Fitzpatrick, ed., *The Writings of George Washington, from the Original Manuscript Sources, 1745–1799* (Washington, D.C.: Government Printing Office, 1934), 12:277.

36. Curtis J. Morgan, Jr. "'A merchandise of small Wares': Nathanael Greene's Northern Apprenticeship, 1775–1780," in Gregory D. Massey and Jim Piecuch, eds., *General Nathanael Greene and the American Revolution in the South* (Columbia: University of South Carolina Press), 47.

37. *Ibid.*, 49.

38. Greene to Col. Jeremiah Wadsworth, August 12, 1780, in Showman, *Papers*, 6:201.

39. Golway, *Washington's General*, 226.

40. Washington to Greene, October 14, 1780, in Showman, *Papers*, 6:385–386.

41. Greene to Washington, October 16, 1780, in Showman, *Papers*, 6:396.

42. Greene to Catherine Greene, October 15 or 16, 1780, in Showman, *Papers*, 6:397–398.

43. *Ibid.*

44. Greene to Washington, April 22, 1779, in Showman, *Papers*, 3:423.

45. Greene to John Mathews, October 3, 1780, in Showman, *Papers*, 6:336n.

46. *Ibid.*, 335.

47. Showman, *Papers*, 6:xvi.

48. *Ibid.*

49. General Greene's orders, December 5, 1780, in Showman, *Papers*, 6:527n.

50. *Ibid.*, 527.

51. Greene to General Edward Stevens, December 1, 1780, in Showman, *Papers*, 6:512–513.

52. *Ibid.*

53. *Ibid.*

54. Miecislaus Haiman, *Kosciuszko in the American Revolution* (New York: The Polish Institute of Arts and Sciences, 1975), 104–105.

55. Greene to Col. Edward Carrington, December 4, 1780, in Showman, *Papers*, 6:516–517.

56. *Ibid.*

57. *Ibid.*

58. *Ibid.*, 517n.

59. Charles Konigsberg, "Edward Carrington, 1748–1810: 'Child of the Revolution': A Study of the Public Man in Young America" (Ph.D. diss., Princeton University, 1966), 59.

60. Edward Carrington to Greene, December 6, 1780, in Showman, *Papers*, 6:537.

61. *Ibid.*

62. Greene to North Carolina Board of War, December 7, 1780, in Showman, *Papers*, 6:548–550.

63. *Ibid.*, 551n.

64. Lawrence Babits, "Greene's Strategy in the Southern Campaign, 1780–1781," *Air Force Journal of Logistics* (Winter 1984): 9.

65. Brigadier General Thomas R. Phillips, ed. *Roots of Strategy: The 5 Greatest Military Classics of All Time* (Harrisburg: Stackpole Books, 1985), 324.

66. David K. Wilson, "'Against the tide of misfortune': Civil-Military Relations, Provincialism, and the Southern Command in the Revolution," in Gregory D. Massey and Jim Piecuch, eds., *General Nathanael Greene and the American Revolution in the South* (Columbia: University of South Carolina Press, 2012), 74.

67. Greene to Jefferson, December 6, 1780, in Showman, *Papers*, 6:530–531.

68. *Ibid.*

69. Greene to Governor Abner Nash, December 6, 1780, in Showman, *Papers*, 6:533–534.

70. Greene to Henry Knox, December 7, 1780, in Showman, *Papers*, 6:547.

71. Greene to Horatio Gates, December 8, 1780, in Showman, *Papers*, 6:553.

72. Gates to Greene, December 15, 1780, in Showman, *Papers*, 6:583n.

73. Morgan, "A Merchandise of small Wares," 42.

74. *Ibid.*

75. *Ibid.*, 43.

76. Thayer, *Nathanael Greene*, 282.

77. *Ibid.*

78. Thomas G. Frothingham, *Washington: Commander in Chief* (Boston: Houghton Mifflin, 1930), 326.

79. *Ibid.*, 327.

80. Greene to Marion, December 4, 1780, in Showman, *Papers*, 6:519–520.

81. James R. McIntyre, "Nathanael Greene: Soldier-Statesman of the War of Independence in South Carolina," in Massey and Piecuch, eds. *General Nathanael Greene*, 175.

82. John Buchanan, "'We must endeavor to keep up a Partizan War': Nathanael Greene and the Partisans," in Massey and Piecuch, eds. *General Nathanael Greene*, 120.

83. Greene, *Life of Nathanael Greene*, 3:70.

84. Greene to Washington, December 7, 1780, in Showman, *Papers*, 6:545n.

85. Greene to Reed, January 9, 1781, in William B. Reed, *Life and Correspondence of Joseph Reed* (Philadelphia: Lindsay and Blakiston, 1847), 2:344.

86. Ward, *War of the Revolution*, 2:750.

87. Greene to Daniel Morgan, December 16, 1780, in Showman, *Papers*, 6:589–90.

88. *Ibid.*

89. *Ibid.*

90. Ward, *War of the Revolution*, 2:751.

91. Thayer, *Nathanael Greene*, 296.

92. Babits, "Greene's Strategy," 11.

93. Robert Pugh, "The Cowpens Campaign and the American Revolution" (Ph.D. diss., University of Illinois, 1951), 181.

94. *Ibid.*, 180.

95. *Ibid.*, 178–179.

96. Edwin C. Bearrs, *Battle of Cowpens: A Documented Narrative and Troop Movement Maps* (Johnson City, TN: The Overmountain Press, 1996), 3.

97. Don Higginbotham, *Daniel Morgan: Revolutionary Rifleman* (Chapel Hill: University of North Carolina Press, 1961), 40.

98. Don Higginbotham, *War and Society in Revolutionary America: The Wider Dimensions of Conflict* (Columbia: University of South Carolina Press, 1988), 143.

99. Higginbotham, *Daniel Morgan*, 210.

100. Bearrs, *Battle of Cowpens*, 4.

101. Tarleton, *A History of the Campaigns*, 213.

102. Greene to General Robert Howe, December 29, 1780, in Showman, *Papers*, 7:17.

103. *Ibid.*

104. *Ibid.*, 18.

105. Greene to Ezekiel Cornell, December 29, 1780, in Showman, *Papers*, 7:21.

106. *Ibid.*

107. Greene to Colonel John Marshel, December 30, 1780, in Showman, *Papers*, 7:25.

108. *Ibid.*

109. Pugh, "Cowpens Campaign," 174–175.

110. Cornwallis to Clinton, January 6, 1781, in Willcox, *American Rebellion*, 485.

111. Carrington, *Battles of the American Revolution*, 527.

112. *Ibid.*, 528.

113. Tarleton, *A History of the Campaigns*, 209.

114. Pugh, "Cowpens Campaign," 210.

115. Lawrence E. Babits, *A Devil of a Whipping: The Battle of Cowpens* (Chapel Hill: University of North Carolina Press, 1998), 51.

116. Bearrs, *Battle of Cowpens*, 5.

117. Pugh, "Cowpens Campaign," 213.

118. Bearrs, *Battle of Cowpens*, 5.

119. Babits, *Devil of a Whipping*, 52.

120. *Ibid.*

121. Tarleton, *A History of the Campaigns*, 214.

122. Pugh, "Cowpens Campaign," 222.

123. Tarleton, *A History of the Campaigns*, 215.

124. Dennis Trammell R10672 (pension, Dec. 10, 1833, M804, Roll 2408).

125. Rev. James Hodge Saye, *Memoirs of Major Joseph McJunkin: Revolutionary Patriot* (Greenwood, SC: Greenwood Index-Journal, 1925), 32–34.

126. Thomas Young, "The Memoir of Major Thomas Young," *Orion Magazine* 3 (October–November 1843): n.p.

127. *Ibid.*

128. Babits, *Devil of a Whipping*, 66.

129. James Kelly, S1544 (pension, April 28, 1835, M804, Roll 1466).

130. Babits, *Devil of a Whipping*, 63.

131. Tarleton, *A History of the Campaigns*, 215.

132. Charles Stedman, *The History of the Origin, Progress, and Termination of the American War* (London: J. Murray, 1794), 2:321.

133. J.B.O. Landrum, *Colonial and Revolutionary History of Upper South Carolina* (Greenville: Shannon & Co., Printer and Binders, 1897), 278.

134. Babits, *Devil of a Whipping*, 72.

135. *Ibid.*, 66.

136. Pugh, "Cowpens Campaign," 245.

137. Landrum, *Upper South Carolina*, 279.

138. Pugh, "Cowpens Campaign," 246.

139. Babits, *Devil of a Whipping*, 77.

140. Lee, *Memoirs*, 2:175.

141. *Ibid.*, 76.

142. Landrum, *Upper South Carolina*, 280.

143. Bearrs, *Battle of Cowpens*, 19.

144. *Ibid.*, 22.

145. Young, "Memoir," n.p.

146. Babits, *Devil of a Whipping*, 79.

147. Pugh, "Cowpens Campaign," 236.

148. Morgan to Greene, January 19, 1781, in Bearrs, *Battle of Cowpens*, 122–123.

149. Shaw, *Life & Travels*, 31–32.

150. Henry Wells, S11712 (pension, January 29, 1834, M804, Roll 1415).

151. Stedman, *American War*, 321.

152. *Ibid.*

153. Babits, *Devil of a Whipping*, 91.

154. Pugh, "Cowpens Campaign," 261.

155. Saye, *Memoirs*, 32–34.

156. Babits, *Devil of a Whipping*, 92–93.

157. Roberts, *Revolutionary Soldier*, 57.

158. *Ibid.*

159. Morgan to Greene, January 19, 1781, in Showman, *Papers*, 7:122–123.

160. Morgan to Greene, January 19, 1781, in Showman, *Papers*, 7:153.

161. *Ibid.*, 154.

162. Stedman, *American War*, 322.

163. *Ibid.*, 323–324.

164. Tarleton, *A History of the Campaigns*, 218.

165. Morgan to Greene, January 19, 1781, in Showman, *Papers*, 7:155.

166. Moultrie, *Memoirs of the American Revolution*, 2:257.

167. Jones, "Journal of Alexander Chesney," 22.

168. Stedman, *American War*, 324.

169. *Ibid.*

170. *Ibid.*, 325.

171. Bearrs, *Battle of Cowpens*, 44.

172. Wells, Jan. 29, 1834, pension statement, revwarapps.org.

173. James Wright to Lord George Germain, January 25, 1781, in Davies, *Documents*, 15:45.

Chapter 5

1. Greene to Abner Nash, January 7, 1781, in Showman, *Papers*, 7:62.

2. *Ibid.*

3. *Ibid.*

4. Greene to Sumter, January 8, 1781, in Showman, *Papers*, 7:75.

5. Greene to Col. John Cox, January 9, 1781, in Showman, *Papers*, 7:81.

6. Greene to Hamilton, January 10, 1781, in Showman, *Papers*, 7:88.

7. Col. James Phillips to Greene, January 10, 1781, in Showman, *Papers*, 7:93.

8. Cornwallis to Clinton, December 3, 1780, in Saberton, *Cornwallis Papers*, 3:26.

9. *Ibid.*

10. Cornwallis to Clinton, December 4, 1780, in Saberton, *Cornwallis Papers*, 3:28.

11. Clinton to Cornwallis, December 13, 1780, in Saberton, *Cornwallis Papers*, 3: 32.

12. Cornwallis to Clinton, December 22, 1780, in Saberton, *Cornwallis Papers*, 3: 29.

13. *Ibid.*

14. Greene to unidentified person, January 23, 1781, in Showman, *Papers*, 7:175–76.

15. *Ibid.*

16. Lawrence Babits and Joshua Howard, *Long, Obstinate and Bloody: The Battle of Guilford Courthouse* (Chapel Hill: University of North Carolina Press, 2009), 11.

17. Saberton, *Cornwallis Papers*, 4:3*n*.

18. Buchanan, *Road to Guilford Courthouse*, 334–335.

19. Cornwallis to Germain, March 17, 1781, in Saberton, *Cornwallis Papers*, 4:12.

20. Pancake, *Destructive War*, 157.

21. Lossing, *Pictorial Field-Book of the Revolution*, 2:395*n*.

22. Buchanan, *Road to Guilford Courthouse*, 337.

23. Tarleton, *History of the Campaigns*, 222–223.

24. Morgan to Greene, January 23, 1781, in Showman, *Papers*, 7:178.

25. Scheer and Rankin, *Rebels and Redcoats*, 434.

26. *Ibid.*, 435.

27. Buchanan, *Road to Guilford Courthouse*, 338–339.

28. Babits and Howard, *Long, Obstinate and Bloody*, 15.

29. O'Hara to the Duke of Grafton, April 20, 1781, in Rogers, "Letters," 174.

30. Cornwallis to Germain, March 17, 1781, in Saberton, *Cornwallis Papers*, 4:13.

31. Higginbotham, *War of Independence*, 368.

32. O'Hara to Duke of Grafton, April 20, 1781, in Rogers, "Letters," 174.

33. Stedman, *American War*, 2:332.

34. Greene to Campbell, January 30, 1781, in Nathanael Greene letterbook, 1781, George Bancroft collection, Manuscripts and Archives Division, New York Public Library, Astor, Lenox, and Tilden Foundations.

35. Greene to Samuel Huntington, January 31, 1781, in Showman, *Papers*, 7:226.

36. *Ibid.*, 225.

37. Greene to the officers commanding the Militia in the Salisbury district of North Carolina, January 31, 1781, in Showman, *Papers*, 7:227.

38. *Ibid.*

39. William A. Graham, *General Joseph Graham and His Papers on North Carolina Revolutionary History* (Raleigh: Edwards & Broughton, 1904), 289.

40. Buchanan, *Road to Guilford Courthouse*, 344.

41. *Ibid.*

42. *Ibid.*

43. Babits and Howard, *Long, Obstinate and Bloody*, 18.

44. Robert Henry, *Narrative of the Battle at Cowan's Ford, February 1, 1781* (Greensboro: D. Schenk, 1891), 10; Captain David Vance, *Narrative of the Battle of King's Mountain* (Greensboro: D. Schenk, 1891).

45. Henry, *Narrative*, 11.

46. Roger Lamb, *An Original and Authentic Journal of Occurrences During the late American War* (Dublin: Wilkinson & Courtney, 1809), 343.

47. Henry, *Narrative*, 12.

48. Lamb, *Original and Authentic Journal*, 344.

49. Scheer and Rankin, *Rebels and Redcoats*, 438.

50. Graham, *General Joseph Graham*, 294.

51. Henry, *Narrative*, 14.

52. *Ibid.*

53. Babits and Howard, *Guilford Courthouse*, 22.

54. Tarleton, *A History of the Campaigns*, 263.

55. Stedman, *American War*, 329*n*.

56. Babits and Howard, *Long, Obstinate and Bloody*, 24.

57. A.R. Newsome, ed., "A British Orderly Book, 1780–1781, Part 3," *The North Carolina Historical Review* 9, no. 3 (1932): 293.

58. *Ibid.*, 297.

59. Scheer and Rankin, *Rebels and Redcoats*, 438.

60. Greene to Huger, February 1, 1781, in Showman, *Papers*, 7:231.

61. Huger to Greene, February 1, 1781, in Showman, *Papers*, 7:233.

62. Major Ichabod Burnet to Col. Henry Lee, February 2, 1781, in Showman, *Papers*, 7:234.

63. *Ibid.*

64. Greene to Captain Joseph Marbury, February 2, 1781, in Showman, *Papers*, 7:235.

65. *Ibid.*

66. Seymour, "Journal of the Southern Expedition," 13.

67. Scheer and Rankin, *Rebels and Redcoats*, 439.

68. Greene to Huger, February 5, 1781, in Showman, *Papers*, 7:252.

69. *Ibid.*

70. Greene to the Commanding Officer of the Guilford Militia, February 5, 1781, in Showman, *Papers*, 7:253.

71. Greene to the Officer Commanding the Militia in the Rear of the Enemy, February 6, 1781, in Showman, *Papers*, 7:254.

72. Babits and Howard, *Long, Obstinate and Bloody*, 27.

73. Fries, *Records of the Moravians*, 4:1742.

74. Buchanan, *Road to Guilford Courthouse*, 352.

75. Proceedings of a Council of War, February 9, 1781, in Showman, *Papers*, 7:261–262.

76. *Ibid.*, 262.

77. Graham, *Morgan*, 355.

78. Greene to Washington, February 9, 1781, in Showman, *Papers*, 7:267–269.

79. Greene to Baron Steuben, February 10, 1781, in Showman, *Papers*, 7:281.

80. Greene to Abner Nash, February 9, 1781, in Showman, *Papers*, 7:265.

81. Buchanan, *Road to Guilford Courthouse*, 354.

82. Cornwallis to Germain, March 17, 1781, in Saberton, *Cornwallis Papers*, 4:14.

83. Scheer and Rankin, *Rebels and Redcoats*, 439.

84. Babits and Howard, *Long, Obstinate and Bloody*, 31.

85. *Ibid.*, 30.

86. W. Carroll Headspeth and Spurgeon Compton, *The Retreat to the Dan* (South Boston: South Boston News, 1975), 16.

87. Seymour, "Journal of the Southern Expedition," 296.

88. *Ibid.*

89. Ramsey, *American Revolution*, 2:236.

90. Williams to Greene, February 11, 1781, in Showman, *Papers*, 7:283.

91. Buchanan, *Road to Guilford Courthouse*, 357.

92. Lee, *Memoirs*, 1:278–279.

93. Williams to Greene, February 13, 1781, in Showman, *Papers*, 7:285–86.

94. Lee, *Memoirs*, 1:289.

95. *Ibid.*, 291.

96. *Ibid.*

97. Greene to Williams, Feb-

ruary 14, 1781, in Showman, *Papers*, 7:287.

98. *Ibid.*

99. Lee, *Memoirs*, 1:293.

100. Ichabod Burnet to Benjamin Walker, February 15, 1781, in Showman, *Papers*, 7:287.

101. Tarleton, *A History of the Campaigns*, 229.

102. Cornwallis to Germain, March 17, 1781, in Saberton, *Cornwallis Papers*, 4:15.

103. Otho Williams to Elie Williams, February 15, 1781, *in Otho Holland Williams Papers*, MS 908, Reel 1, Maryland Historical Society.

104. Greene to Steuben, February 15, 1781, "Greene letterbook, 1781."

105. Lee, *Memoirs*, 1:294–96.

106. *Ibid.*, 296.

107. Pancake, *Destructive War*, 172.

108. Greene to NC Legislature, February 15, 1781, in Showman, *Papers*, 7:290.

109. *Ibid.*

110. Greene to Steuben, February 15, 1781, "Greene letterbook, 1781."

111. Greene to Abner Nash, February 17, 1781, in Showman, *Papers*, 7:304.

112. *Ibid.*, 306.

113. Washington to Greene, February 17, 1781, in Showman, *Papers*, 7:308.

114. *Ibid.*

115. Greene to Steuben, February 18, 1781, in Showman, *Papers*, 7:311.

116. *Ibid.*

117. *Ibid.*

118. Pancake, *Destructive War*, 174.

119. Dennis M. Conrad, "Nathanael Greene and the Southern Campaigns, 1780–1783" (Ph.D. diss., Duke University, 1979), 138.

Chapter 6

1. Otho Williams to Elie Williams, February 21, 1781, *Williams Papers*.

2. Cornwallis to Germain, March 17, 1781, in Saberton, *Cornwallis Papers*, 4:15.

3. Buchanan, *Road to Guilford Courthouse*, 359.

4. Cornwallis to Rawdon, February 21, 1781, in Ross, *Correspondence*, 1:84.

5. *Ibid.*

6. *Ibid.*

7. Stedman, *American War*, 2:335.

8. A.R. Newsome, ed., "A British Orderly Book, 1780–1781, Part 4," *The North Carolina Historical Review* 9, no. 4 (1932): 373.

9. *Ibid.*

10. O'Hara to Duke of Grafton, 20 April 1781, in Rogers, "Letters," 176–177.

11. Stedman, *American War*, 332–333.

12. Tarleton, *History of the Campaigns*, 233.

13. Greene, *Nathanael Greene*, 3:179.

14. Pickens to Greene, February 19, 1781, in Showman, *Papers*, 7:320.

15. Buchanan, *Road to Guilford Courthouse*, 362.

16. Greene to Caswell, February 20, 1781, in Showman, *Papers*, 7:321.

17. Lewis Morris, Jr., to General Lewis Morris, February 19, 1781, in Henry Steele Commager and Richard B. Morris, *The Spirit of 'Seventy-Six: The Story of the American Revolution as Told by Participants* (Edison: Castle Books, 1967), 1162.

18. Lee to Greene, February 23, 1781, in Showman, *Papers*, 7:336.

19. Buchanan, *Road to Guilford Courthouse*, 362.

20. Lee, *Memoirs*, 1:305.

21. Arnold W. Kalmanson, "Otho Williams and the Southern Campaign of 1780–1782" (master's thesis, Salisbury State University), 57.

22. Pickens to Greene, February 26, 1781, in Showman, *Papers*, 7:358.

23. Stedman, *American War*, 2:334.

24. Babits and Howard, *Long, Obstinate, and Bloody*, 42.

25. Greene to Campbell, February 24, 1781, in Showman, *Papers*, 7:341.

26. Lawson to Greene, February 24, 1781, in Showman, *Papers*, 7:344.

27. Lock to Greene, February 24, 1781, in Showman, *Papers*, 7:345.

28. Malmedy to Burnet, February 24, 1781, in Showman, *Papers*, 7:345.

29. Tarleton, *A History of the Campaigns*, 234.

30. Greene, *Nathanael Greene*, 3:183.

31. Cornwallis to Germain, March 17, 1781, in Saberton, *Cornwallis Papers*, 4:16.

32. Greene, *Nathanael Greene*, 3:185.

33. Buchanan, *Road to Guilford Courthouse*, 365.

34. Kalmanson, "Otho Williams," 57.

35. Greene, *Nathanael Greene*, 3:187.

36. William Campbell to Greene, March 2, 1781, in Showman, *Papers*, 7:380.

37. Greene to Abner Nash, March 6, 1781, in Showman, *Papers*, 7:402.

38. *Ibid.*

39. *Ibid.*

40. Lamb, *Original and Authentic Journal*, 348.

41. Buchanan, *Road to Guilford Courthouse*, 367.

42. O'Hara to Duke of Grafton, April 1781, in Rogers, "Letters," 177.

43. Williams to Greene, March 7, 1781, in Showman, *Papers*, 7:407.

44. *Ibid.*

45. Buchanan, *Road to Guilford Courthouse*, 367.

46. *Ibid.*

47. Williams to Greene, March 7, 1781, in Showman, *Papers*, 7:407–408.

48. Charles Magill to Thomas Jefferson, March 10, 1781, in Julian P. Boyd, ed., *The Papers of Thomas Jefferson* (Princeton: Princeton University Press, 1952), 5:115.

49. Captain William Pierce, Jr., to General John Butler, March 4, 1781, in Showman, *Papers*, 7:388.

50. Pickens to Greene, March 5, 1781, in Showman, *Papers*, 7:399.

51. Greene to Pickens, March 8, 1781, in Showman, *Papers*, 7:410.

52. Greene to Joseph Reed, *Life and Correspondence*, 2:349.

53. Buchanan, *Road to Guilford Courthouse*, 368.

54. Babits and Howard, *Long, Obstinate, and Bloody*, 49.

55. Greene to Lee, March

9, 1781, in Showman, *Papers*, 7:415.

56. *Ibid.*, 416*n*.

57. Greene to Lee, March 14, 1781, in Showman, *Papers*, 7:430.

58. Lee, *Memoirs*, 1:335.

59. Tarleton, *History of the Campaigns*, 270.

60. Babits and Howard, *Long, Obstinate, and Bloody*, 51.

61. Lee, *Memoirs*, 1:337.

62. *Ibid.*

63. Algie I. Newlin, *The Battle of New Garden: The Little-Known Story of One of the Most Important "Minor Battles" of the Revolutionary War in North Carolina* (Greensboro: The North Carolina Friends Historical Society, 1977), 22.

64. Lee, *Memoirs*, 1:338.

65. *Ibid.*

66. Babits and Howard, *Long, Obstinate, and Bloody*, 54.

67. Lee, *Memoirs*, 1:339.

68. Cornwallis to Germain, March 17, 1781, in Saberton, *Cornwallis Papers*, 4:16.

69. Robinson, *William R. Davie*, 32.

70. Patrick K. O'Donnell, *Washington's Immortals: The Untold Story of an Elite Regiment Who Changed the Course of the Revolution* (New York: Atlantic Monthly Press, 2016), 314.

71. Lee, *Memoirs*, 1:342–343.

72. John Hairr, *Guilford Courthouse: Nathanael Greene's Victory in Defeat, March 15, 1781* (Cambridge, MA: Da Capo Press, 2002), 76.

73. Greene to Samuel Huntington, March 16, 1781, in Showman, *Papers*, 7:434.

74. *Ibid.*

75. James Boone Bartholomees, Jr., "Fight or Flee: The Combat Performance of the North Carolina Militia in the Cowpens-Guilford Courthouse Campaign, January to March 1781" (Ph.D. diss., Duke University, 1978), 174.

76. Cornwallis to Germain, March 17, 1781, in Saberton, *Cornwallis Papers*, 4:17.

77. Robinson, *William R. Davie*, 32.

78. Lamb, *Original and Authentic Journal*, 361.

79. *Ibid.*

80. Lee, *Memoirs*, 1:343–344.

81. Cornwallis to Germain,

March 17, 1781, in Saberton, *Cornwallis Papers*, 4:18.

82. *Ibid.*

83. Otho Williams to Elie Williams, March 16, 1781, Williams Papers.

84. Greene to Huntington, March 16, 1781, in Showman, *Papers*, 7:439*n*.

85. St. George Tucker to Frances Bland Tucker, March 18, 1781, *Magazine of American History* 7 (September 1881): 40.

86. *Ibid.*,41.

87. Cornwallis to Germain, March 17, 1781, in Saberton, *Cornwallis Papers*, 4:18.

88. John Eager Howard to unknown, 1782, Bayard Papers 1675–1895, MS 109, Box 1, Folder 18, Maryland Historical Society.

89. *Ibid.*

90. Greene to Huntington, March 16, 1781, in Showman, *Papers*, 7:435.

91. Cornwallis to Germain, March 17, 1781, in Saberton, *Cornwallis Papers*, 4:18.

92. *Ibid.*

93. Greene to Huntington, March 16, 1781, in Showman, *Papers*, 7:440*n*.

94. Cornwallis to Germain, March 17, 1781, in Saberton, *Cornwallis Papers*, 4:18–19.

95. *Ibid.*, 19.

96. Buchanan, *Road to Guilford Courthouse*, 380.

97. Stedman, *American War*, 344.

98. *Ibid.*, 347.

99. O'Hara to Duke of Grafton, April 20, 1781, in Rogers, "Letters," 177–78.

100. Bruce E. Burgoyne, ed. and trans., *Enemy Views: The American Revolutionary War as Recorded by Hessian Participants* (Bowie, MD: Heritage Books, 1996), 450.

101. *Ibid.*

102. General Greene's Orders, March 16, 1781, in Showman, *Papers*, 7:431.

103. Greene to Samuel Huntington, March 16, 1781, in Showman, *Papers*, 7:435.

104. Greene to Lee, March 19, 1781, in Showman, *Papers*, 7:454.

105. Cornwallis to Clinton, April 10, 1781, in Willcox, *American Rebellion*, 508–509.

106. Greene to Lillington,

March 26, 1781, in Showman, *Papers*, 7:469.

107. O'Hara to Duke of Grafton, April 20, 1781, in Rogers, "Letters," 178.

108. Cornwallis to Clinton, April 10, 1781, in Willcox, *American Rebellion*, 508–509.

109. Craig to Cornwallis, March 22, 1781, in Saberton, *Cornwallis Papers*, 4:27.

110. O'Hara to Duke of Grafton, April 20, 1781, in Rogers, "Letters," 178.

111. William Dickson to Robert Dickson, November 30, 1784, in James O. Carr, ed., *The Dickson Letters* (Raleigh: Edwards & Broughton, 1901), 15.

112. Cornwallis to Clinton, April 10, 1781, in Willcox, *American Rebellion*, 508–509.

113. Stedman, *American War*, 353.

114. State of the troops at Wilmington, April 15, 1781, in Saberton, *Cornwallis Papers*, 4:142–144.

115. Cornwallis to Germain, April 18, 1781, in Saberton, *Cornwallis Papers*, 4:106.

116. *Ibid.*

117. Cornwallis to Major General Phillips, April 10, 1781, in Ross, *Correspondence*, 1:87.

118. *Ibid.*

119. *Ibid.*

120. Cornwallis to Clinton, April 10, 1781, in Saberton, *Cornwallis Papers*, 4:110–111.

121. Cornwallis to Germain, April 18, 1781, in Saberton, *Cornwallis Papers*, 4:106.

122. Tarleton, *A History of the Campaigns*, 281.

123. *Ibid.*, 283.

124. Cornwallis to Germain, April 23, 1781, in Willcox, *American Rebellion*, 511.

125. *Ibid.*, 511–512.

126. Greene to Washington, March 29, 1781, in Showman, *Papers*, 7:481.

Chapter 7

1. Greene to Samuel Huntington, March 30, 1781, in Conrad, et al., *The Papers of Nathanael Greene* (Chapel Hill: University of North Carolina Press, 1995), 8:7–8.

2. Greene to Sumter, March 30, 1781, in Conrad, *Papers*, 8:12.

3. *Ibid.*
4. Greene to Steuben, April 6, 1781, in Conrad, *Papers*, 8: 61*n*.
5. Thayer, *Nathanael Greene*, 335.
6. *Ibid.*, 336.
7. Cornwallis to Phillips, April 24, 1781, in Willcox, *American Rebellion*, 512.
8. *Ibid.*
9. Greene, *Nathanael Greene*, 230.
10. Greene to Samuel Huntington, April 22, 1781, in Conrad, *Papers*, 8:130.
11. *Ibid.*
12. Seymour, "Journal of the Southern Expedition," 380.
13. Sumter to Greene, April 7, 1781, in Conrad, *Papers*, 8:66.
14. Greene to Sumter, April 14, 1781, in Conrad, *Papers*, 8:94.
15. Greene to Sumter, April 19, 1781, in Conrad, *Papers*, 8:119.
16. Greene to Lee, April 22, 1781, in Conrad, *Papers*, 8:133.
17. Sumter to Greene, April 25, 1781, in Conrad, *Papers*, 8:149.
18. *Ibid.*
19. Greene to Huntington, April 22, 1781, in Conrad, *Papers*, 8:131–132.
20. *Ibid.*
21. Greene, *Nathanael Greene*, 240.
22. Thayer, *Nathanael Greene*, 341.
23. Greene, *Nathanael Greene*, 241.
24. *Ibid.*, 243.
25. *Ibid.*
26. Robinson, *William R. Davie*, 43.
27. Pancake, *Destructive War*, 193.
28. Henry Lumpkin, *From Savannah to Yorktown: The American Revolution in the South* (Lincoln, NE: toExcel Press, 1987), 179.
29. *Ibid.*
30. Pancake, *Destructive War*, 195.
31. John Eager Howard to unknown, 1782, *Bayard Papers, 1672–1895*, MS 109, Box 1, Folder 18, Maryland Historical Society.
32. Stedman, *American War*, 356.
33. Pancake, *Destructive War*, 196.

34. Lumpkin, *Savannah to Yorktown*, 180.
35. Stedman, *American War*, 357.
36. Greene to Huntington, April 27, 1781, in Conrad, *Papers*, 8:155.
37. *Ibid.*, 158*n*.
38. Greene to Huntington, April 27, 1781, in Conrad, *Papers*, 8:156–157.
39. Lumpkin, *Savannah to Yorktown*, 183.
40. Pancake, *Destructive War*, 198.
41. Greene to Huntington, April 27, 1781, in Conrad, *Papers*, 8:158*n*.
42. *Ibid.*
43. Greene to Sumter, April 30, 1781, in Conrad, *Papers*, 8:176–177.
44. Greene to Reed, May 4, 1781, in Conrad, *Papers*, 8:201.
45. Greene to Reed, August 6, 1781, in Reed, *Correspondence*, 2:362.
46. Anne King Gregoire, *Thomas Sumter* (Columbia: R.L. Bryan, 1931), 155.
47. Rawdon to Cornwallis, April 25, 1781, in Saberton, *Cornwallis Papers*, 4:179.
48. Rawdon to Cornwallis, April 26, 1781, in Saberton, *Cornwallis Papers*, 4:180.
49. Stedman, *American War*, 361.
50. *Ibid.*
51. *Ibid.*
52. Greene to Marion, April 27, 1781, in Conrad, *Papers*, 8:160–161.
53. Greene to Marion, May 6, 1781, in Conrad, *Papers*, 8:211.
54. Marion to Greene, May 6, 1781, in Conrad, *Papers*, 8:214–215.
55. *Ibid.*
56. Greene to Marion, May 9, 1781, in Conrad, *Papers*, 8:230–231.
57. Ward, *War of the Revolution*, 2:811.
58. Captain Nathaniel Pendleton to Gen. Thomas Sumter, 10 May 1781, in Conrad, et al., *PNG*, 8:236.
59. Ward, *War of the Revolution*, 2:811.
60. Gray, "Observations," 157.
61. *Ibid.*, 158.
62. Jerome A. Green, *Ninety-Six: A Historical Narrative*

(Denver: National Park Service, 1978), 120.
63. *Ibid.*, 120.
64. Lossing, *Pictorial Fieldbook*, 2:484.
65. Pancake, *Destructive War*, 210.
66. Lumpkin, *Savannah to Yorktown*, 194.
67. Ward, *War of the Revolution*, 2:817.
68. *Ibid.*
69. Lee, *Memoirs*, 1:353.
70. Greene to Lee, May 22, 1781, in Conrad, *Papers*, 8:291–292.
71. Greene to Lafayette, May 23, 1781, in Conrad, *Papers*, 8:300.
72. Lee, *Memoirs*, 2:98.
73. Roderick MacKenzie, *Strictures on Lt. Col. Tarleton's "History of the Campaigns of 1780 and 1781, in the Southern Provinces of North America"* (London: Printed for the Author, 1787), 147.
74. *Ibid.*, 148.
75. Haiman, *Kosciuszko*, 112.
76. MacKenzie, *Strictures*, 148.
77. Haiman, *Kosciuszko*, 112.
78. Green, *Ninety Six*, 131.
79. MacKenzie, *Strictures*, 150.
80. *Ibid.*, 150–151.
81. Cruger to Rawdon, 31 May 1781, in Saberton, *Cornwallis Papers*, 5:282.
82. Cruger to Rawdon, 3 June 1781, in Saberton, *Cornwallis Papers*, 5:282.
83. Ward, *War of the Revolution*, 2:818.
84. MacKenzie, *Strictures*, 152.
85. Russell Weigley, *The Partisan War: The South Carolina Campaign of 1780–1782* (Columbia: University of South Carolina Press, 1970), 59.
86. Alexander Garden, *Anecdotes of the American Revolution* (Charleston: A.E. Miller, 1828), 65.
87. Green, *Ninety Six*, 142.
88. Greene to Huntington, June 9, 1781, in Conrad, *Papers*, 8:363–364.
89. Ward, *War of the Revolution*, 2:820.
90. *Ibid.*
91. Green, *Ninety Six*, 149.
92. MacKenzie, *Strictures*, 156.

93. Pancake, *Destructive War*, 212–213.
94. Lee, *Memoirs*, 1:375.
95. *Ibid.*
96. Lee, *Memoirs*, 1:376.
97. *Ibid.*
98. MacKenzie, *Strictures*, 159.
99. Pancake, *Destructive War*, 213.
100. Lee, *Memoirs*, 1:377.
101. Lumpkin, *Savannah to Yorktown*, 204.
102. Lee, *Memoirs*, 1:378.
103. *Ibid.*, 1:377.
104. Greene to Pickens, June 19, 1781, in Conrad, *Papers*, 8:415.
105. *Ibid.*
106. Lee. *Memoirs*, 1:378.
107. Greene's Orders, June 20, 1781, in Conrad, *Papers*, 8:418–419.
108. Lee, *Memoirs*, 1:378.
109. *Ibid.*, 379.
110. *Ibid.*, 379.
111. Pancake, *Destructive War*, 215.
112. Marion to Greene, July 7, 1781, in Conrad, *Papers*, 8:505.
113. Lee, *Memoirs*, 1:387.
114. Pancake, *Destructive War*, 215.
115. McCrady, *South Carolina in the Revolution*, 296.
116. Pickens to Lee, November 25, 1811, *Draper Microfilm*, VV, 1:108.
117. Greene, *Nathanael Greene*, 3:320.
118. Greene to Samuel Huntington, June 20, 1781, in Conrad, *Papers*, 8:423n.
119. *Ibid.*
120. Greene to Jefferson, June 27, 1781, in Conrad, *Papers*, 8:463–464.
121. *Ibid.*
122. Greene to Huntington, June 20, 1781, in Conrad, *Papers*, 8:421.
123. Lee, *Memoirs*, 2:158.
124. Moore, *Diary of the American Revolution*, 2:462.
125. Stedman, *American War*, 2:376.
126. Greene, *Greene*, 3:335–336.
127. Green, *Ninety Six*, 177.
128. Greene to Reed, May 4, 1781, in Reed, *Correspondence*, 2:352–353.
129. Reed to Greene, June 16, 1781, in Conrad, *Papers*, 8:396.
130. *Ibid.*

131. *Ibid.*
132. *Ibid.*
133. Greene to Reed, August 6, 1781, in Reed, *Correspondence*, 2:362.
134. *Ibid.*,363.
135. *Ibid.*
136. *Ibid.*
137. *Ibid.*

Chapter 8

1. Dennis M. Conrad, Roger N. Parks, Martha J. King, eds., *The Papers of Nathanael Greene* (Chapel Hill: University of North Carolina Press), 9: xi.
2. *Ibid.*
3. *Ibid.*, xvii.
4. Greene to Pickens, July 15, 1781, in Conrad, *Papers*, 9:11–12.
5. *Ibid.*, 12n.
6. Governor Rutledge to Gen. Marion, August 7, 1781, in R.W. Gibbes, *Documentary History of the American Revolution* (Columbia: Banner Steam-Power Press, 1853), 3:124.
7. Greene to Mathews, July 18, 1781, in Conrad, *Papers*, 9:39.
8. Greene to Wade Hampton, July 30, 1781, in Conrad, *Papers*, 9:107n.
9. Greene to Pickens, July 30, 1781, in Conrad, *Papers*, 9:109.
10. *Ibid.*
11. Headnote on the Dog Days Expedition, in Conrad, *Papers*, 9:13.
12. *Ibid.*
13. Sumter to Greene, July 15, 1781, in Conrad, *Papers*, 9:17.
14. *Ibid.*, 17–18.
15. Marion to Greene, July 19, 1781, in Conrad, *Papers*, 9:47–48.
16. Headnote, in Conrad, *Papers*, 9:16.
17. Greene to Sumter, July 25, 1781, in Conrad, *Papers*, 9:55.
18. Greene to Sumter, July 21, 1781, in Conrad, *Papers*, 9:56.
19. Greene to Marion, August 10, 1781, in Conrad, *Papers*, 9:159.
20. Greene to Balfour, August 26, 1781, in Conrad, *Papers*, 9:250–251.

21. Greene's Proclamation, August 26, 1781, in Conrad, *Papers*, 9:252.
22. *Ibid.*
23. *Ibid.*, 253.
24. Lee, *Memoirs*, 2:251.
25. Patrick O'Kelley, *Unwaried Patience and Fortitude: Francis Marion's Orderly Book* (West Conshohocken, PA: Infinity Publishing, 2006), 544.
26. *Ibid.*, 545.
27. Lee, *Memoirs*, 1:464.
28. Greene to Thomas McKean, September 11, 1781, in Conrad, *Papers*, 9:328–329.
29. Jim Piecuch, "The Evolving Tactician: Nathanael Greene at the Battle of Eutaw Springs," in Massey and Piecuch, eds., *Nathanael Greene*, 226–227.
30. Lee, *Memoirs*, 1:464.
31. Ward, *War of the Revolution*, 2:827.
32. Greene to Thomas McKean, September 11, 1781, in Conrad, *Papers*, 9:329.
33. Lumpkin, *Savannah to Yorktown*, 214.
34. O'Kelley, *Unwaried Patience*, 545.
35. Joseph Brown Turner, ed. *The Journal and Order Book of Captain Robert Kirkwood of the Delaware Regiment of the Continental Line*, Part 1: A Journal of the Southern Campaign 1780–1782 (Wilmington: The Historical Society of Delaware, 1910), 23.
36. Greene, *Greene*, 3:388–389.
37. O'Kelley, *Unwaried Patience*, 546.
38. Lumpkin, *Savannah to Yorktown*, 216.
39. Pancake, *Destructive War*, 217–218.
40. Greene to McKean, September 11, 1781, in Conrad, *Papers*, 9:328.
41. Otho Williams account, in Gibbes, *Documentary History*, 2:146.
42. *Ibid.*, 148.
43. *Ibid.*,329.
44. Otho Williams account, in Gibbes, *Documentary History*, 2:148.
45. *Ibid.*
46. Lee, *Memoirs*, 1: 468–469.
47. *Ibid.*, 469.
48. Ward, *War of the Revolution*, 2:832.
49. Stewart to Cornwallis,

September 9, 1781, in Gibbes, *Documentary History*, 2:138.

50. Otho Williams account, in Gibbes, *Documentary History*, 2:153.

51. *Ibid.*, 154.

52. Otho Williams account, in Gibbes, *Documentary History*, 2:152.

53. *Ibid.*, 155.

54. Greene to McKean, September 11, 1781, in Conrad, *Papers*, 9:332.

55. *Ibid.*, 337n.

56. Stewart to Cornwallis, September 9, 1781, in Gibbes, *Documentary History*, 2:138.

57. Ward, *War of the Revolution*, 2:834.

58. Stewart to Cornwallis, September 9, 1781, in Gibbes, *Documentary History*, 2:138.

59. *Ibid.*, 139.

60. Lee, *Memoirs*, 2:300.

61. *Ibid.*, 300–301.

62. Weigley, *Partisan War*, 68.

63. Lee, *Memoirs*, 1:475.

64. Greene to McKean, September 11, 1781, in Conrad, *Papers*, 9:332.

65. *Ibid.*, 338n.

66. Otho Williams account, in Gibbes, *Documentary History*, 2:157.

67. Stedman, *American War*, 2:381.

68. Cornwallis to Clinton, April 23, 1781, in Saberton, *Cornwallis Papers*, 4:112.

69. Cornwallis to Phillips, April 24, 1781, in Saberton, *Cornwallis Papers*, 4:116.

70. *Ibid.*

71. Townsend to Cornwallis, April 14, 1781, in Saberton, *Cornwallis Papers*, 5:320.

72. Balfour to Cornwallis, May 21, 1781, in Saberton, *Cornwallis Papers*, 5:275.

73. Saberton, *Cornwallis Papers*, 4:103.

74. Tarleton, *A History of the Campaigns*, 285.

75. Cornwallis to Balfour, May 3, 1781, in Saberton, *Cornwallis Papers*, 4:176.

76. *Ibid.*

77. Tarleton to Cornwallis, May 4, 1781, in Saberton, *Cornwallis Papers*, 4:155.

78. *Ibid.*, 286.

79. Tarleton to Cornwallis, May 5, 1781, in Saberton, *Cornwallis Papers*, 4:158.

80. Tarleton, *A History of the Campaigns*, 287–288.

81. Arnold to Cornwallis, May 12, 1781, in Saberton, *Cornwallis Papers*, 4:151–152.

82. Cornwallis to Phillips, May 14, 1781, in Saberton, *Cornwallis Papers*, 4:152–153.

83. Arnold to Cornwallis, May 16, 1781, in Saberton, *Cornwallis Papers*, 4:153.

84. Tarleton, *A History of the Campaigns*, 293.

85. Cornwallis to Clinton, May 26, 1781, in Saberton, *Cornwallis Papers*, 5:89.

86. John Graves Simcoe, *Simcoe's Military Journal: A History of the Operations of a Partisan Corps called The Queen's Rangers* (New York: Bartlett & Welford, 1844), 218.

87. S.R. Mealing, "Simcoe, John Graves," in *Dictionary of Canadian Biography*, vol. 5, University of Toronto/Universite Laval, 2003, http://biographi.ca/en/bio/simcoe_john_graves_5E.html. (accessed September 20, 2018).

88. Tarleton, *A History of the Campaigns*, 294–295.

89. Balfour to Cornwallis, May 21, 1781, in Saberton, *Cornwallis Papers*, 5:277.

90. *Ibid.*, 278.

91. Balfour to Cornwallis, June 7, 1781, in Saberton, *Cornwallis Papers*, 5:287.

92. Cornwallis to Rawdon, May 20, 1781, in Saberton, *Cornwallis Papers*, 5:287.

93. Richard Henry Lee to Arthur Lee, June 4, 1781, in James Curtis Ballagh, ed., *Letters of Richard Henry Lee* (New York: Macmillan, 1914), 2:229–31.

94. Simcoe, *Journal*, 217.

95. *Ibid.*, 220–221.

96. *Ibid.*, 223.

97. Tarleton, *A History of the Campaigns*, 296.

98. *Ibid.*, 297.

99. *Ibid.*

100. Sir Henry Clinton, *Observations on Earl Cornwallis' Answer to Sir Henry Clinton's Narrative* (London: J. Debrett, 1783), 101.

101. Clinton to Cornwallis, June 11, 1781, in Saberton, Cornwallis Papers, 5:96.

102. *Ibid.*, 5:97.

103. Cornwallis to Clinton, July 8, 1781, in Saberton, *Cornwallis Papers*, 5:116.

104. Clinton to Cornwallis, July 21, 1781, in Saberton, *Cornwallis Papers*, 5:139–143.

105. Robert Middlekauff, *The Glorious Cause: The American Revolution, 1763–1789* (New York: Oxford University Press, 2005), 583.

106. O'Hara to the Duke of Grafton, 20 October 1781, in Rogers, "Letters," 179.

Chapter 9

1. Greene to Colonels Shelby and John Sevier, September 16, 1781, in Conrad, *Papers*, 9:351.

2. *Ibid.*

3. Greene to Marion, September 17, 1781, in Conrad, *Papers*, 9:359.

4. Greene to Marion, September 19, 1781, in Conrad, *Papers*, 9:375.

5. Colonel Lewis Morris, Jr., to Greene, September 23, 1781, in Conrad, *Papers*, 9:387.

6. Greene to Colonels Shelby and Sevier, October 11, 1781, in Conrad, *Papers*, 9:442.

7. *Ibid.*

8. *Ibid.*, 442–443n.

9. Greene to Col. William Davies, October 18, 1781, in Conrad, *Papers*, 9:451.

10. Pancake, *Destructive War*, 236.

11. Ward, *War of the Revolution*, 2: 837.

12. Greene to McKean, October 25, 1781, in Conrad, *Papers*, 9:482.

13. *Ibid.*, 483.

14. Greene to Washington, October 25, 1781, in Conrad, *Papers*, 9:485.

15. Golway, *Washington's General*, 292.

16. Pancake, *Destructive War*, 236.

17. Greene to Griffith Rutherford, October 18, 1781, in Conrad, *Papers*, 9:452.

18. Greene to Griffith Rutherford, October 20, 1781, in Conrad, *Papers*, 9:457.

19. *Ibid.*

20. Washington to Greene, October 31, 1781, in Conrad, *Papers*, 9:505.

21. Pancake, *Destructive War*, 236.

22. Greene to Marion,

November 15, 1781, in Conrad, *Papers*, 9:577–578.

23. Thayer, *Nathanael Greene*, 386.

24. Marion to Greene, November 30, 1781, in Conrad, *Papers*, 9:641–642.

25. *Ibid.*

26. Ward, *War of the Revolution*, 2:838.

27. Greene to Williams, December 2, 1781, in Conrad, *Papers*, 9:649.

28. Marion to Greene, November 30, 1781, in Conrad, *Papers*, 9:642–643*n*.

29. *Ibid.*, 643.

30. Thayer, *Nathanael Greene*, 387.

31. Greene to Rutledge, December 3, 1781, in Conrad, *Papers*, 10:4.

32. *Ibid.*

33. Greene to Lee, December 7, 1781, in Conrad, *Papers*, 10:13.

34. Greene to Rutledge, December 9, 1781, in Conrad, *Papers*, 10:22.

35. Golway, *Washington's General*, 296.

36. Pancake, *Destructive War*, 237.

37. Greene to Rutledge, January 21, 1782, in Conrad, *Papers*, 10:229–230*n*.

38. Ward, *War of the Revolution*, 2:839.

39. Lee, Memoirs, 1:525–526.

40. *Ibid.*, 541.

41. Thayer, *Nathanael Greene*, 393.

42. Lee to Greene, December 20, 1781, in Conrad, *Papers*, 10:84.

43. Greene to Lee, December 21, 1781, in Conrad, *Papers*, 10:85.

44. *Ibid.*

45. Greene to Rutledge, January 16, 1781, in Conrad, *Papers*, 10:206.

46. *Ibid.*, 209*n*.

47. Pancake, *Destructive War*, 238.

48. Lee to Greene, January 26, 1782, in Conrad, *Papers*, 10:264–65.

49. Greene to Lee, January 27, 1782, in Conrad, *Papers*, 10:269.

50. Gregory D. Massey, *John Laurens and the American Revolution* (Columbia: University of South Carolina Press, 2000), 212.

51. Charles Royster, *Light-Horse Harry Lee and the Legacy of the American Revolution* (New York: Alfred A. Knopf, 1981), 52.

52. Lee to Greene, January 29, 1782, in Conrad, *Papers*, 10:283.

53. Greene to Lee, February 18, 1782, in Conrad, *Papers*, 10:378.

54. *Ibid.*, 380*n*.

55. Massey, *John Laurens*, 212.

56. Pancake, *Destructive War*, 238–239.

57. Klein, *Unification of the Slave State*, 121.

58. Greene to Reed, February 27, 1782, in Conrad, *Papers*, 10:414.

59. *Ibid.*

60. Golway, *Washington's General*, 299.

61. Joseph Lee Boyle, ed., "The Revolutionary War Diaries of Captain Walter Finney," *South Carolina Historical Magazine* 98, no. 2 (1997): 136.

62. Major Ichabod Burnet to Charles Pettit, April 12, 1782, in Conrad, *Papers*, 11:38.

63. General Greene's Orders, April 20, 1782, in Conrad, *Papers*, 11:80.

64. Robert Morris to Greene, April 24, 1782, in Conrad, *Papers*, 11:113.

65. Burnet to Pettit, April 12, 1782, in Conrad, *Papers*, 11:40*n*.

66. Thomas Farr to Greene, May 20, 1782, in Conrad, *Papers*, 11:225.

67. *Ibid.*, 228n.

68. Ian R. Christie, *The End of North's Ministry 1780–1782* (New York: St. Martin's Press, 1958), 371.

69. *Ibid.*

70. Farr to Greene, May 20, 1782, in Conrad, *Papers*, 11:229*n*.

71. *Ibid.*, 234n.

72. Greene to Washington, July 11, 1782, in Conrad, *Papers*, 11:436

73. *Ibid.*, 436*n*.

74. Lee. Memoirs, 1:563.

75. *Ibid.*, 565.

76. Thayer, *Nathanael Greene*, 405.

77. *Ibid.*, 409.

78. Lee, Memoirs, 1:573.

79. Thayer, *Nathanael Greene*, 233.

80. Golway, *Washington's General*, 308.

81. Greene to Catharine Greene, August 4, 1783, in Parks, *Papers*, 13:83.

82. Reverend William Gordon to Greene, February 26–March 3, 1783, in Conrad, *Papers*, 12:489–90.

83. Reed to Greene, March 14, 1783, in Conrad, *Papers*, 12:518.

84. Warner Mifflin to Greene, October 21, 1783, in Parks, *Papers*, 13:157–58.

85. Greene to Mifflin, November 1783, in Parks, *Papers*, 13:192.

86. Greene to Catharine Greene, June 2, 1775, in Showman, *Papers*, 1:83.

87. *Ibid.*, 310.

88. Dr. Benjamin Rush to Greene, September 16, 1782, in Conrad, *Papers*, 11:667.

89. Robert Morris to Greene, June 28, 1785, in Parks, *Papers*, 13:545.

90. Greene to Williams, September 17, 1782, in Conrad, *Papers*, 11:669.

91. Greene to Marion, August 9, 1782, in Conrad, *Papers*, 11:510.

92. Gregory D. Massey, "Independence and Slavery: The Transformation of Nathanael Greene," in Gregory D. Massey and Jim Piecuch, eds., *General Nathanael Greene and the American Revolution in the South* (Columbia: University of South Carolina Press, 2012), 253.

93. Greene to Catharine Greene, April 14, 1785, in Parks, *Papers*, 13:493.

94. Golway, *Washington's General*, 313.

95. Greene to Lincoln, February 2, 1783, in Conrad, *Papers*, 12:402.

96. *Ibid.*

97. Greene to Morris, February 2, 1783, in Conrad, *Papers*, 12:404–405.

98. Conrad, *Papers*, 12:xv.

99. Statement of John Banks, February 15, 1783, in Conrad, *Papers*, 12:446.

100. Statement of Anthony Wayne and Col. Edward Carrington, February 15, 1783, in Conrad, *Papers*, 12:447–48.

101. Conrad, *Papers*, 12:xvi.

102. Thayer, *Nathanael Greene*, 416.

103. *Ibid.*, 417.

104. Conrad, *Papers*, 12:xvi

105. Thayer, *Nathanael Greene*, 417.

106. Conrad, *Papers*, 12:xvii.

107. Massey, "Independence and Slavery," 254.

108. Greene, *Nathanael Greene*, 3:532–536.

109. *Charleston Evening Gazette*, June 23, 1786, vol. 2, no. 299.

110. Harold C. Syrett, ed., *The Papers of Alexander Hamilton* (New York: Columbia University Press, 1962), 5:347–348.

111. Lafayette to Jefferson, August 30, 1786, in Julian P. Boyd, ed., *The Papers of Thomas Jefferson* (Princeton: Princeton University Press, 1954), 10:311.

112. Henry Knox to George Washington, October 23, 1786, in W.W. Abbot, ed., *The Papers of George Washington*, Confederation Series (Charlottesville: University of Virginia Press, 1995), 4:302.

113. Washington to Rochambeau, July 31, 1786, in Abbot, *Washington Papers*, 4:180.

114. Johnson, *Sketches*, 2:422.

115. William Gordon, *The History of the Rise, Progress, and Establishment, of the Independence of the United States of America: Including an Account of the Late War and of the Thirteen Colonies, from their Origin to that Period* (Freeport: Books for Libraries Press, 1969), 407.

116. Francis Vinton Greene, *The Revolutionary War and the Military Policy of the United States* (New York: Charles Scribner's Sons, 1911), 257–258.

117. J.W. Fortesque, *A History of the British Army* (London: Macmillan, 1911), 3:409.

Chapter 10

1. Wilson, *Southern Strategy*, 62.

2. *Ibid.*

3. Smith, *Loyalists and Redcoats*, 79.

4. *Ibid.*, 115.

5. Ira D. Gruber, "Britain's Southern Strategy," in W. Robert Higgins, ed., *The Revolutionary War in the South: Power, Conflict and Leadership* (Durham: Duke University Press, 1979), 218.

6. Andrew Jackson O'Shaughnessy, *The Men Who Lost America: British leadership, the American Revolution, and the Fate of the Empire* (New Haven: Yale University Press, 2013), 355.

7. Gruber, "Southern Strategy," 228.

8. *Ibid.*, 219.

9. Dauphinee, "Cornwallis and the Loyalists," 64.

10. O'Shaughnessy, *The Men Who Lost America*, 355.

11. *Ibid.*

12. Dauphinee, "Cornwallis and the Loyalists," 65.

13. Christie, *North's Ministry*, 173.

14. Shy, *Numerous and Armed*, 211–212.

15. Cornwallis to Lieutenant Colonel Kirkland, November 13, 1780, in Ross, *Correspondence*, 1:70.

16. O'Shaughnessy, *The Men Who Lost America*, 356.

17. Gruber, "Southern Strategy," 237.

18. Shy, *Numerous and Armed*, 213.

19. O'Shaughnessy, *The Men Who Lost America*, 354.

20. Joel Anthony Edward, "A Comparative Evaluation of British and American Strategy in the Southern Campaign of 1780–1781" (master's thesis, U.S. Army Command and General Staff College, 2002), 93.

21. Charles C. Mann, "America, Found and Lost," *National Geographic* (May 2007): 53.

22. Shy, *Numerous and Armed*, 212.

23. *Ibid.*, 213.

24. Lumpkin, *Savannah to Yorktown*, 251.

25. *Ibid.*, 251–252.

26. *Ibid.*, 249.

27. *Ibid.*, 250.

28. Page Smith, *Reflections on the Nature of Leadership* (Washington, D.C.: The Society of the Cincinnati, 1982), 29.

29. Morgan, "A Merchandise of small Wares," 49.

30. *Ibid.*, 50.

31. Buchanan, "We must endeavor to keep up a partisan War," 120.

32. McIntyre, "Soldier-Statesman," 176.

33. John Oller, *The Swamp Fox: How Francis Marion Saved the American Revolution* (New York: Da Capo Press, 2016), 103.

34. Greene to Marion, December 4, 1780, in Showman, *Papers*, 6:520.

35. Frothingham, *Washington*, 326.

36. McIntyre, "Soldier-Statesman," 179.

37. *Ibid.*,184.

38. John R. Maass, "'With humanity, justice and moderation': Nathanael Greene and the Reconciliation of the Disaffected South," in Massey and Piecuch, eds., *Nathanael Greene*, 199.

39. Greene to Marion, December 12, 1781, in Conrad, *Papers*, 10:38.

40. Greene to Weedon, October 1, 1782, in Conrad, *Papers*, 12:4.

41. Maass, "With humanity," 207.

42. McIntyre, "Soldier-Statesman," 185.

43. Wilson, "Against the tide of misfortune," 78.

44. Gaillard Hunt, ed., *Journals of the Continental Congress, 1774–1789* (Washington, D.C.: Government Printing Office, 1912), 21:784.

45. Greg Brooking, "'I am an independent spirit, and confide in my own resources': Nathanael Greene and His Continental Subordinates, 1780–1781," in Massey and Piecuch, eds., *Nathanael Greene*, 88.

46. Greene to Anthony Wayne, July 24, 1781, in Conrad, *Papers*, 9:75.

47. Brooking, "I am an independent spirit," 100.

48. *Ibid.*, 107.

49. Dennis M. Conrad, "General Nathanael Greene: An Appraisal," in Massey and Piecuch, eds., *Nathanael Greene*, 8.

50. Greene to Anne-Cesar, Chevalier de La Luzerne, April 28, 1781, in Conrad, *Papers*, 8:168.

51. Greene to Washington, June 22, 1781, in Conrad, *Papers*, 8:441.

52. Conrad, "Greene: An Appraisal," 12.

53. *Ibid.*, 14.

54. Piecuch, "The Evolving Tactician," 217.

55. Higginbotham, *The War of Independence*, 373.

56. James Kirby Martin, "No Way Out: Lord Cornwallis, the Siege of Yorktown, and America's Victory in the War for Independence," *Perspectives on America's Wars* 31, 2012, www.gilderlehrman.org.

57. *Ibid.*
58. O'Shaughnessy, *The Men Who Lost America*, 261.
59. *Ibid.*, 262.
60. Franklin Wickwire and Mary Wickwire, *Cornwallis: The American Adventure* (Boston: Houghton Mifflin, 1970), 176.
61. Lamb, *Original and Authentic Journal*, 381.
62. *Ibid.*
63. O'Shaughnessy, *The Men Who Lost America*, 268.
64. *Ibid.*, 285.
65. Washington to Cornwallis, October 18, 1781, in Saberton, *Cornwallis Papers*, 6:114.
66. Troop return, October 18, 1781, in Saberton, *Cornwallis Papers*, 6:117.
67. Cornwallis to Clinton, October 20, 1781, in Saberton, *Cornwallis Papers*, 6:127.
68. O'Shaughnessy, *The Men Who Lost America*, 365.
69. "News," *Public Advertiser*, January 11, 1782, 17th–18th Century Burney Collection Newspapers. Gale Document Number Z2001174348.
70. "News," *Whitehall Eve-*

ning Post, January 22–24, 1782, 17th–18th Century Burney Collection Newspapers. Gale Document Z2001613342.
71. Cornwallis to Clinton, October 20, 1781, in Saberton, *Cornwallis Papers*, 6:127.
72. Benjamin Franklin Stevens, ed., *The Campaign in Virginia 1781: An exact Reprint of Six Rare Pamphlets on the Clinton–Cornwallis Controversy with Very Numerous Important Unpublished Manuscript Notes by Sir Henry Clinton K.B.* (London: Charing Cross, 1888), 6.
73. Willcox, *American Rebellion*, 523.
74. *Ibid.*, 523–524.
75. *Ibid.*, 535.
76. *Ibid.*, 536.
77. Cornwallis to Alexander Ross, January 15, 1783, in Ross, *Correspondence*, 1:144.
78. Stevens, *Campaign in Virginia*, 80–83.
79. *Ibid.*, 169.
80. *Ibid.*, 308.
81. Cornwallis to Clinton, October 15, 1781, in Saberton, *Cornwallis Papers*, 6:4–5.

82. *Ibid.*, 6:41.
83. King George III to Cornwallis, March 28, 1782, in Ross, *Correspondence*, 1:136–37.
84. Cornwallis to Alexander Ross, February 23, 1786, in Ross, *Correspondence*, 1:208.
85. Franklin B. Wickwire and Mary B. Wickwire, *Cornwallis: The Imperial Years* (Chapel Hill: University of North Carolina Press, 2012), 17–18.
86. Cornwallis to Sir. W. Fawcett, August 12, 1787, in Ross, *Correspondence*, 1:268–69.
87. O'Shaughnessy, *The Men Who Lost America*, 367.
88. Cornwallis to Ross, July 1, 1798, in Ross, *Correspondence*, 2:356.
89. Cornwallis to Ross, July 9, 1798, in Ross, *Correspondence*, 2:360.
90. O'Shaughnessy, *The Men Who Lost America*, 370.
91. Don Higginbotham, "Reflections on the South in the American Revolution," *The Journal of Southern History* 73, no. 3 (2007): 669.
92. *Ibid.*

Bibliography

Considering the enormous number of resources consulted in writing this work, this bibliography contains resources that were consulted which we felt were the most useful for this voluminous subject. We have left out those sources that have provided minor flourishes to the narrative that have already been documented in the endnotes.

Books and Articles

Adams, Charles Francis. *The Works of John Adams, Second President of the United States: With a Life of the Author, Notes and Illustrations.* 10 vols. Boston: Little, Brown, and Company, 1852.

Anscombe, Francis Charles. *I Have Called You Friends: The Story of Quakerism in North Carolina.* Boston: The Christopher Publishing House, 1959.

Babits, Lawrence. *A Devil of a Whipping: The Battle of Cowpens.* Chapel Hill: University of North Carolina Press, 1998.

Babits, Lawrence, and Joshua Howard. *Long, Obstinate, and Bloody: The Battle for Guilford Courthouse.* Chapel Hill: University of North Carolina Press, 2009.

Bearrs, Edwin C. *Battle of Cowpens: A Documented Narrative and Troop Movement Maps.* Johnson City, TN: The Overmountain Press, 1996.

Blackwelder, Ruth. "The Attitude of the North Carolina Moravians Toward the American Revolution." *The North Carolina Historical Review* 9, no. 1 (1932): 1–21.

Boatner, Mark Mayo III. *Encyclopedia of the American Revolution.* New York: David McKay, 1966.

Borick, Carl. *A Gallant Defense: The Siege of Charleston, 1780.* Columbia: University of South Carolina Press, 2003.

Boyd, William K., ed. *Some Eighteenth-Century Tracts Concerning North Carolina.* Raleigh: Edwards & Broughton, 1927.

Brannon, Rebecca. *From Revolution to Reunion: The Reintegration of South Carolina Loyalists.* Columbia: University of South Carolina Press, 2016.

Brooking, Greg. "'I am an independent spirit, and confide in my own resources': Nathanael Greene and His Continental Subordinates, 1780–1781." In *General Nathanael Greene and the American Revolution in the South.* Edited by Gregory D. Massey, and Jim Piecuch. Columbia: University of South Carolina Press, 2012.

Brown, Richard Maxwell. *The South Carolina Regulators.* Cambridge: The Belknap Press of Harvard University, 1963.

Buchanan, John. *The Road to Guilford Courthouse: The American Revolution in the Carolinas.* New York: John Wiley & Sons, Inc., 1997.

_____. "'We must endeavor to keep up a Partizan War': Nathanael Greene and the Partisans." In *General Nathanael Greene and the American Revolution in the South.* Edited by Gregory D. Massey, and Jim Piecuch. Columbia: University of South Carolina Press, 2012.

_____. *South Carolina: A History.* Columbia: University of South Carolina Press, 1998.

Carrington, Henry B. *Battles of the American Revolution, 1775–1781.* New York: A.S. Barnes, 1876.

Christie, Ian R. *The End of North's Ministry, 1780–1782.* New York: St. Martin's Press, 1958.

Conrad, Dennis M. "General Nathanael Greene: An Appraisal." In *General Nathanael Greene and the American Revolution in the South.* Edited by Gregory D. Massey, and Jim Piecuch. Columbia: University of South Carolina Press, 2012.

Conway, Stephen. "From Fellow-Nationals to Foreigners: British Perceptions of the Americans, circa 1739–1783." *The William and Mary Quarterly* 59, no. 1 (2002): 65–100.

Crow, Jeffrey J. "Liberty Men and Loyalists:

Disorder and Disaffection in the North Carolina Backcountry." In *An Uncivil War: The Southern Backcountry during the American Revolution.* Edited by Ronald Hoffman, Thad Tate, and Peter Albert. Charlottesville: University of Virginia Press, 1985.

Davies, K.G., ed. *Documents of the American Revolution, 1770–1783.* 21 vols. Dublin: Irish University Press, 1972–1981.

Davis, Robert Scott, Jr. "Thomas Pinckney and the Last Campaign of Horatio Gates." *The South Carolina Historical Magazine* 86, no. 2 (1985): 75–99.

Draper, Lyman C. *King's Mountain and its Heroes: History of the Battle of King's Mountain, October 7th, 1780, and the Events Which led to It.* Cincinnati: Peter G. Thomson, Publisher, 1881.

Dunn, Richard S. *Sugar and Slaves: The Rise of the Planter Class in the English West Indies, 1624–1713.* Chapel Hill: University of North Carolina Press, 1972.

Edgar, Walter. *Partisans and Redcoats: The Southern Conflict That Turned the Tide of the American Revolution.* New York: William Morrow, 2001.

Ekirch, Roger A. "'A New Government of Liberty': Herman Husband's Vision of Backcountry North Carolina, 1755." *The William and Mary Quarterly* 34, no. 4 (1977): 632–646.

_____. *"Poor Carolina": Politics and Society in Colonial North Carolina, 1729–1776.* Chapel Hill: University of North Carolina Press, 1981.

_____. "Whig Authority and Public Order in Backcountry North Carolina." In *An Uncivil War: The Southern Backcountry during the American Revolution.* Edited by Ronald Hoffman, Thad Tate and Peter Albert. Charlottesville: University of Virginia Press, 1985.

Flexner, James Thomas. *George Washington in the American Revolution.* Boston: Little, Brown, 1967.

Fortesque, J.W. *A History of the British Army.* 13 vols. London: Macmillan, 1899–1930.

Fries, Adelaide L., ed. *Record of the Moravians in North Carolina.* 13 vols. Raleigh: Edwards & Broughton, 1922–1969.

Frothingham, Thomas G. *Washington: Commander in Chief.* Boston: Houghton Mifflin, 1930.

Golway, Terry. *Washington's General: Nathanael Greene and the Triumph of the American Revolution.* New York: Henry Holt, 2006.

Gordon, William. *The History of the Rise, Progress, and Establishment of the Independence of the United States of America: Including an Account of the Late War and of the Thirteen Colonies, from their Origin to that Period.* Freeport: Books for Libraries Press, 1969, reprint.

Graham, William A. *General Joseph Graham and His Papers on North Carolina Revolutionary History.* Raleigh: Edwards & Broughton, 1904.

Gray, Robert. "Colonel Robert Gray's Observations on the War in Carolina." *South Carolina Historical and Genealogical Magazine* 11, no. 3 (1910): 139–159.

Green, E.R.R. "The Scotch-Irish and the Coming of the Revolution in North Carolina." *Irish Historical Studies* 7, no. 26 (1950): 77–86.

Green, Jerome A. *Ninety-Six: A Historical Narrative.* Denver: National Park Service, 1978.

Greene, Francis Vinton. *The Revolutionary War and the Military Policy of the United States.* New York: Charles Scribner's Sons, 1911.

Greene, George Washington. *The Life of Nathanael Greene, Major-General in the Army of the Revolution.* 3 vols. Freeport: Books for Libraries Press, 1972, reprint.

Greene, Jack P. "Independence, Improvement, and Authority: Toward a Framework for Understanding the Histories of the Southern Backcountry During the Era of the American Revolution." In *An Uncivil War: The Southern Backcountry During the American Revolution.* Edited by Ronald Hoffman, Thad Tate, and Peter Albert. Charlottesville: University of Virginia Press, 1985.

Gregg, Alexander. *History of the Old Cheraws.* New York: Richardson, 1867.

Gregoire, Anne King. *Thomas Sumter.* Columbia: The R.L. Bryan Company, 1931.

Gruber, Ira D. "Britain's Southern Strategy." In *The Revolutionary War in the South: Power, Conflict and Leadership.* Edited by W. Robert Higgins. Durham: Duke University Press, 1979.

_____. *John Peebles' American War: The Diary of a Scottish Grenadier, 1776–1782.* Mechanicsburg: Stackpole Books, 1998.

Haiman, Miecislaus. *Kosciuszko in the American Revolution.* New York: The Polish Institute of Arts and Sciences, 1975.

Hairr, John. *Guilford Courthouse: Nathanael Greene's Victory in Defeat, March 15, 1781.* Cambridge: Da Capo Press, 2002.

Headspeth, W. Carroll, and Spurgeon Compton. *The Retreat to the Dan.* South Boston: South Boston News, Inc., 1975.

Higginbotham, Don. *Daniel Morgan: Revolutionary Rifleman.* Chapel Hill: University of North Carolina Press, 1961.

_____. *War and Society in Revolutionary America: The Wider Dimensions of Conflict.* Columbia: University of South Carolina Press, 1988.

_____. *The War of Independence: Military Attitudes, Policies, and Practice, 1763–1789.* New York: Macmillan, 1971.

Hoffman, Ronald. "The 'Disaffected' in the Revolutionary South." In *The American Revolution: Explorations in the History of American Radicalism.* Edited by Alfred F. Young. Dekalb: Northern Illinois University Press, 1976.

James, William Dobein. *A Sketch of the Life of Brig. Gen. Francis Marion.* Charleston: Gould and Milet, 1821.

Johnson, George Lloyd. *The Frontier in the Colonial South: South Carolina Backcountry, 1736–1800.* Westport: Greenwood Press, 1997.

Jones, Rufus M. *The Quakers in the American Colonies.* London: Macmillan, 1911.

Joselit, Jenna Weissman. *Immigration and American Religion.* New York: Oxford University Press, 2001.

Kars, Marjoleine. *Breaking Loose Together: The Regulator Rebellion in Pre-Revolutionary North Carolina.* Chapel Hill: University of North Carolina Press, 2002.

Kay, Marvin L. Michael, and Lorin Lee Carey. "Class, Mobility, and Conflict in North Carolina on the Eve of the Revolution." In *The Southern Experience in the American Revolution.* Edited by Jeffrey J. Crow, and Larry E. Tise. Chapel Hill: University of North Carolina Press, 1978.

Klein, Rachel N. "Ordering the Backcountry: The South Carolina Regulation." *The William and Mary Quarterly* 38, no. 4 (1981): 661–680.

_____. *Unification of a Slave State: The Rise of the Planter Class in the South Carolina Backcountry, 1760–1808.* Chapel Hill: University of North Carolina Press, 1990.

Landrum, J.B.O. *Colonial and Revolutionary History of Upper South Carolina.* Greenville: Shannon & Co., Printer and Binders, 1897.

Lee, Wayne. "Restraint and Retaliation: The North Carolina Militias and the Backcountry War of 1780–1782." In *War and Society in the Revolution.* Edited by John Resch, and Walter Sargent. Dekalb: Northern Illinois University Press, 2007.

Lossing, Benson J. *The Pictorial Field-Book of the Revolution.* 2 vols. Rutland: Charles E. Tuttle, 1972, reprint.

Lumpkin, Henry. *From Savannah to Yorktown: The American Revolution in the South.* Lincoln, NE: ToExcel Press, 1987.

Maass, John. "'With humanity, justice and moderation': Nathanael Greene and the Reconciliation of the Disaffected South." In *General Nathanael Greene and the American Revolution in the South.* Edited by Gregory D. Massey, and Jim Piecuch. Columbia: University of South Carolina Press, 2012.

Massey, Gregory D. "Independence and Slavery: The Transformation of Nathanael Greene." In *General Nathanael Greene and the American Revolution in the South.* Edited by Gregory D. Massey, and Jim Piecuch. Columbia: University of South Carolina Press, 2012.

_____. *John Laurens and the American Revolution.* Columbia: University of South Carolina Press, 2000.

McCrady, Edward. *The History of South Carolina in the Revolution, 1780–1783.* New York: Macmillan, 1902.

_____. *The History of South Carolina Under the Royal Government, 1719–1776.* New York: Macmillan, 1897.

McIntyre, James R. "Nathanael Greene: Soldier-Statesman of the War of Independence in South Carolina." In *General Nathanael Greene and the American Revolution in the South.* Edited by Gregory D. Massey, and Jim Piecuch. Columbia: University of South Carolina Press, 2012.

Meriwether, Robert L. *The Expansion of South Carolina, 1729–1765.* Kingsport: Southern Publishers, 1940.

Middlekauff, Robert. *The Glorious Cause: The American Revolution, 1763–1789.* New York: Oxford University Press, 2005.

Moody, T.W. "The Ulster Scots in Colonial and Revolutionary America." *Studies: An Irish Quarterly Review* 34, no. 133 (1945): 85–94.

_____. "The Ulster Scots in Colonial and Revolutionary America, Part II." *Studies: An Irish Quarterly Review* 34, no. 134 (1945): 211–221.

Moore, Peter N. "The Local Origins of Allegiance in Revolutionary South Carolina: The Waxhaws as a Case Study." *The South Carolina Historical Magazine* 107, no. 1 (2006): 26–41.

Morgan, Curtis F., Jr. "'A merchandise of small Wares': Nathanael Greene's Northern Apprenticeship, 1775–1780." In *General Nathanael Greene and the American Revolution in the South.* Edited by Gregory D. Massey, and Jim Piecuch. Columbia: University of South Carolina Press, 2012.

Nadelhaft, Jerome. *The Disorders of War: The Revolution in South Carolina.* Orono: University of Maine at Orono Press, 1981.

Nelson, Paul David. *General Horatio Gates: A Biography.* Baton Rouge: Louisiana State University Press, 1976.

_____. "Horatio Gates in the Southern Department, 1780: Serious Errors and A Costly Defeat." *The North Carolina Review* 50, no. 3 (1773): 256–272.

_____. "Major Horatio Gates as a Military Leader: The Southern Experience." In *The Revolutionary War in the South: Power, Conflict and Leadership.* Edited by W. Robert Higgins. Durham: Duke University Press, 1979.

Newlin, Algie I. *The Battle of New Garden: The Little-Known Story of One of the Most Important "Minor Battles" of the Revolutionary War in North Carolina.* Greensboro: North Carolina Friends Historical Society, 1995.

Nobles, Gregory H. "Breaking into the Backcountry: New Approaches to the Early American Frontier, 1750–1800." *The William and Mary Quarterly* 46, no. 4 (1989): 641–670.

O'Donnell, Patrick K. *Washington's Immortals: The Untold Story of an Elite Regiment Who Changed the Course of the Revolution.* New York: Atlantic Monthly Press, 2016.

O'Kelley, Patrick. *Unwaried Patience and Fortitude: Francis Marion's Orderly Book.* West Conshohocken, PA: Infinity Publishing, 2006.

Oller, John. *The Swamp Fox: How Francis Marion Saved the American Revolution.* New York: Da Capo Press, 2016.

O'Shaughnessy, Andrew Jackson. *The Men Who Lost America: British Leadership, the American Revolution, and the Fate of the Empire.* New Haven: Yale University Press, 2013.

Pancake, John S. *This Destructive War: The British Campaign in the Carolinas, 1780–1782.* Tuscaloosa: University of Alabama Press, 1985.

Phillips, Thomas R., ed. *Roots of Strategy: The 5 Greatest Military Classics of All Time.* Harrisburg: Stackpole Books, 1985.

Piecuch, Jim. "The Evolving Tactician: Nathanael Greene at the Battle of Eutaw Springs." In *General Nathanael Greene and the American Revolution in the South.* Edited by Gregory D. Massey, and Jim Piecuch. Columbia: University of South Carolina Press, 2012.

_____. "Incompatible Allies: Loyalists, Slaves and Indians in Revolutionary South Carolina." In *War and Society in the Revolution.* Edited by John Resch, and Walter Sargent. Dekalb: Northern Illinois University, 2007.

Powell, William S., ed. *North Carolina Through Four Centuries.* Chapel Hill: University of North Carolina Press, 1989.

_____. *The Regulators in North Carolina: A Documentary History, 1759–1776.* Raleigh: State Department of Archives and History, 1971.

Ramsay, David. *The History of the American Revolution.* 2 vols. Philadelphia: R. Aitkin & Son, 1789.

Reed, William B., ed. *Life and Correspondence of Joseph Reed.* Philadelphia: Lindsay and Blakiston, 1847.

Royster, Charles. *Light-Horse Harry Lee and the Legacy of the American Revolution.* New York: Alfred A. Knopf, 1981.

_____. *The Revolutionary People at War: The Continental Army and American Character, 1775–1783.* New York: W.W. Norton, 1979.

Sappington, Roger E. "North Carolina and the Non-Resistant Sects during the American Revolution." *Quaker History* 60, no. 1 (1971): 29–47.

Scheer, George, and Hugh Rankin. *Rebels and Redcoats: The American Revolution Through the Eyes of Those Who Fought and Lived It.* New York: DaCapo Press, 1957.

Shy, John. *A People Numerous and Armed: Reflections on the Military Struggle for American Independence.* New York: Oxford University Press, 1976.

Simcoe, John Graves. *Simcoe's Military Journal: A History of the Operations of a Partisan Corps called The Queen's Rangers.* New York: Bartlett & Welford, 1844.

Smith, Page. *Reflections on the Nature of Leadership.* Washington, D.C.: The Society of the Cincinnati, 1982.

Smith, Paul H. *Loyalists and Redcoats: A Study in British Revolutionary Policy.* Chapel Hill: University of North Carolina Press, 1964.

Stedman, Charles. *The History of the Origin, Progress, and Termination of the American War.* 2 vols. London: J. Murray, 1794.

Stevens, Benjamin Franklin, ed. *The Campaign in Virginia 1781: An Exact Reprint of Six Rare Pamphlets on the Clinton-Cornwallis Controversy with Very Numerous Important Unpublished Manuscript Notes by Sir Henry Clinton K.B.* London: Charing Cross, 1888.

Tarleton, Banastre. *A History of the Campaigns of 1780 and 1781, in the Southern Provinces of North America.* Dublin: Colles, Exshaw, et al., 1787.

Thayer, Theodore. *Nathanael Greene: Strategist of the American Revolution.* New York: Twayne, 1960.

Thorne, Dorothy Gilbert. "North Carolina Friends and the Revolution." *The North Carolina Review* 38, no. 3 (1961): 323–340.

Turner, Frederick Jackson. *The Frontier in American History.* Tucson: University of Arizona Press, 1997, reprint.

Uhlendorf, Bernhard A., ed. and trans. *The Siege of Charleston, With an Account of the Province of South Carolina: Diaries and Letters of Hessian Officers from the von Jungken Papers in the William L. Clements Library.* Ann Arbor: University of Michigan Press, 1938.

Ward, Christopher. *The War of the Revolution,* vol 2. Edited by John Richard Alden. New York: Macmillan, 1952.

Ward, Harry. *The War for Independence and the Transformation of American Society.* London: UCL Press, 1999.

Weigley, Russell F. *The Partisan War: The South Carolina Campaign of 1780–1782.* Columbia: University of South Carolina Press, 1970.

Weir, Robert. *Colonial South Carolina.* New York: KTO Press, 1983.

Whittenberg, James P. "Planters, Merchants and Lawyers: Social Change and the Origins of the North Carolina Regulation." *The William and Mary Quarterly* 34, no. 2 (1977): 215–238.

Wickwire, Franklin, and Mary Wickwire. *Cornwallis: The American Adventure.* Boston: Houghton Mifflin, 1970.

_____. *Cornwallis: The Imperial Years.* Chapel Hill: University of North Carolina Press, 2012.

Willcox, William B., ed. *The American Rebellion.* New Haven, CT: Yale University Press, 1954.

_____. *Portrait of a General: Sir Henry Clinton in the War of Independence.* New York: Alfred A. Knopf, 1962.

Wilson, David K. "'Against the tide of misfortune': Civil-Military Relations, Provincialism, and the Southern command in the Revolution." In *General Nathanael Greene and the American Revolution in the South.* Edited by Gregory D. Massey, and Jim Piecuch. Columbia: University of South Carolina Press, 2012.

_____. *The Southern Strategy: Britain's Conquest of South Carolina and Georgia, 1775–1780.* Columbia: University of South Carolina Press, 2005.

Manuscripts and Other Printed Primary Sources

Abbot, W.W., et al., ed. *The Papers of George Washington.* 22 vols. Charlottesville: University of Virginia Press, 1987-.

Baldwin, Samuel. "Diary of Events, In Charleston, SC, from March 20th to April 20th, 1780." *New Jersey Historical Society* 1, 1845–1846. Newark: Daily Advertiser, 1847.

Boston Chronicle, December 5–12, 1768. In *The Colonial South Carolina Scene: Contemporary Views, 1697–1774.* Edited by H. Roy Merrens. Columbia: University of South Carolina Press, 1977.

Boyd, Julian P., ed. *The Papers of Thomas Jefferson.* 43 vols. Princeton: Princeton University Press, 1950–2017.

Burgoyne, Bruce E., ed. and trans. *Diaries of Two Ansbach Jaegers.* Westminster: Heritage Books, 2007.

_____, ed. and trans. *Enemy Views: The American Revolutionary War as Recorded by Hessian Participants.* Bowie: Heritage Books, 1996.

Carr, James O., ed. *The Dickson Letters.* Raleigh: Edwards & Broughton, 1901.

Chesney, Alexander. "A Journal of Alexander Chesney, A South Carolina Loyalist in the Revolution and After." Edited by E. Alfred Jones. *The Ohio State University Bulletin* 26, no. 4 (1921): 1–56.

Chestnutt, David R., and C. James Taylor, eds. *The Papers of Henry Laurens.* 16 vols. Columbia: University of South Carolina Press, 1968–2003.

Clark, Walter, ed. *The State Record of North Carolina.* 26 vols. Winston: M.L. & J.C. Stewart, 1886–1907.

Clinton, Sir Henry. *Observations on Earl Cornwallis' Answer to Sir Henry Clinton's Narrative.* London: J. Debrett, 1783.

Coleman, Charles Washington, Jr. "The Southern Campaign, 1781, from Guilford Court House to the Siege of York." *Magazine of American History* 7 (1881): 210–216.

Commager, Henry Steele, and Richard B. Morris, eds. *The Spirit of 'Seventy Six: The Story of the American Revolution as Told by Participants.* Edison: Castle Books, 1967.

Dann, John C., ed. *The Revolution Remembered: Eyewitness Accounts of the War for Independence.* Chicago: University of Chicago Press, 1980.

Diary of Captain von der Malsburg, Lidgerwood Collection, Morristown National Historical Park, *Hessian Documents of the American Revolution, 1776–1783.* Fiche Number 333, in the collections of the David Library of the American Revolution.

Ewald, Johann. *Diary of the American War: A Hessian Journal.* Edited and translated by Joseph P. Tustin. New Haven: Yale University Press, 1979.

Finney, Walter, and Joseph Lee Boyle, ed. "The Revolutionary War Diaries of Captain Walter Finney." *South Carolina Historical Magazine* 98, no. 2 (1997): 126–152.

Fitzpatrick, John C., et al., ed. *The Writings of George Washington, from the Original Manuscript Sources, 1745–1799.* 39 vols. Washington, D.C.: Government Printing Office, 1931–1944.

Francis Marion to Benjamin Lincoln, 5 March 1780. *Benjamin Lincoln Papers,* microfilm edition, 16 reels. Boston: Massachusetts Historical Society, 1967.

Garden, Alexander. *Anecdotes of the American Revolution.* Charleston: A.E. Miller, 1828.

Gibbes, R.W., ed. *Documentary History of the American Revolution.* 3 vols. Columbia: Banner Steam-Power Press, 1853–1857.

Hawes, Lilla Mills, ed. *Lachlan McIntosh Papers in the University of Georgia Libraries.* Athens: University of Georgia Press, 1968.

Henry, Robert. *Narrative of the Battle at Cowan's Ford, February 1, 1781.* Greensboro: D. Schenk, 1891.

Hooker, Richard. J., ed. *The Carolina Backcountry on the Eve of the Revolution: The Journal of Charles Woodmason, Anglican Itinerant.* Chapel Hill: University of North Carolina Press, 1953.

Hunt, Gaillard, ed. *Journals of the Continental Congress, 1774–1789.* 34 vols. Washington, D.C.: Government Printing Office, 1904–1937.

Kolb, Wade, and Robert Weir, eds. *Captured at Kings Mountain: The Journal of Uzal Johnson, A Loyalist Surgeon.* Columbia: University of South Carolina Press, 2011.

Lamb, Roger. *An Original and Authentic Journal of Occurrences during the Late American War.* Dublin: Wilkinson & Courtney, 1809.

Lee, Henry. *Memoirs of the War in the Southern Department of the United States.* New York: University Publishing Company, 1869.

Lee, Richard Henry. *Letters of Richard Henry Lee.* 2 vols. Edited by James Curtis Ballagh. New York: Macmillan, 1914.

Lincoln, General Benjamin. *Letter to Commodore Abraham Whipple, January 30, 1780.* Abraham Whipple Collection. MSS 802, Box 1, Folder 1, Rhode Island Historical Society.

MacKenzie, Roderick. *Strictures on Lt. Col. Tarleton's "History of the Campaigns of 1780 and 1781, in the Southern Provinces of North America."* London: Printed for the Author, 1787.

Moore, Frank. *Diary of the American Revolution: From Newspapers and Original Documents.* 2 vols. New York: Charles Scribner's, 1860.

Moss, Bobby Gilmer, ed. *The Journal of Alexander Chesney.* Roanoke Rapids: Scotia-Hibernia Press, 2002.

Moultrie, William. *Memoirs of the American Revolution, So Far as It Related to the States of North Carolina and South Carolina, and Georgia.* 2 vols. New York: David Longworth, 1802.

Newsome, A.R., ed. "A British Orderly Book, 1780–1781: III." *The North Carolina Historical Review* 9, no. 3 (1932): 273–298.

_____. "A British Orderly Book, 1780–1781: IV" *The North Carolina Historical Review* 9, no. 4 (1932): 366–392

O'Hara, Charles. "Letters of Charles O'Hara to Duke of Grafton." Edited by George C. Rogers. *South Carolina Historical Magazine* 65, no. 3 (1964): 158–180.

Robinson, Blackwell P., ed. *The Revolutionary War Sketches of William R. Davie.* Raleigh: Department of Cultural Resources, 1976.

Ross, Charles, ed. *Correspondence of Charles, First Marquis Cornwallis.* 3 vols. London: John Murray, 1859.

Saberton, Ian, ed. *The Cornwallis Papers: The Campaigns of 1780 and 1781 in The Southern Theatre of the American Revolutionary War.* 6 vols. Uckfield: The Naval and Military Press Ltd., 2010.

Salley, A.S., Jr., ed. *Col. William Hill's Memoirs of The Revolution.* Columbia: The Sate Company, 1921.

Saye, James Hodge. *Memoirs of Major Joseph McJunkin: Revolutionary Patriot.* Greenwood: Greenwood Index-Journal, 1925.

Seymour, William. "A Journal of the Southern Expedition, 1780–1783." *The Pennsylvania Magazine of History and Biography* 7, no. 3 (1883): 286–298.

Shaw, John Robert. *A Narrative of the Life & Travels of John Robert Shaw.* Lexington: Daniel Bradford, 1807.

Showman, Richard, et al., ed. *The Papers of General Nathanael Greene.* 13 vols. Chapel Hill: University of North Carolina Press, 1976–2005.

Sparks, Jared, ed. *Correspondence of the American Revolution: Being Letters of Eminent Men to George Washington, From the time of his Taking Command of the Army to the End of his Presidency.* 4 vols. Boston: Little, Brown and Co., 1853.

Syrett, Harold C., and Jacob E. Cooke, eds. *The Papers of Alexander Hamilton.* 27 vols. New York: Columbia University Press, 1961–1987.

Turner, Joseph Brown, ed. *The Journal and Order Book of Captain Robert Kirkwood of the Delaware Regiment of the Continental Line, Part 1: A Journal of the Southern Campaign, 1780–1782.* Wilmington: The Historical Society of Delaware, 1910.

United States. Continental Army. Southern Department. Continental Army Southern Department Records, 1778–1790. (34/201 OvrSz) South Carolina Historical Society, April 15, 1780.

Vance, Captain David. *Narrative of the Battle of King's Mountain.* Greensboro: D. Schenk, 1891.

Williams, Otho Holland. "A Narrative of the Campaign of 1780." In *Sketches of the Life and Correspondence of Nathanael Greene.* Edited by William Johnson. Charleston: A.E. Miller, 1822.

_____. *The Otho Holland Williams Papers 1747–1794.* MS 908, 3 reels. Maryland Historical Society.

Dissertations, Theses and Unpublished Works

Bartholomees, James Boone, Jr. "Fight or Flee: The Combat Performance of the North

Carolina Militia in the Cowpens-Guilford Courthouse Campaign, January to March 1781." Ph.D. diss., Duke University, 1978.

Brannon, Rebecca. "Reconciling the Revolution: Resolving Conflict and Rebuilding Community in the Wake of Civil War in South Carolina." Ph.D. diss., University of Michigan, 2007.

Bulger, William T. "The British Expedition to Charleston, 1779–1780." Ph.D. diss., University of Michigan, 1957.

Conrad, Dennis M. "Nathanael Greene and the Southern Campaigns, 1780–1783." Ph.D. diss., Duke University, 1979.

Dauphinee, Andrew. "Lord Charles Cornwallis and the Loyalists: A Study in British Pacification During the American Revolution, 1775–1781." Master's thesis, Temple University, 2011.

Edward, Joel Anthony. "A Comparative Evaluation of British and American Strategy in the Southern Campaign of 1780–1781." Master's thesis, U.S. Army Command and General Staff College, 2002.

Hughes, Kaylene. "Populating the Backcountry: The Demographic and Social Characteristics of the Colonial South Carolina Frontier, 1730–1760." Ph.D. diss., Florida State University, 1985.

Kalmanson, Arnold W. "Otho Holland Williams and the Southern Campaign of 1780–1782." Master's thesis, Salisbury State University, 1990.

Konigsberg, Charles. "Edward Carrington, 1748–1810: 'Child of the Revolution': A Study of the Public Man in Young America." Ph.D. diss., Princeton University, 1966.

Pugh, Robert. "The Cowpens Campaign and the American Revolution." Ph.D. diss., University of Illinois, 1951.

Index